CLEO

"Possibly the next *Marley & Me, Cleo* by Helen Brown is an honest and un-mawkish true story of ordinary people re-building their lives after a tragedy, with the help of a kitten. Even non-cat-lovers will be moved."
—**Good Housekeeping**

"This is an absolute must gift for yourself or a cat-loving friend."
—**Cat World**

"A buoyant tale, heartfelt and open."
—**Booklist**

"Helen Brown's remarkable memoir threatened to break my heart, but she didn't break my heart at all—she opened it."
—**Beth Hoffman**, *New York Times* bestselling author of *Saving CeeCee Honeycutt*

"Lively and admirably unsentimental . . . a salutary reminder of the gratitude we humans owe to our companion animals."
—**Daily Mail**

"Helen Brown's *Cleo* is not just a tender story about a cat and a family facing the world again after a family bereavement. It's also an epic, genuinely moving, funny, and ultimately uplifting. Don't be surprised to find yourself smiling through tears after reading it."
—**Witi Ihimaera**, author of *The Whale Rider*

"To say that gifts of inspiration, hope, and pure love emanate out of every page would be an understatement."
—Leukaemia Foundation

"A heartwarming, tear-stained ride told with great charm and humor."
—Jillian Devon, *North & South*

JONAH

"An intimate memoir about one woman and her relationships with her cat and her family . . . [Brown] writes eloquently about the bonds that exist between women of all ages . . . a pleasant and moving story of love and identity among mothers, daughters, and felines."
—*Kirkus Reviews*

"Journalist and humorist Brown shares her experiences with breast cancer, a rebellious daughter, and a rambunctious cat in this sequel to *Cleo*, told with unflinching candor and Aussie-tinged wit. Her life 'ruled by a cat,' Brown reprises her first book's theme: Cats have the power to help heal human suffering. Brown's voice is alternately, and appropriately, lighthearted and solemn, her vulnerability evident as Jonah, a stunning Siamese, provides love, friendship, and is the 'listener, healer, the companion who never judged.' Having courageously faced down fear, loss, and mortality, Brown realizes she has learned much along the way."
—*Publishers Weekly* (starred review)

"It takes a remarkable feline to help a family put things in perspective and impart the kinds of life lessons one can't always learn from a two-footed guru. Candid, genuine, and unaffected, Brown's touching memoir celebrates the affirmational power of animal companions to help humans navigate life's most challenging moments."
—*Booklist*

"Oh, what a delightful read this is!"
—*The Booksellers*

"This book follows Helen Brown's *Cleo*, the wonderful memoir of the cat who healed her family during a time of many changes. This new memoir is another wonderful book by Helen Brown. It is genuine and honest. Cat fanciers will especially enjoy Jonah and his own way of healing."
—*McGuffey's Reader*

"Author Helen Brown has a wonderful sense of humor and that shows abundantly here, despite that she writes about scary things mixed with the ubiquitous awww-inspiring pet-and-me stories . . . This is one of those books you leave on the table so it's handy when you want to return to it—which will be often. Whether your kiddies or kitties have two legs or four, this is a book you'll pounce on."
—**The Bookworm**

"In the midst of a series of life's upheavals—Brown's son getting married, one of her daughters exploring life in a Buddhist monastery, and a breast cancer diagnosis for Brown herself—she wound up bringing home a wonderful and utterly crazy Siamese kitten. This book revolves around Jonah, the quirky and strong-willed feline . . . A good bi-species memoir."
—**Sparkle the Designer Cat**

"I found this book incredibly hard to put down. Brown writes with humor, compassion and honesty about her struggles with her illness, her daughter, and her rambunctious cat. This is a story of love and family—both two- and four-legged—with all the challenges and imperfections that are part of life. The lessons Helen Brown learns along the way about letting go and having faith are nothing short of inspirational."

"Funny and poignant . . . a beautiful, well-written story."
—Bookshelf Bombshells

"I picked up this book with joy, having loved Brown's earlier bestselling memoir *Cleo*. You don't have to be an ailurophile to love this book, but you probably will be by the time you finish it."
—Hudson Valley News

"Heartwarming . . . Brown's story of how she learns to let go and embrace change is both inspiring and moving."
—Modern Cat

"*Cleo* was an international bestseller. With its honesty and wisdom, the tale of how a scrappy black kitten helped the author's family heal following the death of one of her young sons struck a universal chord with cat lovers. As is often the case with blockbusters, a sequel is in order . . . *Jonah* is irrepressibly appealing. A heartwarming tale, a page turner."
—Best Friends

BONO

TUMBLEDOWN MANOR

"If you loved Helen Brown in her bestselling memoir, *Cleo*, you'll love her all over again as the author of *Tumbledown Manor*. She takes on fiction with as much spunk as her heroine, Lisa Trumperton, who leaves a failed marriage and takes on a new life. As usual, Helen Brown is warm, wise, and witty. Prepare for a treat."
—**Kristin von Kreisler**, best-selling author of
An Unexpected Grace

"Brown, author of bestselling memoirs *Cleo* and *Jonah*, writes with empathy and humor in her first novel, about finding new love and purpose in middle age."
—*Booklist*

Books by Helen Brown

Cleo

Jonah

Bono

Cleo and Rob

Tumbledown Manor

MICKEY

THE CAT WHO RAISED ME

HELEN BROWN

CITADEL PRESS
Kensington Publishing Corp.
www.kensingtonbooks.com

CITADEL PRESS BOOKS are published by

Kensington Publishing Corp.
900 Third Avenue
New York, NY 10022

ISBN: 978-0-8065-4184-6

First trade paperback printing: April 2024

ISBN: 978-0-8065-4185-3 (e-book)

10 9 8 7 6 5 4 3 2 1

Printed in the United States of America

For our daughter Katharine, who (along with Jonah, of course) has been asking me to tell this story for ages. And to Lydia and baby Alice, for surrounding us with joy and kindness through challenging times. Stand tall in your light.

Contents

CONTENTS

AUTHOR'S NOTE: HOW IT BEGAN

The walls are dappled with gold as I settle at my battered yellow desk. Summer's running out of steam. The tree outside my window will soon shed her leaves. A lanky Siamese cat bounds through the door and lands with a thud on my lap. Jonah yawns and emits a sleepy purr, as if to say "Okay, I'm here. You can start now."

Under Jonah's supervision, I've written books about three remarkable cats—Cleo, Bono, and (of course) Jonah himself. Each of these extraordinary felines guided me through difficult times, teaching me about resilience and joy. There's so much to thank them for, including the ability to savor the miracle of simply being alive.

My connection to felines stems back a long way to a gray tabby. I called him Mickey. He's the one who started it all. Back when I was twelve years old and embarking on a bumpy year of adolescence, he became my first friend and love.

A polydactyl with extra toes on his front paws, Mickey listened and never laughed. With supreme wisdom he guided me through loneliness and the awkwardness of my shape-shifting body. He was the only one I could share my dreams with.

While there was no shortage of affection in our flamboyant household, my parents and older siblings were engrossed in their own dramas. I felt lost, unseen—until the gentle tabby offered the love and encouragement I craved. Mickey sustained my connection to the warm flow of life. In many ways, he helped raise me through that year. More than a friend, Mickey was my feline parent.

Here in my study, Dad's tenderly composed photos beam down from the shelf above my computer. Beach holidays and Christmases glow in vintage hues. I remember the day Dad handed me his precious Canon camera. Heavier than it looked, it wobbled as I clicked the shutter button. Mickey's eyes are half-closed and his fur blurs around the edges. It's a close-up. Too close. A terrible photo, but the only one I have of Mickey.

Grief becomes a familiar companion as we travel through life. The pang of loss for Mum, Dad, and my brother Jim has become part of my being. Those larger-than-life personalities left gaps no one would dare fill. Loved ones, pets included, are never entirely "lost," however. They seep deep into our core of being and remain part of who we are.

These days, I have a deeper appreciation of the way families ebb and flow through decades. When my daughter Lydia gave birth to a baby girl eighteen months ago, I wept with joy.

With dark flashing eyes, young Alice has a familiar passion for music and nature. She's fascinated by animals, among them a long-haired cat who's a regular visitor to her backyard. Unlike many felines, this handsome tan and white fellow isn't afraid of toddlers. Hearing Alice's chuckles of delight as he dips his nose in her palm, I have an inkling he may become her Mickey.

Through all life's changes, cats are a constant. A second encounter with breast cancer was an unexpected claw swipe last year. After my lumpectomy, Jonah launched into nurse mode again, curling up beside me on the bedcovers. Once I was strong enough, he urged me upstairs to my study to complete the story of Mickey's lasting impact.

There's never been a simple place and time in history. Living under a snow-capped mountain in 1960s provincial New Zealand, we were all too aware of tensions between Russia and the US. Our world could evaporate in a mushroom cloud any time. The Vietnam War was practically on our doorstep.

Even closer, in the Pacific Ocean, France and other nations were conducting nuclear tests.

At the same time, inside our shabby castle we heard whispers of exciting trends from overseas—the miniskirt, the Beatles, and something called The Pill. *Castle* was one way to describe our home, perched on a mound in a secretive valley. With double tiers of lacy verandas and a gothic tower, some called it a wedding cake. Others, more accurately, a folly (*"a costly, generally nonfunctional building erected to enhance a natural landscape,"* thanks, *Encyclopedia Britannica*).

However other people saw us, I'm grateful Noeline and Bill (who was christened Athol) Blackman dared to be different in a society that demanded conformity. Their haphazard but well-meaning parenting allowed freedoms that would be considered scandalous today.

Welcome to my twelve-year-old world, as I remember it, and some of the people who loomed large back then. In order to write this memoir, I've had to massage a few timelines. I hope friends, family, and fact checkers will understand some characters and events required embellishment, while others were trimmed and, in a few cases, created from composites.

Meantime, let me take you on a quick tour of our dwelling's dilapidated wooden splendor. The musky aroma of my pet mice wafts down the ladder from the tower. Strains of Tom Jones's song "It's Not Unusual" ooze from under my sister Mary's bedroom door (she has a portable record player, which I'm jealous of, because she's a full-grown teenager).

Downstairs in his museum, my big brother Jim (not loving his last year of high school) runs a magnifying glass over the papery remains of an embalmed python. On the other side of the kitchen, in the living room sitting at the upright Bechstein piano, our glamorous mother reaches for an elusive high note in preparation for the Operatic Society's *The King and I* auditions.

Outside, Dad strolls across the vast, sloping top lawn, hedge clippers in hand, whistling Mahler's *Songs of a Wayfarer*. Our dog, Fritz, a mixed breed mostly resembling a dachshund, prances at his heels.

Dad pauses at a stately totara tree and strokes its lichen-laden trunk. He breathes in the cool, moist air. Heavy with the aroma of damp earth and freshly cut grass, it's the smell of New Zealand. My father takes a rumpled handkerchief from his shorts pocket and gazes across the bottom lawn. A more athletic family than ours would play tennis down there on the luscious green rectangle lined with blue hydrangeas. We are not that way inclined.

Everywhere Dad turns, things pester for attention. Grass nags to be mown, weeds beg to be pulled, vegetables ache to be sprayed (with DDT, the pesticide of choice of that era). A 60-foot ladder rises from the dahlia bed to precipitous eaves above the top veranda. He's barely started painting the house.

As if he doesn't have enough to worry about running the coal gasworks and trying to persuade the town to source natural gas from under the sea. My father dabs his brow and wanders past blushing camellias and brazen azaleas toward the basement arch. Stooping to avoid bumping his head, he disappears under the arch into the shadows. The darkroom door closes with a clunk, leaving Fritz to whine outside.

A thrush emits an arpeggio of *tooktooktooks* from the totara tree. Fritz, teeth bared, tail flying, yaps after the bird. It soars above him, *tooktooktook*, echoing across the valley as the bird sails past my upstairs bedroom window.

That's me in there perched on the pastel pink candlewick bedspread, the chunky girl with startling yellow curls. Alone, as usual. No one understands how desperately I need to be prima ballerina in the Sadler's Wells Ballet Company, London. Or why I can't do math. There has to be someone who understands, a friend. Just for me . . .

It all began on a wet dismal day when my father knocked on my bedroom door and invited me to take a ride with him . . .

Chapter One

LUCKY
CAT

"Just who I was looking for," Dad said with a smile. "Get dressed. There's someone I want you to meet."

"Where are we going?" I asked, trotting after him through the rain to the sky-blue Ford Zephyr parked in the basement.

I shook the rain off my face and slid onto the front bench seat beside him. My cheeks sizzled. I couldn't remember the last time I'd been allowed to take Mum's place next to him in the car. My father never had time to take me anywhere on my own.

"You'll see," he said, clunking the driver's door and adjusting his rearview mirror.

Dad gunned the motor and clunked the steering wheel gear stick. I felt a glow of importance as he stretched his arm across the seatback behind me. The reassuring aroma of coal wafted from his tweed jacket, his paisley cravat, and his wild dark hair. It permeated the car. I sheltered my eyes as we reversed into watery daylight.

"Ready?" he said, positioning the car at the top of our precipitous driveway.

I couldn't believe he was up for it. Not in this weather. I nodded and held my breath.

Dad shunted the gear lever into neutral and let the car inch toward the top of the driveway. We were barely moving—until gravity took hold and sent us plummeting streetwards. I gripped my stomach as we rocketed past a blur of privet hedging. My thighs wobbled. A nanosecond before we burst onto the street, Dad honked the horn to warn any hapless pedestrians below.

He was ridiculously proud of our secondhand family sedan. It wasn't flashy like the fin-tailed American cars that swam like sharks across the pages of *National Geographic*. With rounded curves and a smiling chrome radiator grille, it beamed out at the world through circular headlights. Unlike a shark, it lumbered about like a benevolent seal.

"Phew!" I said, adjusting the wide orange headband Mum made for my twelfth birthday.

I glanced up at the dilapidated folly we lived in. High above the ornate verandas and vertiginous eaves, the tower jutted like a freshly sharpened pencil into the mist.

When we reached the street corner, Dad took a right and coaxed the car up Cutfield Road. We craned our necks for a glimpse of the mountain. It was sulking behind a gray shroud.

I couldn't fathom who Dad was taking me to meet. The worst scenario would be a math tutor, but I was pretty sure they couldn't afford one of those. There was a strong possibility I'd done something wrong.

"Are we going to church?"

Amusement rippled across his lips.

"Where's your eyepatch?" he asked as the Zephyr rumbled past the wrought iron hospital gates.

"At home." I said, toes curling inside my sandals. I'd forgotten it in the rush.

"I hear Dr. Hughes thinks you mightn't need another operation."

My relationship with Dr. Hughes was complex. In retrospect I wonder if the elf-like surgeon was an enabler of what today might be considered an unhealthy obsession with medically approved self-harm.

"That's not what he told me," I said.

Dr. Hughes was one of the few adults who treated me as an equal. It was a relief having him take responsibility for *correcting* my physical failings. A medical landscaper of the human form, he pruned my imperfections, clearing the path for me to rival the world's greatest ballerina, Margot Fonteyn.

Though surgery was no fun, I figured it was worth the investment. From the experience of losing my tonsils and adenoids, and then the first eye operation, I'd discovered that blood and pain were short-lived inconveniences. Once home from hospital, I'd revel in blissful weeks of parental indulgences. Mum would deliver meal trays to my bedside while Dad stroked my forehead and told stories about the olden days when firemen rode horses. Somber with concern, the two of them morphed into ideal parents, reading books aloud in their best dramatic voices. I wanted it to go on forever.

The operation to tighten my eye muscles (to stop alarming people when they spiraled in opposite directions) was only half successful. When I was tired, my left eye wandered around like a lost sheepdog.

"Are you keeping up your eye exercises?" Dad asked.

Mum had clearly talked him over to her side.

"See that lamppost?" I said, squinting till the pole melted and formed an identical twin. "There's two of them, right?"

Dad said nothing. He crunched the gear stick and pointed the car at the restless steely sea.

My spirits plummeted as we pulled up outside the gasworks. Poised on a cliff just outside town, the yellow brick cube glared down at the ocean through tiny windows. Everyone knew the gas industry was on its knees. The only person in denial was the gasworks manager, Dad.

"Wait here." he said, flicking up his jacket collar and springing out of the car. "Won't be long."

Splashing through the downpour, chin tucked into his jacket, feet splayed out, he resembled an overgrown penguin. My father was immortal, solid as the mountain. But as he paused at the coke stacks and glanced up at the gasometer, a devastating thought hit me; Dad might not always be here.

A feeling of tenderness for my father coursed through my limbs. It was so powerful I had to open a little drawer inside my head and shut it away with all the other feelings that had nowhere to go.

Dad disappeared inside the gasworks building. I waited and watched mist rise from the sea. The curve of coastline and the Devon Street shops dissolved into silvery clouds. Beyond them, haze engulfed the distant port and sugar loaves.

Rain decided to have a competition with the waves thundering on the cliffs below. It tap danced on the roof, louder and louder, until it drummed the roaring waves into submission.

My thigh tickled. I glanced down to see a militant ant marching across my lap.

"Where did *you* come from?"

I scraped the tiny creature onto my palm.

Furious, the ant waved its miniscule legs. I was a million times its size, but it was up for the fight. The struggle between weak and strong was never-ending.

"Good for you," I said, setting the insect respectfully onto the dashboard.

Dad was famously absentminded. I wondered if he'd forgotten me.

As I reached for the door handle, he emerged from the gasworks. Oblivious to the downpour, he hunched over a rectangular shape sheltered in the folds of his jacket. Rivulets streamed down his polyester shirt as he sprinted toward me and tugged the passenger door open.

"Take care of this," he said, thrusting a wooden fruit box onto my lap.

The box was heavier than it looked. It was covered by a damp brown blanket that reeked of coal. An intriguing mound rose from the blanket's center. Dad slammed the door and sprinted to the driver's side.

Curious, I touched the mound. It flattened and became

still, as if it was trying hard not to be noticed. Emboldened, I ran my hand over the ridges of what felt like a bony spine. It was alive.

"Go on," Dad said as he slid into the driver's seat. "Take a look."

I raised a corner of the blanket. To my astonishment, a cheddar cheese nose-tip rose from the shadows. I gasped and extended a trembling finger. The cheddar cheese withdrew and made itself invisible.

Dad beamed at me, his blue eyes brimming with affection.

From the blanket came a timid meow.

"A kitten!"

An uncontrollable sensation surged down my arms. The young animal was helpless and alone in the world.

"Please don't be frightened," I whispered, lifting the blanket.

A skinny feline shivered onto his front feet. His coat was pale gray marked with dark brown stripes. The fur was matted with dried-up mud. A cobweb hung like a suspension bridge between his ears.

His imperfections only made my love for him stronger.

"What do you think of him?" I'd forgotten Dad was there.

The kitten's scrawny neck was barely strong enough to carry the weight of his head. One of his eyes, the left one, was glued shut.

"He's the best kitten in the world!"

"He could do with a clean-up," Dad said, smiling. "Did you notice something different about him?"

My father leaned across and draped the kitten's front paws over his fingers. To my amazement, each foot had an extra toe, attached to it like an afterthought. The extra toes made his feet wider.

"It's like he's wearing slippers. Is he deformed?"

"No, he's polydactyl. The old sailors loved them. They said a ship would never sink with one of these fellows on board. Polydactyls are lucky cats."

I ached to hold the animal's warmth and feel his softness, but he wasn't ready for that.

"Hello, lucky cat," I whispered, proffering my hand. "Where did he come from, Dad?"

The feline sniffed my fingers and retreated into the blanket's folds.

"Ginger found him hanging around the back of the coke pile."

The stoker Ginger had never struck me as an animal lover. I had yet to learn tenderness can flow from unlikely streams.

"He reckons this one belonged to a pack of wild cats that was poisoned last week."

My chest tightened. The horror was unthinkable.

I gasped. "Who would poison a whole family of cats?"

"People are capable of great cruelty," my father replied. "They can be worse than animals sometimes."

"Like in The War?"

Silence ballooned between us. Dad never talked about World War II, let alone why he'd stayed behind.

"Anyhow, this little fellow survived," he said, lifting the mood. "He's timid. Maybe that's what saved him."

"Do you think he was too nervous to follow the others and eat poison?"

"Could be."

"Are you sure he's a boy?"

"Ginger says so."

I raised the corner of the blanket again. Ribs jutted out from under the animal's fur. A scrawny excuse for a tail curved around his back legs.

It had been a long time since this cat had known love. Probably never had.

But his markings were beautiful.

"What happened to his eye?" I asked.

"Who knows? Maybe lost in a fight."

The Zephyr coughed to life.

"Can I keep him? *Please?*"

Dad clunked the gears into action. The wipers yawned and stretched across the windscreen.

"I haven't spoken to your mother about it. We'll have to wait and see."

"*Really?* I can keep him!"

Dad maintained the silence of the wise. I clutched the fruit box to my chest and lifted the blanket for another look.

"You're beautiful!" I breathed.

The kitten shook his tattered ears and beamed back at me through a single golden eye. Flecked with silver and circled with a smooth dark outline, it shimmered like the sun. In that instant, the kitten and I recognized each other. Our souls were meshed together in eternity.

A single thought clouded this moment of bliss. My glamorous, highly strung mother had an aversion to cats. She claimed they got on her Nerves. Everyone in our house lived in fear of Mum's Nerves. The Nerves, if they felt like it, could take over her entire being and destroy a weekend.

If Mum found out about the new kitten, she and the Nerves would probably kill all three of us.

Chapter Two

BLESSING IN HIDING

Our mother had no quarrel with birds and fish (*Look at the feathers! Those colors are enough to make a person believe in a higher being.*) Or farm animals (*useful*). She occasionally tossed our rambunctious dog, Fritz, a tennis ball. Even my white mice were tolerated, providing they stayed up the ladder inside the tower.

She loathed only two species. Her fear of rats was pathological. The plump rodents who lurked around the incinerator behind the clothesline were a source of terror. One glimpse and she'd gallop back inside the house, clutching her apron, screaming, *"Rat! Rat!"*

In a logical world, a woman who hated rats would warm to their natural predator. But Mum disliked felines almost as much. Cats, she said, were selfish, spiteful creatures that belonged only in barns.

"Let's not tell her," I said, tugging the headband elastic that was burrowing into a soft spot behind my ear.

"She is in a fragile state," Dad said.

"Her Nerves again?"

"No," he said, as the car toiled up the hill past the hospital. "The audition."

Mum lived and breathed for the annual Operatic Society productions. Glamorous parts were always taken by self-entitled sopranos, leaving our mother and her luscious contralto voice to scavenge for so-called character roles. These were usually evil, wounded women destined to suffer unspeakable humiliation or death. Mum claimed not to care. According to her, villains were more interesting.

Our family heaved a collective sigh of relief whenever she scored a part in a production, even if it meant she occasionally forgot to feed us.

"There's a contralto in *The King and I*?"

"Not exactly," Dad said. "The king's wife, Lady Thiang, is a mezzo soprano."

"Won't Geraldine go for it?"

Our next-door neighbor, Geraldine, was Mum's best friend and nemesis rolled into one. As the only *creative* women in the valley, they were conjoined by their devotion to the Arts. Unusual for their generation, both had held actual jobs before they were married. Inside her head, Mum was still a journalist. Likewise, Geraldine clung to her former identity as a professional actress, which gave her a dangerous edge with auditions. Geraldine was also a pedigreed mezzo soprano.

"Not necessarily," Dad said. "Your mother's convinced she has enough time to train herself to reach the high G."

"That's three whole notes out of her range."

I'd been listening to Mum's rich contralto since the womb. Keeping up with her vocal triumphs, knowing the difference between her chest notes and the dreaded high ones, was my way of maintaining intimacy with her.

"She needs to focus. Perhaps we'll keep this little chap a secret in the meantime."

I loved the idea of Dad and I having a secret.

The mound under the blanket remained motionless. The kitten seemed to be listening to our conversation. I rested my hand on the sharp edge of his spine. He cowered deeper into the box. The poor thing was petrified.

"Do you think it's his first time in a car?"

"He's feral. He won't have been this close to humans before. All these sounds and smells are new to him."

I lowered my face over the blanket.

"You're okay, boy," I whispered. "I'll look after you."

It was a miracle that this half-grown feline had escaped the mass murder of his family. I wanted to wrap him in my arms and protect him from wicked poisoners forever.

"Look at *that!*" Dad said, braking at Cutfield Road.

A vast white triangle rose against the freshly painted sky. Mount Taranaki towered above the windscreen and glistened before us. Its clefts and crevices stood out like veins on the body of an ancient god. All-knowing, ethereal, the near perfect cone claimed the soul of every creature who lived in its shadow. Generations of humans passed under its eternal gaze. The mountain witnessed all their weakness and vanity through their piteously short lifespans. And chose not to care.

Like every deity, Mount Taranaki demanded respect. Those who forgot to pay homage suffered punishment. Almost every winter, climbers tumbled down crevasses or froze to death on the Cone of Catastrophe. Dad occasionally helped out on rescue missions.

"I saw a couple fools in tennis shoes up there last weekend," he said, shaking his head. "They thought they were going to summit."

The Zephyr shuddered at the thought and hurtled down the hill. The cat swayed under the blanket and scrabbled to regain balance as we spun around the corner into Bracken Street.

"Those extra toes are coming in handy," Dad said, straightening the wheel.

Narrow and secluded with a short street carved up its middle, our glen was a mystical haven. Trees and ferns, dark green in their winter coats, bowed with moisture. Wooden houses scattered over the gentle concave slopes and oozed lazy spirals of smoke rose from their chimneys. Tucked away from the rest of the town, our glen was a miniature kingdom apart.

Across the road from our place, Mrs. Dooley was pegging sheets out on her line. Mum discouraged me from going over there, but I liked Mrs. Dooley. I curled my fingers in a surreptitious wave. Mrs. Dooley hoisted the washing basket on her hip and raised her free arm in reply.

A sage green Morris Minor crouched like a tortoise on the street outside our place. A good omen. Aunt Lila and Nana were paying one of their impromptu visits. Mum would be too busy wielding teacups, pretending to be in control of everything, to notice our stowaway.

Rising from rolling lawns and damp bush, our home seemed more unworldly than ever. Everybody had an opinion about our abode. Some called it a haunted house, others a fairy-tale castle. People said we must be rich, posh, or insane to live there. None of it was true, except maybe the last. By 1960s provincial New Zealand standards, we were the other side of normal.

Threads of mist coiled around the tower. Sprawled over four levels, if you included the basement and tower, the elaborate wooden folly gazed across the glen through hundreds of small rectangular windowpanes—and offered a million places to hide a cat.

Though I'd lived there since birth, I hadn't managed to explore all its nooks and crannies. I wasn't brave enough to squeeze through the manhole into the roof space above the upstairs bathroom, for instance—or creep into the darkest corners of the basement, where there was rumored to be an old well. Our walls were steeped in secrets. People were hardly going to notice an extra one with four feet and a cheese wedge nose-tip.

"What do you think of the new color?" Dad asked.

After months of death-defying ladder work, he'd only half-finished the Herculean task of painting the weatherboards. Mum oversaw the color palate, as usual. Her solution to modernizing any type of period woodwork was to smother it in pastel-shaded enamel paint.

"Not sure about the lime green."

"Chartreuse, your mother calls it."

I appreciate my parents' bravado even more today. In a conventional town in a remote little country that worshipped at the monogrammed slippers of Victorian Britain, they dared to stand out. And paint their castle lime green.

I clutched my cargo as we roared up the driveway and slid to a halt in the basement.

Dad helped me out of the car with the box, which was more unwieldy than it looked. Strains of Rodgers and Hammerstein drifted from the living room piano above our heads.

We exchanged glances.

"You go first," I said.

"Actually, I should see how those prints are drying," Dad said, striding toward his basement darkroom. "Ten minutes should do it."

Mum's voice rose above the piano. She was in good form.

I had two options for smuggling the cat inside. The most direct route involved passing Dad's darkroom, heading outside past the fishpond, darting across the front lawn, and climbing the top flight of steps. Though our front door had an imposing brass handle, it was never locked (except when we went away on holiday and left the key under the doormat). From there, the stowaway and I could step into the entrance hall. We'd then sprint across the threadbare oriental carpet, up the stairs, around the dog leg under the giant stained-glass window, onto the landing, and into my bedroom.

If, however, the living room door was open, we'd be in full view of our visitors and the piano.

The back door was a safer option. Clasping the box and its occupant, I teetered out from under the house, up the path along the side of the house, past the clothesline to the back steps.

"What have we here?"

I froze and looked up.

"Don't tell anyone!"

A conspiratorial smile settled on Aunt Lila's lips. With her sparse short hair and offhand manner, my aunt unnerved some people, but I adored her. Funny and kind, she had a mind sharper than a dentist's probe. More importantly, she could be trusted.

"Here," she said, easing the box from my hands. "Where are we taking this?"

In those days, it was universally acknowledged that a woman who sidestepped marriage and motherhood was a failure. Simultaneously pitied, patronized, and feared, my maiden aunt hovered on the fringes of adult society. Had she been born fifty years later, I imagine she would have flourished as an accomplished scientist or academic of some sort, an independent woman challenging the patriarchy.

Her attention focused on the box, she pivoted toward my brother's museum off the kitchen.

"Not *that* way!"

The adults called her Violet, which was her real name. They expected her to make sandwiches and pour tea for them while keeping her opinions to herself. Lila's role, they believed, was to feed and care for the matriarch. Our aunt did much more than that. She escorted Nana on extensive North Island tours, visiting the nine adult children, who were mostly on farms. Lila offered the thirty-two grandchildren an open invitation to stay during school holidays. As a quiet sideline (and to save her sanity, no doubt), she bet on horses and played bridge and killer lawn bowls.

Lila stopped and turned. I followed her herringbone tweed trousers down the back hall and up the stairs. When we reached the landing, she sank into the big old armchair, dyed bright crimson during one of Mum's home decorating binges.

"Let's take a look," she said, settling the box on her knees.

I knelt beside her as she raised a corner of the blanket. The cat and Lila locked gazes.

Lila saw the world differently from other people. She seldom spoke. When she did, I listened.

"Hmm," she said, after a long pause. "A wise old soul."

"You think so?"

"Handsome coat. He could do with fattening up, though."

I pointed out the extra toes.

"You're joining a fine tradition," Lila said. "The author Ernest Hemingway loved polydactyl cats. Maybe you'll be a writer, too, some day."

Having failed my last spelling test, I was convinced nothing was less likely.

"How do you think this one lost his eye?"

"He may not have lost it," she said. "It could be an infection. Once he gets to know you better, he might let you bathe it."

"How would I do that?"

"Just dab the eye with a soft cloth dipped in warm water," Lila said. "You'll need to tame him first."

"Tame?"

I'd never tamed anything. The white mice took a chunk out of me whenever they had a chance.

"If you're kind to him, he might learn to trust you. Don't rush things. What are you going to call him?"

I studied the cat. He was too fragile and frightened to be called anything bouncy.

"There's an "M" on his forehead," I said. "How about Mickey?"

"That's a fine name," Lila said.

I leaned over to christen Mickey with a pat, but he slithered out of my reach. He sprang out of the box and disappeared under the chair.

I dropped to the floor, lifted the chair's frilly skirt, and peered into the darkness. A single eye beamed back. I moaned in disappointment.

"Give it time," Lila said. "He could turn out to be a blessing."

"How will I know?"

My aunt crouched beside me. "Sometimes, people don't appreciate a blessing till it's gone."

My aunt could seem sadder than the moon sometimes.

"*Violet!*" Mum's voice echoed up the stairwell. "You're needed at the piano."

Lila and I froze. There wasn't a sound from under the chair.

"Down in a minute!" Lila called.

"What do I do *now*?"

"He'll settle once he's had something to eat and drink," Lila said, standing up and resting her hand on the balustrade. "Why not bring him something from the fridge while we're rehearsing?"

I was reluctant to leave Mickey, but he had to be hungry. I waited for the piano to start up again. After a few introductory chords, Mum's voice launched into an impassioned rendition of the powerful love song "Something Wonderful."

Our mother prided herself on voice projection. From the tones reverberating up the stairwell, I could tell she'd entered a self-hypnotic trance, Lady Thiang inhabiting every cell in her body.

I tiptoed downstairs and past the No Entry sign on the door of Jim's museum. The room was originally for a maid. Mum said she was the only servant left around here these days. Though I thought it unfair Jim had been given his own personal museum *with a lock and key*, I now realize it was an inspired act of parenting on Mum and Dad's part. All teenagers should have a museum of their own. Evil smells wafted from under the door.

The kitchen was quiet, apart from the gurgle of the cream-colored fridge perched on its spindly metal legs. The antiquated fridge ran on gas and, like everything else in our household, had a temperamental streak. If ignored for too long, the appliance erupted and leaked pungent fluid over the vinyl floor. I opened the door and pinched a ball of ground beef and some bacon. After a quick glance over my shoulder, I tiptoed to the crockery cupboard and stole a side plate and saucer. Mickey needed food and drink. I put my head down and crept toward the stairs.

"Going somewhere?"

My brother stepped out of his museum and into my path. His handsome brooding features gave him the air of an elongated James Dean (who, at five feet seven, was seven inches shorter than Jim). Everything about my brother—his looks, his laughter, and his passions for unusual hobbies—seemed magnified, more intense than anyone else. I was too young and intimidated by his moods to understand he was absorbed in pursuit of an identity our society was too ignorant and unevolved to understand.

"No," I said, peering over his shoulder to see if he'd added anything new to his collection. A snakeskin hung on the wall. An armadillo shell cast an eerie shadow. His latest obsession was taxidermy.

"What's that for?" he said, pointing at the meat. "Midnight snack?"

"It's for . . . the mice."

Jim narrowed his gaze and beckoned me into the museum.

"Since when have your mice been carnivores?" he asked, stroking a glassy-eyed ferret that had reportedly died in its sleep.

I balked at the stench of formaldehyde.

"You're hiding an animal, aren't you?" he said.

Chapter Three

DIRT MATTERS

My furtive attempts to coax Mickey out from his bunker under the chair on the landing failed. Though he was sure to emerge some time. I worried he might appear the moment Mum or my brother walked by.

Before going to bed that night, I wedged my door open with a battered copy of *Winnie the Pooh*. Once the household was asleep, I was confident Mickey would creep out and snuggle up with me.

Next morning, I yawned awake, stretched an arm across the candlewick bedspread and fumbled for the crescent shape of a feline.

Rejection hit like the frosty thud of a dumper wave on black sand at Oakura beach.

I had yet to learn that a relationship can't be willed into existence. No matter how much I craved the cat's affection, my control over the outcome was minimal. Whether he chose to return my affection was entirely up to him.

A familiar cacophony wafted up the stairwell. Down in the kitchen, Mum was rattling pans in the kitchen sink. The museum door slammed. My brother was no doubt embarking on some macabre activity. I hitched my flannelette pajama pants and crept onto the landing.

The stained-glass window scattered rainbows across the floorboards. Wind whined through the broken pane Dad hadn't got around to fixing.

A whiff of Brylcreem wafted on a cloud of steam, a sure sign my father was shaved and up a ladder somewhere. With the bathroom next to my bedroom, I had intimate knowledge of family ablutions. Our father was always first in, gasping through a three-minute blast of cold water after his hot shower. The health benefits of cold water and ice baths have only recently been rediscovered. Back then, we regarded his regime a remnant from quaint nineteenth-century notions about manliness.

Eerie silence hovered over the landing. Dust particles danced in a band of sunlight outside Jim's bedroom. Surely Mickey hadn't scaled the ladder inside his door? White mice would make a delicious breakfast for a cat . . .

I sprawled on the floor in front of the chair and lifted its outrageous skirt. Darkness gave way to shapes. A spider drifted like a circus performer on a rope. Deeper in the gloom, a yellow marble rested against the back chair leg.

"You've got a kitten, don't you?" a voice said.

I banged my head against the edge of the chair and looked up. Mary.

"Owwww!" I said, rubbing the hot spot on my forehead. "Don't tell Mum! Or Jim. He's looking for animals to stuff."

Dark curls framed my sister's face. She gazed down at me through soft hazel eyes. Mary was like Dad in many ways. Reserved and thoughtful, she never said the first thing that came into her head. She even looked like our father sometimes.

"It's okay," she said.

"I can't find him."

"The kitten? I saw him just now," she said, sinking to her knees beside me. "He's at the back there. See?"

Squinting into the darkness, I could make out the curve of a spine, the matching peaks of ears. The yellow marble was actually his one eye, cautiously surveying his adopted space.

"Mickey!" I cried, almost bursting with relief and happiness.

The cat pretended not to hear.

"Isn't he beautiful?"

"I can't tell," Mary replied with her usual tact. "Has he got a sandbox?"

"A what?"

"Well, you're putting food *into* him, right?"

"Oh . . . I see!"

I'd been thinking of Mickey as a mobile teddy bear, not an animal with plumbing needs.

Mary stood up and rubbed her knees. I admired her long skinny legs and olive skin.

"Put some clothes on," she said. "We'll find something."

Since Mary had become a teenager, she'd stopped playing dolls with me and developed bewildering obsessions. When she wasn't shut away listening to the Beach Boys, she was across the street watching *Dr. Kildare* on TV at Melissa's house.

My chest thudded with excitement. Maybe Mickey would bring us close and make us best friends again. I hurried to my room and dived into my playsuit and pink cardigan.

Almost every thread we wore was made by Mum. People never said, "I love you," unless they were drunk or looney. Emotions were kept bottled like peaches in Mum's pantry. We were expected to follow the rules set by repressed British imperialists. Making our clothes was Mum's way of wrapping us in love, yet the care and labor she poured into those garments was taken for granted. My sister and I longed for machine-made outfits from C.C. Ward's or Farmers on Devon Street.

Mary escorted me downstairs, out the front door, down the top flight of concrete steps, across the lawn to the fishpond. We ducked under the archway, past Dad's darkroom door and into the depths of the basement.

Under the house was a scary place. Reeking of masculinity, it resembled a deranged giant's playground. Old paint buckets, rags and newspapers, glass jars and gardening gear were strewn through the shadows. In the filtered light beside the darkroom, planks of timber piled on top of each other. According to Dad, they were left over from the house's construction back in the early 1900s. Old man Curtis insisted on having the timber stacked and dried on the ridge above the glen for three years before the builders even started. Sour, harsh smells wafted from the darkness beyond the woodpiles. At night, ghostly wails rose from its bowels. Under the house was a place to avoid, unless I had to retrieve my bike.

Mum's heels tap-tapped over the kitchen linoleum overhead.

"Wait here," Mary said, disappearing into a crevice behind a woodpile.

After what felt like a school term, she clambered back into the daylight. She was clutching an old shoe box. My sister shook dust from her hair and handed me the prize.

"You'd better line it with something," she said, pointing at a heap of yellowing newspapers.

I tugged a *Daily News* from the bottom of the pile. KENNEDY SHOT DEAD. The memory of that November day three years earlier sent a shiver down my neck. I placed the dead president on top of a large paint can and smoothed his smiling face. Dad's words echoed inside my head. *People can be capable of great cruelty.*

Mary grabbed a crisp new edition and patted BRIDE OF THE YEAR FINALISTS—MORE RADIANT THAN EVER into the shoe box.

"Where's the sand?"

"I'll think of something," she said.

A yellow hula hoop drooped off a nail. A battered dolls' pram lay on its side next to a pyramid of old bricks.

We crawled out under the camellia bushes below the dining room window.

"Dig," Mary said.

"In *this?* It's not sand!"

"Go on."

I sank my hands into the sticky, volcanic soil. The radiant brides beamed out from the newspaper inside the box. I felt a guilty thrill smothering them with clumps of earth.

"Anyone seen Fritz?"

We stopped dead still. Deep and theatrical, the voice was unmistakable.

"Not for ages," Mary called up to Mum on the veranda. Our dog was often off on adventures.

Mum's heels clicked over the wooden slats. "What are you girls up to?"

Resplendent in a yellow satin kimono, our mother peered down at us. Her lips were vivid red, her prominent eyes circled with black liner and flicked up at the edges. Layers of stage makeup flattened her complexion, which highlighted her chiseled cheekbones. An elaborate black wig teetered over her charcoal brows. Scarlet toenails peeked from her gold high-heeled evening sandals. A cigarette smoldered in her hand.

"Just a game," Mary said.

"That so?" Mum said, leaning over the balustrade and tapping ash over the camellia bushes.

"Yes, it's called Buried Treasure," I said, trying to sound offhand.

"She's going to bury plastic soldiers from the Weet-Bix packet in there," Mary added. "Then we'll have a competition to see who can find them first."

"I see," our mother said, narrowing her eyes and inhaling. "Like a Christmas pudding?"

My sister nodded. I loved her more than the moon.

"What do you think?" Mum said, raising her arms and twirling in a spiral of smoke. "Is this not the first wife of the king of Siam?"

"What about Geraldine?" I asked. "Isn't she getting the part?"

Our mother squared her shoulders.

"Haven't you heard *the news*?"

Barely able to conceal her glee, Mum explained Geraldine was out of the picture because she'd taken on too much. Already swamped in little children, all three of them recently adopted, our neighbor had just accepted a job teaching home economics at the Intermediate School.

"Didn't she say she wanted Lady Thiang more than anything?"

Our mother replied with a melodramatic shrug.

In the oppressive pre-feminist era, *taking on too much* was scandalous behavior for a housewife. Among the suspects were ones who didn't have dinner on the table on the dot of six P.M., forgot to put curlers in their hair and insisted on joint bank accounts with their husbands. Punishments ranged from exclusion from afternoon tea parties to cool stares over cake stands at school galas.

"There's only one Lady Thiang in town now," Mum said, flapping her butterfly sleeves and floating to the front door.

"Oh, and by the way, I'll need help with meals this week. Mary, you've got homework, so that means you, Helen," she said, pointing the cigarette like a wand. "What's that lump on your forehead? Did you bump into something?"

"No."

"Doesn't look too serious," she said, drifting into the shadows. "And mind my Czar Japonica. It brings the first flowers of spring. Strong and yet so fragile."

The Czar Japonica upstaged all the other camellia bushes in Mum's garden. With vivid pink flowers and yellow stamens blazing against dark shiny leaves, the shrub shared some of her attributes. Though vigorous, tall, and generous in display, the spectacular blooms wilted when cut and brought inside.

Mary brushed mud off her knees and strode up the front steps two at a time.

"Hey! Where you going?" I called.

"I've got a history test on Tuesday."

A typical youngest child, I was a master at avoiding responsibility. I was conveniently blind to many things—including the extent to which my sister watched over me.

Once the reassuring sound of piano notes wafted from the living room window, I heaved the shoe box upstairs to the landing. Hard as I tried, the thing was too big and unwieldy to squeeze underneath the armchair's skirt.

I was left with no choice but to carry it, along with its earthy contents, into my bedroom and hide it in the dusty cave underneath my wire-woven mattress. Taking care of an illegal cat was proving more arduous than imagined.

After checking the coast was clear, I tiptoed back onto the landing and slid bacon leftovers under the chair.

I had no idea of Mickey's culinary preferences. A few hours later, the bacon was gone, though the cat continued to cower under the landing chair. Heartened that he was at least eating, I peeked under my bed.

Mickey may have been a recluse, but he knew what a litterbox was for.

Chapter Four

WHERE FAIRIES COME FROM

As I sit here at my desk while Jonah flosses his teeth on the edge of the computer screen, I'm tempted not to tell you about the fairies. It would be simpler to sidestep the subject and relieve you of any concern I might have forgotten to take my medication.

However, experience has taught me that overlooking the fairies would be unwise, possibly even dangerous.

Let's not waste time getting into an argument about the existence of fairies. I'm not even sure that's the right word for them. The ones I knew didn't look like picture book fairies with tutus, wings, and wands. More abstract than that, they were a visceral source of benevolent power and light. If that sounds strange, it's probably worth mentioning that much of human life is governed by invisible forces.

Not so long ago, I was asked to give a talk in one of Tokyo's largest bookstores. The host invited me to stand on a platform in front of a huge poster-sized photo of the Bracken Street house.

When I pointed out my upstairs bedroom and explained how magical beings visited me there at night, the audience became transfixed. Unnerved by the intense atmosphere in the room, I sensed things needed lightening up. I shrugged and added the fairies were probably a figment of my imagination.

As the translator's voice faded, the audience looked alarmed. The room emitted a single gasp as the poster toppled off its hinges and crashed on the floor behind me.

I should have known. Magical entities demand a lifetime's respect.

Anyone who's been in a relationship with non-physical beings understands how powerful they can be. Looking back, I'm sure they were involved with Mickey's arrival. He was a manifestation of the love they knew I hungered for.

My relationship with fairies had unlikely beginnings. I was about eight years old when Mum decreed my sister needed her own bedroom. It shouldn't have been a big deal. Mary had put up with me longer than most big sisters would.

We'd shared the gracious airy room off the top veranda since the dawn of time. It was a beautiful bedroom. Tall French doors opened on a balcony that curved past Jim's bedroom window to another set of doors leading to the room our parents shared.

In the mornings, sunlight stripes played across the bright green curtains. Outside, beyond the balcony a broad ribbon of sea flattened itself against the horizon. Ships' horns echoed from the port, as if they couldn't bear to leave our part of the world. When I woke and saw my sister across the room, her dark hair spilled like seaweed over her pillow, my world was complete.

More than a big sister, Mary had nursed me through sleepless nights with chicken pox, measles, the tonsillectomy and the first eye operation. At bedtime, she'd switch on the big old radio and we'd listen to the comedy show *Life With Dexter*. If I was still awake after thirty minutes, she'd turn the radio off, and spring into her bed. She was my queen.

The little room was more a cupboard than a bedroom. Like Jim's museum, it was probably designed for a homesick servant girl. Tucked next to the bathroom across the landing, it had a high ceiling shaped to echo the roofline's angles. Double windows, each with twelve small rectangular panes, overlooked the street as it sloped up to the dead end, and the vertiginous zigzag beyond. It offered a great view of wooden houses across the street and neighbors' gardens unfurling in vivid mosaics below.

Mum let me choose the wallpaper for my new room. An arrangement of trees rambling over a pale background looked fun and breezy in the pattern book. Once up on the walls, it took on a new sinister life, sprawling from floor to ceiling in a tangle of vegetation.

Everything in the room was secondhand and dotted with wood borer, but that didn't matter. We hadn't heard of IKEA. Mum *updated* everything with her paintbrush. A pastel blue wardrobe loomed over the foot of my bed and filtered dim reflections through a tall, mildewed mirror. The kidney-shaped glass tabletop on my bedside dresser flaunted an exuberant floral skirt. A wind-up alarm clock crouched on top of a pile of library books.

On my first night, I invented nightmares so I could run to my parents' bed and wedge between their warm limbs. Their tolerance waned. Dad escorted me back to my cupboard and spoke sternly.

The following night, abandoned in the depths of the creepy wallpaper forest, I ran out of ideas. I pulled the top sheet up to my chin and studied the ceiling. A globular tear formed in the corner of my good eye.

Something glinted high in the corner above the door. At first, I thought it was the tear, but the light winked again, more brightly this time. It wasn't from the streetlight below, or the milk truck that rattled through the glen before dawn. This was different, a sparkly conglomeration of energy.

As nights passed, the presence relaxed and expanded across the ceiling. Thousands of effervescent particles swirled and became a shimmer, twinkling with goodwill. Mesmerized, I watched the twinkling light waft down toward me.

I lay still as the ecstatic force enveloped me in sensations of love and joy, tinged with a happy kind of mischief. It was glorious. I had no idea where the presence came from, but it was powerful and empathic. It seemed to have seeped down from the mountain, through damp native forests and crystal streams into my room.

Before long, the shimmering particles and I started communicating. Not in words, but in thoughts. I asked if they were actual fairies. They didn't deny it.

The magical beings and I reached an arrangement. If I unscrewed my window latch last thing at night, they would glide the window open the following day at 7:10 A.M. on the dot. It worked a treat.

Every morning, I woke to a wave of cool air combing my cheek, accompanied by a gentle scraping sound. I'd roll over just in time to watch the window glide open, seemingly of its own accord. The alarm clock's spindly hands pointed at ten past seven. Exactly.

It was a miracle, and one I chose to keep secret for many years. Decades later, some new owners of the house kindly let me take a tour. It had all been beautifully renovated inside and out. When we reached my old bedroom, and I asked if fairies were still opening the window, the owner assured me it had been fitted with a new lock.

Chapter Five

IN SEARCH
OF SOUL

Mickey roosted under the chair on the landing day and night. Though I was hurt by his rejection, I recognized that his retiring nature made him an ideal fugitive. Mum was too engrossed in Lady Thiang to notice anything. Fritz was away on another of his extended jaunts.

Like any normal family of that time, we ate red meat three times a day, so there was no shortage of ground beef and sausages in the fridge. Every morning, I waited for Jim to ride off on his bike to Boys' High. Once the coast was clear, I went into the kitchen and sneaked leftovers. The pattern was repeated after school, without hitch so far.

Tension mounted in our household as audition day loomed.

My mother's voice rose over the whistle of the pressure cooker as she put all her passion into Lady Thiang's signature song. She was determined to master it. She looked up, noticed me, and asked, "Where is my crown prince?"

"The usual," I said, shaking frozen peas into boiling water.

"Tell him dinner is about to be served in the Royal Hall."

I banged on the museum door.

Wednesday night dinners were always in the dining room, which, paradoxically, was on the opposite side of the house from the kitchen.

Condensation streamed down the kitchen windows as I loaded the trolley with serving dishes. Carrots and potatoes from Dad's garden sweated under their lids.

"What's this?" I asked, lifting a scrap of wrinkled paper from the kitchen table.

"Throw it away," Mum said.

I smoothed the paper.

"It's the cast list for *The King and I.*"

"Have you set the table?"

"Ages ago," I said, clearing my throat to read aloud. "*Lady Thiang is the most glamorous role in the production. As the king's chief wife, she's looked up to and admired by all the wives and children.*"

Mum wrangled the pressure cooker lid open with a hiss.

"*Powerful and determined, she's the only one with enough authority to persuade Anna to visit the dying king* . . . Wow, Mum. This sounds like you!"

"Take the trolley through, will you?"

"*Our producer is looking for someone with a strong mezzo voice and exceptional acting abilities. This role is made for a young performer, who* . . ."

"*Dinner's ready!*" Mum bellowed. Sweat gleamed on her forehead.

"What's wrong?" I asked, pouring the peas into a bowl.

"I'm hardly a spring chicken, am I?" she said, slapping the corned beef on a platter.

"But you *are!*"

"Really?" she said, a coquettish smile forming on her cupid bow lips.

"Everyone at school says you're the youngest Mum," I said, wielding the trolley toward the door.

"Is that so?"

Mum raised her head and tilted it slightly to one side. It was the perfect angle for a spotlight to catch her high cheekbones, the Hollywood eyelids—every aspect of her beautiful face.

"You're right," she said. "The role's made for me."

I wheeled the trolley through to the dining room. Jim's tropical fish tank bubbled in an alcove next to Dad's new record turntable with speakers the size of small houses. The water in the aquarium was murky. One of the fish was a suspected cannibal.

Presiding over his usual spot at the head of the table, Dad rasped his carving knife across the sharpener with crisp, regular strokes. Mary sat quietly under the Van Gogh print Mum had cut out of a book and framed. *The Church of Auvers* had an eerie gothic tower like our place. Van Gogh's sky was oppressive. On the path leading to the church, a woman was bent in despair.

"I smelled a gas leak outside Collier's music shop today," Mary said.

The town gas pipes were ancient. The slightest earth tremor cracked their arthritic joints, so they emitted toxic odors above ground. Dad had trained us to suss out a leak from fifty paces.

"I smelled it, too," I added.

Mary rolled her eyes.

"I *did*!"

"Thank you, girls," Dad said. "I'll look into it tomorrow. And remember, if any of your friends or their parents smell gas, ask them to report it immediately. Because—"

"We know," Mary said. "It's poisonous."

"With any luck, it won't be for much longer," Dad said. "Once we get natural gas reticulated, it won't be so dangerous."

My father was the only person on Earth who used the word *reticulate*. Whenever I asked what it meant and he started talking about networks of pipes carrying natural gas underground, possibly through the entire North Island someday, I'd stifle a yawn and wonder if my white mice needed their bowls topping up. Six months later I'd have to ask what reticulate meant again. He never took offense at my lack of interest. Reticulation was so fascinating to him; he'd lecture a fence post about the subject if it was willing to listen.

Mum swept in, a fresh coat of scarlet on her lips, her dark

hair sculptured from an afternoon in rollers. If I could grow up to be half as glamorous, I thought, my life would be complete.

"Who should we invite to opening night?" she said, placing the corned beef in front of Dad with a flourish.

"We're not starting till everyone's here," Dad said, then turned to me. "Where's your brother?"

"Veronica from the *Daily News* is a definite," Mum went on. "I suppose we could ask poor Geraldine along, if she can bear to see me in the role. Though I suppose she *could* learn a thing or two from my interpretation . . ."

Jim burst into the room and plunked himself on the chair next to mine. His school uniform was wrinkled, the shorts coated in dust. His fingernails were dark crescents.

"Wash your hands, young man," Dad said.

Jim thrust his hands in the air and stormed out. Remembering my fugitive, I smuggled a slice of meat into the pocket of my bellbottoms.

"Did you know," Mum said, settling into her seat. "*The King and I* has several roles for children?"

"Wow!" I said, almost choking on my potatoes. "Do they dance?"

"No. The royal children do a little march for the King and that's about it. You can come along and audition with me if you like."

"I'd *love* to!" My dream of dancing on stage was about to come true.

"Not you, dear," Mum said, slicing into her corned beef, which could just as well been my liver. "They're looking for dark-haired children. Besides, you're having surgery, Helen, aren't you? I meant *you*, Mary."

My sister looked as if she was about to have a molar pulled.

"I'm too tall," Mary pleaded. "All the kids in the movie were little."

I was away at school camp when *The King and I* movie

with Yul Brynner and Deborah Kerr was in town. It left a
vital gap in my musical theater knowledge.

"The show's running for a week and it won't finish till ten
thirty at night. They need children who're old enough to stay
up till the king dies in the last scene."

Jim slunk back into his seat.

"It's all very exciting," Dad said, "but do you have a
Plan B?"

"What do you mean?" Mum asked, taken aback.

"Well, if for some reason the audition doesn't work out?"
he said, pouring white sauce over his corned beef.

Mum blanched and raised a hand to her throat like an operatic heroine who'd been stabbed.

"Eric says the part's mine for the taking."

"Yes, but things change fast in the artistic world. How
about reviving your journalistic career? You always say they
were the best four years of your life."

A dreamy expression drifted across her face. Mum was
about to float off on one of her monologues.

"Can I feed the fish?" I asked.

"I was just twenty-one when I won the nation's most pres-
tigious singing competition," she said. "It was unheard of for
a contralto to win anything, let alone first prize. They gave
me a diamond ring. I was about to sail for Europe and further my vocal studies. Then the war came . . ."

"You told us before," I said, tapping flakes into the fish
tank.

"The men went overseas to fight and left their day jobs behind. For the first time, a woman could step up and have a
real vocation. It was marvelous."

The flakes spiraled on the oily surface.

"Are there any fish left in here?"

Dad shot me a warning look.

"I'll get dessert," Mary said, standing to scrape plates and
load them on the trolley.

"I could hardly believe my luck when I landed that job on

the *Hawera Star*," Mum went on. "They trained me to produce serious journalism, not just cake recipes for the women's page. I covered court cases, council meetings. I even interviewed families of soldiers who'd died."

Dad focused on a bubble in the wallpaper above the doorway. Jim chewed his thumbnail.

"At the end of the war, the men came home and wanted their old jobs back. Like every other woman, I obliged and swapped my pay packet for . . . all this."

A familiar, unpleasant feeling settled in my stomach. Living with us was no match for the glorious newsroom. I watched the flakes dissolve and sink into the murk.

"Why don't you ask Veronica for a job?" Dad asked.

Veronica Pentecost was extraordinary. Having dodged motherhood and the employment needs of returning soldiers, she'd glued herself to the subeditors' desk to become one of the most feared and revered news editors in the country. She smoked cigars and could shoot down a cliché at fifty paces.

"Be realistic," Mum said. "There are only two females on the staff besides Veronica. They're both career women with no children. The newspaper's never going to hire me."

Mum lowered her knife.

"Anyway, just wait and see the reviews for Lady Thiang," she said, reaching for a cigarette packet on the sideboard. "This role will set me on a new path."

The phone blared from the bottom of the stairs. Dad frowned and excused himself to handle another dreaded evening call from the gasworks. The pressure was down again, and housewives were complaining they couldn't light their ovens.

I lowered my spoon into Mum's latest culinary discovery—bright pink instant pudding sprinkled with coconut. Mary gave me a gentle kick under the table. She was resting her hand on her chin, with her forefinger pointing discreetly sideways toward the open dining room door.

My heart stopped. A small, feline shape was creeping down the stairs. Tail looped low, ears flattened, it moved like a panther taking stealthy liquid steps.

"I think it's time you and I had trip to town together," Mum said, swiveling her attention to me. "And maybe a little talk."

Mary studied her plate. The figure stopped and looked at us. His saucer eye gleamed through the shadows. Before I could do anything, Mickey put his head through a gap in the balustrade and meowed.

"What's that?" Mum said, startled. "It sounded like a—"

I sat rigid and waited for Jim to blow my cover. He was more interested in something outside the windows, however.

"That laundry door's squeaking again," Dad said, striding back from his phone call. "I'll grease it over the weekend."

"The sky's red," my brother said quietly.

Mum and Dad followed his gaze. The silence was profound, unsettling.

"It's just the sunset," Dad said after a long pause.

"It can't be," Jim said. "The sun went down ages ago."

"May we leave the table?" Mary asked.

"Do you think it's safe for them to go outside?" Mum asked under her breath.

"I don't see why not," Dad replied.

The sweet plastic taste of instant pudding lingered in our mouths as we filed outside to the back garden. The sky was fierce and beautiful, as if an arsonist had poured gasoline over the Milky Way and set it alight. We stood gazing up, awestruck.

"What is it?" I asked.

"Nothing to be afraid of," Dad said, churning coins in his pocket. "It's the Aurora Australis."

I could tell he was lying to protect us from something terrible.

"It's a nuclear test," Jim said.

Dad didn't respond. Thousands of miles away, on the idyllic Pacific atoll of Mururoa, a clear blue sky was turning violent orange. A vast radioactive mushroom was towering into space. The lagoon was seething like a cauldron while coconut trees were flattened by the force of the explosion. It was raining dead fish and mollusks.

French President Charles de Gaulle described the spectacle as "beautiful." After that test, and the many more that followed, radiation levels soared across the Pacific, reaching as far as our homeland. Some of the bombs were 200 times stronger than the ones dropped on Japan during the war.

I needed Mickey.

"It's freezing," I said, leaving them to stare up at the sky.

Sharp yapping echoed from inside the house. Fritz was back. I followed the high-pitched barks to the kitchen.

Up on the counter next to the bread slicer, Mickey was arched like a Halloween cat. Below him, Fritz pranced on his hind legs, barking and snarling. With every bounce, Fritz jumped higher and showed more teeth.

"Down, boy!"

Fritz ignored me. I ran forward to grab Mickey. The cat recoiled and tensed his claws. As I reached for him, everything went into slow motion. Mickey soared over my hands, high above Fritz's snapping jaws. He landed neatly on the vinyl tiles of the counter next to the oven. Fritz stood dumbfounded as Mickey bolted down the hall past the museum. I chased after him, slamming the kitchen door behind me to keep Fritz inside.

Mickey galloped upstairs. Panting after him, I arrived on the landing just in time to see the tip of his tail disappear under the armchair.

I collapsed on the floor and leaned against the chair. Downstairs, voices were laced with apprehension and wonder, interspersed with reassuring sounds from Dad.

This so-called lucky cat was proving to be nothing but trouble.

"I know you're a wild animal, Mickey," I said, taking the slice of corned beef from my pocket. "You don't have to like me."

The meat was squishy and wet with white sauce.

"But you could at least trust me," I said, nudging the beef under the chair.

Downstairs, Dad was shutting Fritz in the laundry. Mickey would be safe for the night.

A hot tear trickled down my cheek.

"Mickey, I can't keep this up much longer. Why do you hate me?"

The chair's skirt rippled. Spellbound, I watched a stripey paw slide out from the shadows to rest on the back of my hand. I didn't move a muscle. With its seven toes, the paw was wide as a mitten, its pads warm and squishy as baked beans on toast. The cat caressed my skin with a gentle squeeze.

I drew a breath as something profound happened. Mickey's soul touched mine.

I am here for you, it said.

Chapter Six

ILLEGALLY BLONDE

Like Mickey, I was a born misfit. For the first two years of life, I was completely bald. People would stop Mum in the street to compliment her on her baby boy. When she corrected them, they shook their heads in bewilderment and asked when I was going to grow hair. As if she knew. It was embarrassing, even for a baby.

When I finally managed to sprout a crop of white curls, people went berserk and said how adorable I was. Their adulation was addictive. That was before my blond tresses mutated to mousey brown. Cuteness and I were parting ways.

Anxious to look my best for dance class, I opened the bathroom cabinet. It was a mess, as usual. On the bottom shelf, a pile of scruffy toothbrushes collapsed over a strangulated tube of Pepsodent. Mum's coral colored Cutex nail polish jostled for position with Bakelite combs, a brush smothered in various shades of hair, a bottle of castor oil, a blue tin of Nivea cream, two packets of Lifebuoy soap, and a tube of Clearasil.

The middle shelf, devoted to Dad's obsession with first aid, featured liniment, ointment, and a collection of rolled-up crepe bandages, the largest being for sprained ankles. I remembered how Dad's hands had trembled with tenderness when he wrapped the big bandage around Mary's ankle after she fell out of the cherry tree on the bottom lawn. Mum took a dinner tray up to her room that night. They treated her like a movie star.

Maybe someday I'd get lucky, fall off my bike, and let them fuss around me like blowflies. Or have the eye operation.

On the third shelf, Fixodent denture cream was squeezed in alongside a Gillette razor, shaving brush and cream, blades, a sticky bottle of Old Spice, a well- rifled packet of Aspro, Nyal decongestant cough mixture *(Breathe freely in two minutes!)*, and a jar of Vick's VapoRub.

I noticed a new addition to the top shelf—a discreet white cardboard box, about the size of a wallet. Mum's name was typed on the front with a prescription from Dr. Forrest. I prized it open. Inside were packets of little while pills, one for every day of the week. I hoped she wasn't seriously sick.

To my relief, the small brown bottle was still hiding in the corner of the top shelf behind the Listerine.

I took it down and examined the skull-and-crossbones label: POISON. It was only peroxide, for heaven's sake.

I poured the clear, sharp-smelling fluid over a comb and scraped it through my hair. My scalp started burning. The bleach was working. Or killing me. My hair darkened with fluid. I covered it with the headband and let it set.

On the way to my bedroom, I made a detour and knelt in front of the chair on the landing.

"You okay, boy?"

A single eye flashed like the new traffic light they'd installed on Devon Street.

Living rough at the gasworks had honed Mickey's survival skills. Against all odds, he'd managed to avoid enemies inside our house for nearly a week.

Mum swept out of their bedroom and tripped over my feet.

"Ow!" she said, flapping her kimono sleeves. "What are you doing down there?"

Hot with panic, I scrabbled for an answer.

"Looking for a marble."

"Haven't you grown out of those things?"

In an era of strictly defined gender roles, it wasn't done for girls to play marbles when they could be putting ribbons in a doll's hair.

"I have actually," I said, willing Mickey to stay still and quiet. "Margaret wants my old ones. She's collecting them."

"You're not still seeing that girl?"

Mum was concerned about my lack of suitable friends. Though I liked most kids my own age, we seldom shared the same interests. To make up for my lack of social skills, Mum once invited a tribe of children I barely knew to celebrate my birthday. The freedom and novelty of the house sent them crazy. They ran screaming up and down the stairs, while I spent most of the party hiding under my bed, where Mickey's litterbox now lurked.

I extended my hand toward Mickey cowering in the darkness under the chair.

"What have you done to your hair?"

"Nothing!" I said, sitting bolt upright and running my fingers through the stiff, damp strands poking out from under the headband.

"Better get a move on. You'll be late."

Back in my room, I glanced in the mirror. Satisfied my hair was a sufficiently vibrant shade of yellow, I slid the headband into place. The dance class girls were bound to be impressed.

The black leotard issued a voiceless challenge. It sucked at my curves. Once I'd wrestled it into place, I pulled the purple shift dress over the top of it. The Op Art shift dress was another of Mum's triumphs. She'd *thrown it together* at her sewing machine after reading an article about the London fashion designer, Mary Quant. My entreaties to raise the hemline above my knees were ignored. According to Mum, I was about to become the first girl in town to wear a dress with no waist, and that was enough.

I shoved a sweater into a string bag and ran downstairs toward the kitchen.

"What's the hurry?" came a masculine voice.

I skidded to a halt outside Jim's museum.

My brother smiled. Not in a good way.

"Where are you off to?"

"Dance class."

"Come in," he said, spreading an arm in pseudo welcome. He never invited me in. It was too good an opportunity to miss. He closed the door behind me. I nearly choked on the smell of chemicals and dead things.

The reputation of my brother's museum was growing. People had started donating bones that might have come from dinosaurs and broken junk that soldiers brought home from the wars. Jim reckoned he'd be able to charge an entrance fee soon.

A stuffed baby alligator, its mouth stuck in a permanent grin, crouched on the big black desk. Its eyes were glassy and cold. An armadillo shell perched on a pole beside a globe of the world. A stuffed python zigzagged across the wall. Shelves were laden with bones, pelts, and jars full of indeterminate forms floating in fluid. Piles of stamp albums, books, and old magazines slumped in a corner under a poster featuring NATIVE BIRDS OF NEW ZEALAND.

I became aware of a third living presence in the room. Mrs. D's son Shane leaned against the sash window. Head tilted, arms crossed, he acknowledged my presence with a nod. Shane had a reputation, which was one step away from being a bad boy. He'd been spotted outside Woolworths smoking cigarettes with motorbike boys, who were automatically bad.

"I didn't know you two were friends," I said, running a

hand through my hair, which was setting to the consistency of straw.

"On and off," Shane replied, turning his gaze to the street outside the window.

"Does Mum know he's here?" I whispered.

"None of your business," Jim said.

"Is that a new jacket?"

My brother's garment was beaten up and wrinkled in the wrong places, like the stuffed animals he kept. He pushed the sleeves up his forearms.

"Yeah. Real leather."

"Where'd you get it?"

"Uncle Fred had it in the war."

"The one who flew bomber planes?"

We had so many uncles it was impossible to keep track of them. Jim nodded.

"He won't be needing it anymore."

Poor Uncle Fred had made the ultimate sacrifice. Like thousands of others, he was just a name on a small-town monument.

"*Helen!*" Mum's voice echoed from the laundry.

Shane scuffed the floor in a lazy rhythm. With his olive skin, half-closed eyes, and parted lips, he looked like Elvis in *Blue Hawaii*. Elvis was too old for me, but I could understand why some people's big sisters went wild over him. Shane must have practiced that pose a million times.

I turned to leave.

"You've got a cat, haven't you?" Jim's question was more of a statement.

I stopped dead as the armadillo's shell.

"No."

"It's all right," Jim said in a voice that was unnaturally warm. "You can trust us."

Shane studied his sneakers. Those boys had enough secrets. They didn't need to steal one of mine. I stood silently while Jim took the python down from the wall and thrust the lifeless head at me.

"Want to touch it?"

I recoiled.

"Go easy on her."

Shane's voice was softer than I'd imagined.

"It's okay," Jim said. "Just having fun."

Big boy fun nearly always involved cruelty. Desperate as I was to make a run for it, I stood firm. If they smelled fear on me, anything could happen.

"What do you want to be when you grow up?" Shane asked.

The inquiry had a genuine ring.

"Ballerina."

The boys exchanged glances. If only I'd lied and said secretary. Or housewife.

"I can just see you in one of those frilly skirts." Jim said, smothering a grin. "What do they call them?"

"Tutus."

The snake clattered onto the desk.

"Look at me, everyone!" Jim said, performing a clumsy pirouette. "I'm Helen the Melon, queen of the elephants, dancing on stage in my little tutu."

Shane buried his chin in his neck. His shoulders trembled. He was laughing.

I ran out the door upstairs to the landing and collapsed in the armchair. Queen of the elephants was bad enough but rhyming my name with a big stupid lump of melon—that was mortifying.

My chest convulsed. I buried my face in the seat cushion and sobbed noiselessly. As I lay stranded facedown, a shipwreck of misery, I sensed a nearby presence.

I stopped crying and lifted my head. Perched on the armrest above me sat a scruffy young cat with an *M* on his forehead.

He gazed down at me through a flecked golden eye.

Mickey's expression was both curious and tender.

Overjoyed, I thrust my hands out to reach him.

He flew into the air and scampered away before I could touch a whisker.

Chapter Seven

COMPARING
CATS

"See you soon," Mum said, planting a kiss on my cheek. We weren't physically demonstrative as a family. Her kiss was almost as surprising as the outfit she was wearing. She usually reserved the green tweed suit (*This old thing? I've had it for twenty years*) and white gloves for hospital visits and the rare airplane flight.

Erasing remnants of her lipstick, I sprinted toward the Scout Hall. A bittersweet aroma of cow dung hovered over a lush paddock hemmed in with barbed wire. The mountain, draped in its glistening winter cloak, was a giant ice cream melting into pale blue sky. No matter what happened in our petty human world, the mountain was always there.

I couldn't wait to see Alma. Our ancient teacher was the most vibrant, graceful person I knew. She moved with puma-like ease. An ocean of steely curls framed a face lined with more joy and sorrow than the inhabitants of our rustic back-water could comprehend. Alma was rumored to have been a ballerina in Budapest before escaping the Nazis. As often happens when the persecuted escape their oppressors, Hungary's loss was her new home's gain. A few other so-called refugees lived in New Plymouth—a physics teacher and his wife, a doctor.

Alma didn't care how anyone looked, let alone the size of their bones. Thick, working men's socks rumpled down from her knees. All she cared about was the music. Under her guidance, we embraced the exuberance of Tchaikovsky, the drama of Dvorak. She directed us to lie on the floor and let symphonies course through our bodies like waves over rock pools. She'd then rewind the tape on her chunky old machine and invite us to stand and let the music guide our dance movements.

We never danced for an audience. Under her passionate guidance, we *became* the thunderstorm in Beethoven's *Pastoral* Symphony; the moonlight rippling on a pond in Chopin's nocturnes.

Running up the ramp, I couldn't wait to step through Alma's invisible window into a world where everything was understood. I hoped there might even be a chance after class to tell her about Mickey, and how worried I was about what Jim and Shane might do to him. I pushed the big heavy door.

"And who's this?" The voice was unfamiliar.

I froze.

The tape recorder machine was in its usual position on the floor, but Alma wasn't there. In her place stood a sharp-angled woman with dark hair permed in concrete waves. Black leotards encased her lean, muscled limbs. The woman fixed me with an appraising eye.

"Well?"

I mumbled my name.

"You're late. From now on, anyone who's late will be locked out of class."

I tore off the shift dress, kicked my sandals into a corner, and joined the dozen or so girls on the floor. Margaret waved. I smiled back. She was the closest I had to a friend.

There was a newcomer amongst the girls. Dainty little Pam Lynch from the clever class at school was a wiz at math. She seemed lost among the other girls. I stood next to her, but not close enough to make her uncomfortable.

"You'll notice a few changes around here." The woman smiled through thin lips. "I've persuaded the Scouts to take other rooms down by the port."

That was when I saw the mirrors. Rows of them down both sides of the hall. They were huge.

"This is going to be a proper dance studio from now on. The landlord's given permission for us to put up barres to stretch on."

I eyed the wooden bannisters running horizontally across the mirrors. What part of us needed stretching? I was already taller than most of my classmates.

"My name is Mrs. Harris," the woman said in enunciated tones. "As you've no doubt heard, Alma is unwell. I'll be taking over her classes from today on."

A boulder tumbled down the mountain slope and settled in my gut. Alma was the healthiest, strongest woman in the world. She couldn't be sick.

"What's wrong with her?" I asked.

The woman swiveled her icy gaze to me. "That's a rude question."

"Can we visit her?" I asked, feeling blood rise to my ears.

"Alma needs rest. She certainly doesn't want visitors. Now, let's start with some exercises. Come along, girls. Line up against the wall and take the barre."

Alma always started with exercises, but they were about pretending to be a bulb working its way through the soil to become a tulip or imagining we were clouds heavy with water that, when the music told us, fell to the floor in sheets of rain. There was never any lining up or taking hold of barres.

"Now rest one hand on the barre and stretch your other arm out as far as it can go," Mrs. Harris said.

Pam tossed her nearly waist-length cascade of chestnut hair. "What happened to your hair?" she asked.

"It's a treatment," I said, patting my scarecrow stiff strands to detract her attention from the flush of embarrassment creeping up my neck.

"Where'd you get that headband?"

"Mum made it," I replied, stretching the fabric to make it wider.

"Thought so," she said, stroking the pastel blue headband that corralled her boisterous tresses. Her band was nylon, narrow compared to mine, and probably a lot more comfortable. "Mine's from C. C. Ward's. You should get one like it."

Mum and Dad were always worrying about money. If I asked for a bought headband, it would only make Mum's eczema worse.

"I don't need a headband from a shop," I said. "I've got a cat."

Pam was impressed. Finally. "What sort?"

It hadn't occurred to me to think of Mickey as a sort.

"He's a . . . tabby."

"Oh," Pam said. "A stray."

"No! He's special."

"Mine's Persian. She's a pedigree. From a breeder in Hamilton. Her name's Scheherazade."

"Mine's got extra toes," I said, trying to keep up. "And he's lucky."

"You've got a cat?" Margaret interjected. "Can I come over to your place tomorrow after school?"

"Silence, girls!" Mrs. Harris snapped. "And you! Tall one in the headband."

Who, me?

"Yes, you. What do you think you're doing? You're the only girl facing the wrong way. Turn around and look at me."

The instructions might as well have been in Arabic. While Mrs. Harris had told us to line up and hold the barre, she hadn't said which way. Scarlet-faced, I stumbled to oblige. The exercises were joyless and painful.

I couldn't have been more relieved when she put on Beethoven's Ninth Symphony for the free dance. The old Scout Hall with its mirrors and girls faded to a blur as I surrendered to the music and hurled about in ecstasy. The music carried me across town to our house and a cavern under the chair on the landing. I felt the warmth of Mickey's presence. The distance between us melted as the music reached its crescendo. Glowing with joy, I slid underneath Mickey's fur and inhabited his body. I was a giant cat, paws raised, tail swishing, claws curved as I arched through the air, baring my teeth and hissing . . .

The tape recorder squealed to a halt.

"Excuse me!" Mrs. Harris shouted. "Girl in the orange headband. Yes, you. Move to the back of the class. You're taking up too much space. I can't see the smaller girls with you writhing about in the front like that."

I was in the front? Alma never talked about fronts and backs—or that anyone might be watching. Wasn't the whole point of creative dance to live in the music and not care what anyone else thought?

At the end of class, Mrs. Harris gathered us in a circle because, she said, she had an exciting announcement. Toward the end of the year, we'd be putting on a grand concert for all our families and friends. Mrs. Harris was going to hire the Memorial Hall with a proper stage. It was going to be a fabulous event.

"We're calling it The Magical Fairy Garden Spectacular," Mrs. Harris said. "And while you've been dancing today, I've made up some wonderful roles for you to play in the concert. Maxine, you can be a nature sprite. Anne, how would you like to be a rosebud?"

The girls bubbled with excitement. For the first time, I noticed how skinny and small they were. As Mrs. Harris swiveled the beacon of her lighthouse gaze to Margaret, my jaw tensed. Margaret was the most dignified person I knew. I'd fight to the death anyone who belittled her just because of her twisted spine.

"And you, Margaret," Mrs. Harris said, gazing down at her attendance sheet with our names on it. "You can be . . . a pixie."

Margaret and I exchanged looks. She accepted the role with equanimity.

"Which leaves us with—" Mrs. Harris turned her attention to me. "I have something special for you."

I waited, hopeful and nervous at the same time.

"Toward the end of the show, there's going to be a massive thunderstorm. Some of the girls will be rain and lightning. You will be the mud puddle."

Mud puddle?

"Yes, you'll have a glorious costume, something glittery on the surface perhaps. I'll send your mother a pattern. It'll be a duet. You can do it with your little friend, the new girl. Pam, how would you like to be the sun sparkling on the mud puddle?"

Pam flicked her tongue across her upper lip.

Chapter Eight

TENUOUS TRUCE

"How was it?" Mum asked as I climbed back in the car. A lilac finger cloud stretched across the mountain and pointed toward our house. I ached to be home with Mickey.

"Alma's sick."

"Oh, yes, I heard."

"What's wrong with her?" I asked, as we drove past rows of tidy wooden houses with crewcut short lawns.

"Cancer," Mum said in a wistful tone as we cruised toward Devon Street.

"Will she get better?"

The traffic light flicked to amber.

"She's had some good innings," Mum said, accelerating through the red light.

I was beginning to understand the way adults could wrap solemn truths in frivolous expressions. Alma wasn't an innings person. She had no interest in baseball or cricket, let alone if her side was batting or not.

"Can we visit her?"

"Oh, she'll have plenty of people hovering around," Mum said, jolting the handbrake.

C. C. Ward's was the closest we had to a department store. Two whole floors were devoted to the clothing requirements of a woman's life, from her first breath to the grave. We paused at a family of shop models in the window. The mannequin Mum wore a long tartan coat. A brown velvet beret flopped over one side of her head. Her vacant smile was focused down on her hands, poised to suggest they were holding an invisible tray.

"I could knit a hat like that," Mum said thoughtfully. "A pair of round needles should do it."

The dad was all manly elegance under his painted brown hair. He clutched a pipe as if it was a pacifier, essential to his mental stability. The toddler in front of him wore a manic grin under her wide-brimmed hat, probably to protect her from polio.

Everyone knew about poliomyelitis. Around the time I was born, many thousands were dying around the world every year. Polio was an invisible assassin that struck at random. A perfectly healthy person might notice a sudden headache, then be paralyzed an hour later. The disease had particularly tragic consequences for children, including our cousin George, who survived with a lifetime limp.

For a long time, people had no idea where polio came from, though it was noticeably virulent in summer. When scientists finally discovered the disease was spread through contaminated food and drink, Mum wasn't convinced. She adhered to the theory that polio was brought about by sunlight bearing down on the napes of children's necks. To protect us, she stitched large handkerchiefs to the backs of our beach hats. We looked ridiculous, but there was no room for negotiation.

Relief was palpable when the polio vaccine rolled into town like a great golden angel. Townsfolk reveled in a glorious knowledge they'd never have to face the horror of a pandemic again. Even though I lined up with all the other kids to receive the drops of sickly pink fluid, Mum insisted I hang onto the handkerchief hat.

A hand-knitted toy rested in the crook of the mannequin toddler's arm. It was a striped brown-and-gray kitten with an *M* embroidered on the forehead. It could have been Mickey, except for the blue eyes.

"Look, Mum! Isn't it cute?"

She offered a distracted smile. Sizing up the beret to make one herself had put her in a good mood. I seized the opportunity to find out if her view on felines had softened.

"Can I have a cat?" The words left the back of my throat in hot little flames.

"Heavens no!" she said, tugging at the cuffs of her white gloves. "Horrible things."

"But what if . . . ?"

"You've already got those smelly mice and a dog."

"Fritz doesn't care about me. And the mice aren't really mine." Technically, they were on loan from Margaret.

"Well, you need to sort that out with your little friend."

Mum's stiletto heels clicked over the tiled mosaic entrance foyer through a forest of cylindrical fabric bolts. I noticed a display of headbands like Pam's gleaming from the haberdashery counter. Sealed inside cellophane wrappers, they were all bland pastel colors.

A clutch of vivid feathers sprouted from a jar. If only I could take the big yellow one home to Mickey.

My hopes lifted as we headed to the back of the store toward the evening and bridal fabrics. Maybe Mrs. Harris had already sent Mum instructions for my costume. I held my breath. *Something glittery* might mean gold lame. I'd die for gold lame, even if it was just a headband.

She turned left and pressed the buzzer for the antiquated elevator. My shoulders dropped. We were heading upstairs to a gold lame desert. I watched the carriage glide down to our level and jerk to a halt. The operator opened the inner door and pushed the metal grate sideways. He smiled at Mum and beckoned us inside.

A large dull hook emerged from his jacket sleeve. When I was younger, I was afraid of him. That was before I noticed the buttery softness in his eyes. The hook wasn't his fault.

Crutches, amputated legs, glass eyes, and wheelchairs weren't unusual among men his age. Often cheerful in public, they behaved as if they didn't expect sympathy from anyone. Even if they'd tried to tell their stories, none of us would have understood their trauma. It was because of the war.

The elevator cabin smelled of ancient linoleum. Perched on his high stool in the corner, the operator closed the door and clanged the grate shut with his good arm. Safely imprisoned, we creaked skywards in silence.

Upstairs at C. C. Ward's, rows of school uniforms marched shoulder to shoulder alongside lines of knitwear and female undergarments. The place had a damp, wooly aroma. Mum sailed out of the elevator toward a woman with hair piled up in graphite beehive. She wore a black cardigan, and a tape measure dangled around her neck.

"An important day for you, young lady," the woman beamed over the top of her half-moon glasses. "Your very first bra."

So that was it. A bra-fitting ambush. The woman nudged me toward a curtained-off cubicle.

"Take your dress off," she said. "And the leotard too."

I backed into a corner of the cubicle and faced forward in case she saw the rip in the back of my panties, thanks to Fritz.

"It's a matter of what you feel comfortable in, dear," the woman said, shaking out a white cotton bra.

She made me turn around, then snapped the thing around my chest and tightened the straps over my shoulders. A shiver of goosebumps crept up my torso.

"There now," she said. "Let's see what Mother thinks."

"Perfect!" Mum said stepping through the curtain. She'd been standing outside listening the whole time.

"Are you sure I need this?" I said, peering down at the shark snouts jutting from my chest. They puckered like balloons short of air.

"We could try going down to a smaller cup size," the woman

said. "But we don't have any triple As in stock. She'll grow into it."

"Don't you love the little blue rose?" Mum asked.

I hadn't noticed the embroidered flower nestling between the two mounds.

"Roses are never blue," I mumbled.

Mum ignored me. She was on an underwear high.

"While we're here, let's fit her for a garter belt. We might as well pick up a pair of stockings too. And while we're at it . . ."

Mum rested her hands on my shoulders and smiled like a game show host about to announce the biggest prize in the world.

"How about a corset?"

"No!" I cried.

The woman and Mum exchanged looks.

"It would do wonders for your silhouette," Mum added.

"No, Mum, *please*!"

"Oh, well," she said, opening her purse and fishing out a bunch of wrinkled pound notes. "Maybe next year."

I wasn't looking forward to July 1967, when our entire nation would be changing to decimal currency. I'd only just got my head around twelve shillings in a pound. Having 100 cents in a dollar was complicated enough. A new corset would only add to the confusion.

The woman put Mum's money in a canister and screwed the lid shut. She connected it to a wire above her head and sent the thing whizzing across the ceiling to an invisible cashier. Minutes later, the canister flew back with a jangle of change in it.

Harnessed like a horse, I stumbled down the stairs, out of C.C. Ward's into the car.

"Can we go home now?" I asked, longing to see Mickey.

"What's the hurry?" Mum said. "Let's get some fresh air." She drove past the clock tower and the Caltex petrol station.

"What would you like to be when you leave school?" she asked as we glided over undulating hills toward the port.

"A bal—"

A vision of Margot Fonteyn appeared in the clouds and shook her head sadly.

"I'd like to teach creative dance, like Alma. Maybe run my own dance studio someday."

Mum didn't object.

"Or maybe I'll get married."

Mum said nothing.

"To a farmer," I added, to cheer her up.

She gave me a skeptical look. "Do you really think you could live on a farm?"

"Yes," I lied. I was scared of our dairy-farming cousins with their calloused hands and infinite silences.

"Whatever you do, don't have sex and get pregnant before you're married. Also, it's vital for a girl to have a career before she gets married," she said, rumbling the car to a halt at the base of Paritutu Rock.

Paritutu was part of an ancient volcano even older than our mountain. Long before humans arrived, it blew up. All that remained was the huge rock, rising like a twisted needle high above us, and the seven Sugarloaf islands nearby. Maori tribes appreciated the fortlike qualities of the rock. They flattened the top, dug pits to store the yams they called *kumara* and scanned the horizon for enemies.

People climbed Paritutu for fun mostly, but every now and then a dad would go up there and shoot himself because he couldn't get over the war.

"I've seen so many women trapped in marriage and unable to escape because they weren't trained to do anything other than housework," Mum added. "My time as a journalist at the *Hawera Star* was—"

"I know. *The best years of your life*," I said. "Do you wish you never married Dad?"

"Of course not!" she said after an uncomfortable pause. "He's . . . wonderful."

"Do you wish you'd never had kids?"

A wistful expression crossed my mother's face.

"Not at all," she said in a tone that wasn't entirely convincing. "A girl must have some skills the world values, that's all. Not just the ability to change diapers."

A majestic wave unfurled and flattened itself on the black iron sand beach below. I opened the passenger door and inhaled the heady aroma of lupines and salt. Slipping out of my sandals, I pushed past flax bushes and scrambled down the sand hill.

"Wait for me!" Mum called, tearing off her gloves and suit jacket.

She slid out of her heels, ran down through the soft dark granules, and took my hand. Laughing, we fell over and tumbled down the dune. It was as if we were girls together. I wanted our time together to last forever.

Mum and I landed breathless on the beach. I stood up, dusted off the sand, and strolled toward a dazzling lime green stream. Rainbow colors played on its surface as it snaked toward the shoreline. Mesmerized by its unworldly beauty, I stepped forward to paddle in the magical water.

"Stop!" Mom called. "Go back and get your sandals."

"Why?" I asked.

"That's overflow from the Ivon Watkins factory up on the hill."

"What's overflow?" I asked. Mom usually approved of anything flaunting fashionable neon colors.

"They're making something for the war in Vietnam. It might be poisonous."

Decades later, I discovered Mum's concern was legitimate. The harmless-looking Ivon Watkins Dow-factory churned out a nasty herbicide called 2,4,5-T for more than 20 years. It contained the dioxin TCDD, a key component of Agent Orange, the notorious defoliant the US military employed in the Vietnam War. The evil concoction has since been linked to cancers and birth defects.

Those behind the factory's construction must have congratulated themselves on building it in such a remote, unquestioning corner of the world. While a senior government official expressed fear that children could die from playing near toxic chemicals flowing from the plant on to Paritutu beach, his protest didn't surface until years after the factory's demolition.

When we arrived home, Jim was out, the museum door locked. Dad and Mary had no idea where he was. I ran up the stairs, two at a time. There was no sign of Mickey under the chair on the landing.

Panting, I opened my bedroom door. The bed was tidier than I'd left it. Someone had plumped the pillow, smoothed the candlewick spread, and folded the eiderdown at the foot of the bed.

Sitting on the eiderdown's satin surface was a small, soft-covered book. The cover featured a photo of a girl with medium-length brown hair and a red headband. Wide and soft, it was the perfect headband. I was sure it didn't hurt her ears.

Blood drained to my toes when I saw the title—*Becoming a Woman*. Sitting on the bed, I turned the pages. The illustrations were bland, the text indecipherable. My eyesight was definitely getting worse.

A tear dropped on the girl's nose. She smiled stupidly back at me. In desperation, I looked up at the corner where the fairies lived. It was too early for them to be out.

As I succumbed to weeping, a small four-legged shadow crept out from under the bed.

"Mickey!"

The cat cringed on all fours and turned to leave.

"Don't run away, boy," I begged, wiping the back of my hand across my nose.

He stopped and tilted his head to one side.

"You've got cobwebs on your ears," I said, breaking into a smile.

Mickey's whiskers quivered. He raised his scruffy tail and pointed the tip toward me.

"Want to be friends?"

The cat gazed up through his single eye and considered the offer.

I patted the eiderdown as an invitation.

To my disbelief, Mickey leaped up beside me and snuggled into my thigh.

Chapter Nine

CATS DO FLY

Cats seldom comply with plans. I expected Mickey to spend all night curled up next to me. When I got up to find my pajamas, however, he leaped off the bed and skedaddled into the shadows.

Disappointed, I fell back on the covers, scrunched my eyes, and watched the light switch morph into two.

I snapped the light off and gazed up at the fairy corner. My pulse quickened. There was a definite shimmer. Trying not to move a muscle, I waited for the magical energy to intensify and spread down the wall.

"Are you awake, dear?"

The fairies vanished. I rolled onto my side and waited for Mum's footsteps to retreat downstairs. A follow-up chat about *Becoming a Woman* was the last thing I wanted.

My fingernails were down to nubs. I chewed around the edge of my little finger. Skin didn't taste so bad.

Maybe the fairies were a fantasy, an optical illusion only surgery could cure. That didn't explain how they could open my window at 7:10 A.M. on request. I reached for the latch and shivered. The nights had been too chilly to leave the window ajar since Mickey's arrival.

After school the next day, Mum was in town working on her Lady Thiang vocal range with Virginia Longford, the region's most famous pianist. Dad was working late at the Queen's Hall adding finishing touches to his gas works stand for the Winter Show. Jim and Mary were out. It was safe for Margaret to come over.

"Let's get this straight," my friend said as I escorted her into my bedroom. "You're keeping the cat a secret from your Mum and your dog but not your dad or sister. Does your brother know about it?"

"Yes, but I want to keep Mickey away from him. He's looking for dead animals to stuff in that museum."

"Good luck with that."

I trusted Margaret more than any kid. She never told fibs for the sake of it.

"Stinks in here," she said.

Margaret helped me retrieve the litterbox and replace the soil with fresh dirt from Mum's camellia garden. As the room's aroma improved, my friend lay on her stomach and slid under the bed to inspect my new lodger.

"How come he's only got one eye?"

"One of them's glued up. I'm going to fix it."

"He's pretty," Margaret said. "We should enter him in the Winter Show. They have a cat section."

Margaret's ideas were always crazy but exciting.

While she was face down, I slid *Becoming a Woman* between my stack of library books. *The Famous Five* were crisp and superior in their British way. Julian, Dick, Anne, George, and their dog Timmy never stopped to wonder if the bad guys really were evil, or just down on their luck. *The Lord of the Rings* was a romp, but I had to skip dozens of pages to avoid tiresome battle scenes. My favorite books featured animals, who were often more noble and giving than humans. My latest find was *The Incredible Journey*, about three pets finding their way home through the Canadian wilderness. Nobody wrote about the lives of ordinary New Zealand girls.

"Doesn't get much fresh air in here, does he?" Margaret said. "Let's take him up the tower."

"What! We can't go up there."

"Why not?"

"How can he get up the ladder?"

The only way to reach the tower was to sneak into Jim's bedroom and climb the rickety old ladder just inside his door.

"Leave it to me," Margaret said.

She was the animal expert.

"What about your mice?" I asked.

"They're *your* mice now."

I couldn't argue. When Margaret had asked me to babysit her four white mice while she was away camping at Rotorua's hot springs with her family, I'd been flattered. The creatures had garnet eyes and sleek, pale bodies. One of them had no tail. We christened that one Tail-less, which we thought incredibly original and hilarious.

Margaret swore the mice were all female. While she was away, however, one of them produced three pinkies. It was all very cute and heartwarming—until the pinkies disappeared, presumably eaten by a parent, or one of their friends. Dad said it was because the cage was too small, and they were overcrowded.

Margaret's mother developed asthma on the camping trip, meaning she could no longer cohabit with pet rodents. To her credit, my Mum didn't complain. I timed it so she was engrossed in reading a script for a play when I told her. Anyway, it was safe enough to assume her silence meant the mice could stay, providing I kept them out of her way.

Dad built a spacious plywood cage with a mesh front and a wheel so the mice could engage in exercise instead of cannibalism. He hung the handsome home from two large hooks on the upstairs veranda wall outside my brother's bedroom.

When Jim grumbled about the smell, the cage and its tenants were relocated to the tower above his bedroom. Though the trapdoor at the top of the ladder created a physical barrier, the cloying sawdust odor wafted down to his room in undiluted glory.

My brother bore the horrible smell with little complaint. In retrospect, I feel guilty for inflicting such olfactory misery on him.

Delighted with their spacious new cage, the mice set about decorating it with babies. Anyone who has stood on a beach watching a tidal wave ripple on the horizon will know how helpless I felt in the face of nature unleashing itself at uncontrollable speed. Horrified, I searched for a culprit. Of the four original mice, only one hadn't produced a litter. Tailless.

"The mice won't care," Margaret said, shaking my pillow out of its case. "Go stand guard."

I tiptoed across the landing and peered through the dimpled amber glass in the top section of Jim's bedroom door. The interior was empty and still.

Margaret appeared next to me, the pillowcase writhing, hissing, and growling in her hand.

"*How did you do that?*"

"Easy."

Once Margaret got a notion in her head, nothing could stop her. I had yet to learn the only way to handle a strong personality is to become one.

"Where is Jim?" she asked.

"School Cadets."

The only disadvantage to being born male was School Cadets. Every Tuesday, all Boys High students were forced to wear ugly khaki uniforms and march about like toy soldiers. They even learned to shoot guns.

I twisted the rattling brass doorknob. The indented floral design was blackened with age. If someone bothered to give it a brisk rub with Brasso, it might have been pretty.

My brother's bedroom was small, about the same size as my own. I wondered if letting him have the museum was our parents' way of compensating for his meager, smelly sleeping arrangements.

Watery beams of sunlight angled onto his sagging bed. Unruly sheets and blankets twisted in the shape of an abstract sculpture.

A portrait of Edmund Hillary glowered down from the pale matchboard walls. Hands resting on his ice axe, the famous mountaineer issued a silent challenge to Jim to be tough, silent, and unemotional. A real Kiwi bloke. The definition of manliness was as merciless and crushing as Mum's meat grinder. Unspeakable punishment awaited any boy who couldn't conform. Something about the picture and the room made me feel sorry for my brother. He didn't even like sports.

"See?" Margaret said, stepping off the top rung of the ladder into the tower and placing the pillowcase on the seagrass matting. "Told you we could do it."

The pillowcase sat motionless at Margaret's feet.

"Ignore Mickey," Margaret said. "He'll come out when he's ready."

I lowered the trapdoor and savored the thrill of being sealed off from the world. The tower room was small and square with windows opening onto the roof of the top veranda. Aside from the mouse cage perched on a box and a pile of moth-eaten cushions, it was empty.

The tower was sacred. You could ask a person anything up there, and they'd tell the truth. Secrets were safe inside its peeling papered walls.

"Does it hurt?" I asked.

"What?"

I'd been in fights with kids who called her a hunchback. The word was too ugly for my beautiful friend. She deserved a more regal name for it.

"Your twisted spine."

"No," she answered, tossing her ponytail over her shoulder.

I regretted asking.

"Sometimes," she added quietly.

I admired her grace and toughness beyond words.

"Do you think there's such a thing as fairies?" I asked.

Amusement rippled across her lips.

"Like the Tooth Fairy?"

"No," I said, chastened. "Something more . . ."

I unlatched the mouse cage to find a new clutch of pinkies writhing on the sawdust. Five of them, about two days old.

"That makes twenty-two," I groaned.

Tail-less lumbered into the wheel and started it spinning, as if the population explosion was nothing to do with him. If I'd isolated him from the start, none of this would have happened.

"At this rate, you'll have 200 by the end of the year," Margaret said.

She opened the window and gazed across the roof to the sea. The pillowcase moved. A cheese nose-tip pushed out of the folds. I ached to gather Mickey up in my arms.

"Ignore him," she said. "He's sussing us out. Will you get in trouble if we draw something on the wallpaper?"

"Probably not. They never come up here." I sensed the cat's interest as I poured birdseed into an upturned peanut butter lid.

Margaret slid a thick blue crayon from her pocket. "Who do you want to kiss?"

"On the lips?" I asked, scraping millet husks into an old paint can. People said looking after mice was easy. It was never-ending toil.

Margaret nodded.

"Friedrich from *The Sound of Music*," I said.

Margaret nearly dropped her crayon. Her face refused to stay straight. "That soppy little kid in the sailor suit? You're kidding!"

"Look!" I said, relieved to have a diversion.

We watched entranced as a small gray and black tiger shuffled, guerrilla style, out of the pillowcase.

"Pretend he's not there," Margaret whispered. "He'll get scared if we make a fuss."

The cat seemed more focused than frightened. He raised his nose and savored the head-spinning perfume of mice and sawdust.

"Who do *you* want to kiss?" I asked.

"One of the Beatles," Margaret said in an offhand way. "They're fab."

If only I'd thought of the adorable mop tops. And to use the word *fab*.

"But not Ringo," she added, flicking her long, slick ponytail. "And probably not George."

Not only could Margaret kiss a Beatle, she had the power to choose which one? She drew a large circle on the wallpaper, filled in with a pair of round eyes, a straight line of a nose, and a smiley mouth.

"Paul's for me," she said, scribbling a fringe and spikes of hair down to the Beatle's shoulders. "You can have John. He's the clever one."

"I'm not having *him*!" I said, surprised by my vehemence.

Mickey winced.

"You're in the clever class. You should like John."

"I'm not *clever*! I can't do math and I can't spell. I'm ordinary."

Startled by my outburst, Mickey scampered to hide behind the cushion pile.

"I'll have Ringo," I mumbled.

"Okay, your turn," Margaret said, thrusting the crayon at me.

Margaret hummed "Yellow Submarine" while I sketched Ringo's puppy dog eyes and prominent nose.

"Have you kissed someone?" Margaret asked.

I shook my head, earlobes on fire.

"It's easy," she said, taking a cushion from the top of the pile and thumping it with her fist.

Margaret placed the mangy old pillow on the floor and knelt in front of it. She smoothed the threadbare velvet and gazed affectionately into its weave.

"I love you, Paul," she whispered. "You're so fab."

Margaret flickered her eyelids and lowered her lips to the fabric.

"Your turn," she said, handing me the cushion.

"You're fab, Ringo," I said, closing my eyes and burying my face in an imaginary Beatle. He smelt moldy and was unresponsive.

"You'll get used to it," Margaret coaxed.

Encouraged, I declared undying love for Ringo and kissed the cushion a second time.

"Look out!" Margaret called.

Mickey sprang out from behind the cushion pile. In a single movement he leaped off his haunches, flew across the room, and landed on top of the mouse cage.

"Mickey, no!" I cried as the cage teetered dangerously on top of the tea chest.

Startled, he jumped. The power of his hind legs propelled the cage into space. As the mesh door swung open, sawdust, mice, and paraphernalia spiraled through the air.

Mickey sat stunned on the floor while two feeding bowls, one water tube, a wheel, a ladder, and twenty-two rodents at various life stages scattered in front of him.

For a moment, nothing moved. Everyone, human and animal, was in silent shock. It was like the aftermath of an explosion.

The cat shook his head as if he'd woken from a dream to find himself surrounded by a mouse buffet.

A mound of sawdust shifted, and a plump brown mouse emerged. Tail-less cleaned his paws meticulously, front and back, then waddled idly toward the upturned feeding trough.

Mickey quivered on his hind legs, pointed his whiskers forward and prepared to pounce.

Without thinking, I grabbed the cat, opened the window, and stepped out onto the roof with him under my arm. I slammed the window shut.

"Can you clean up in there?" I called to Margaret.

She didn't hear. Mickey squirmed out of my grasp and crept across the roof. A passing seagull emitted a squawk. As I leaned back against the window, the roof appeared to be a perfect playground for a young cat.

"That was close!" Margaret said, climbing onto the roof and passing me the tin of millet husk. "What'll we do with this?"

"No need to waste," I said, tossing a handful in the air. A circle of birds gathered on the lawn below and picked over the rejected mouse food.

A voice wafted up from the garden, with a spine-tingling rendition of "Something Wonderful."

"Gee, your Mum's a great singer," Margaret said.

The tone was exquisite.

"She's been working on it. Her chest notes are fine." I was quoting Mum's self-critique.

Then I realized the sound wasn't coming from our place. It wasn't Mum's voice wafting from next door's kitchen window, but Geraldine's golden mezzo.

As our neighbor hit a resounding high note, the birds spooked and scattered.

"Maybe she's *too* good," Margaret said, as a sparrow fluttered past our feet.

Before we could stop him, Mickey lunged at the bird. It swooped and dodged his claws and spun away toward the bamboo. We watched in horror as my precious feline companion sailed against the pale winter sky.

A split second later, paws outstretched, ears flattened, the cat plunged earthward towards Mum's camellia bed.

Stricken with panic, Margaret and I scurried down the ladder, stairs, and front steps out to the garden.

"Mickey! Where are you?"

Across the glen, a blackbird laughed. I fell to my knees and sifted through the undergrowth.

"There he is!" Margaret cried. She pointed to the upper branches of Mum's favorite camellia bush, the Czar Japonica. Perched among the gleaming leaves was the bemused young cat.

"Mickey, are you alright?"

The cat stared quizzically up at a cloud.

I stood on tiptoes and dislodged my pet from his leafy landing pad. For once, he didn't squirm in protest.

If a cat has nine lives, Mickey had just used one of his.

Chapter Ten

WHAT'S NEW, PUSSYCAT?

Candy floss formed a swirl of pink threads in the pan. The machine operator flicked her stick like a magic staff, stirring the strands together. The smell of burned sugar teased my nostrils. Saliva flooded my mouth.

The woman's face settled in lines of concentration. Her eyebrows, plucked out of existence, were replaced by two dark hyphens halfway up her forehead. Toiling over her pot, she was a weary priestess, her world drained of surprises.

"Here you go, love," she said, handing me the stick topped with a trembling peak of promises.

A biscuit moon beamed over the fairgrounds. The mountain glowed like a ghost against an indigo sky. Chatter and laughter filled the air as people lined up for the Ferris wheel and other rides. Sounds of creaking metal, whirring gears, and squeals from the Ghost Train charged the atmosphere with excitement. The entire province was there.

"Roll up! Roll up!" a man called from the Laughing Clowns.

I flipped up the hood of my new red duffle coat. Adorned with elk horn buttons and scarlet satin lining, it was the best coat I'd ever had. The deep, warm pockets were perfect for hiding lollipops, broken pencils, and used bus tickets.

I tore off the first pink cloud of cotton candy. The garish music from the Dodge Cars faded as the sharp sensation of pink sugar melting on my tongue became all consuming.

"Finished already?"

Pam was only halfway through hers.

That was my problem with good things. The more fiercely I loved them, the faster they dissolved in my hands. Or, in this case, mouth. Neon reflections from the Ferris wheel lights winked from a puddle.

"Wanna go on the Dodge Cars?" Margaret asked.

"I'm broke. Let's see how Mickey's getting on."

I felt deeply foolish for allowing Margaret to collect my cat after school and take him to the Winter Show in a box on her bike carrier. I should have been firm with her, but when Margaret made her mind up about something, she was unstoppable. She was determined to put Mickey in the cat show—and Mickey was remarkably cooperative.

"They won't have announced the winner yet," she said.

A blast of heat hit our faces as we entered the Army Hall. I flipped my hood back and joined the throng of townsfolk and farmers milling about in the thick humid air. The walls were adorned with tree fern fronds. Fresh from the bush, the draping branches cast an ethereal elegance over the scene.

Trestle tables covered in newspaper and groaning with home produce and crafts stretched the length of the hall. Acres of jams, preserves, and pies exuded sweet aromas. Knitwear and crochet blankets unfurled in dazzling landslides.

Geraldine waved from across the room and beckoned us over. A patchwork of scones and cakes unraveled on the table before her.

"Would you girls like some fudge?" she asked, patting her floral apron.

"Yes, please!"

"Has your fruitcake won a blue ribbon again this year, Mrs. Taylor?" I asked as she handed us each a delectable square of chocolatey sweetness.

"We're waiting on the judges," Geraldine said, surveying her competition. "How's your mother?"

Mum and Geraldine were always spying on each other. I told her Mum was fine.

"Where's Mickey?" I asked Margaret under my breath.

Margaret pointed to the other end of the hall, where a sign, CAT COMPETITION, was taped to a door. Blood pulsed in my ears as we wove our way through raincoats and tweed skirts. I worried Mickey would be freaking out in these restless surroundings.

The Cat Competition room was small, cool and a peaceful contrast to the main hall. Rows of cages lined the walls.

I hurried past crates labeled SIAMESE, PERSIAN, and BRITISH SHORTHAIR. The Cat Competition seemed like everything else in life. Only self-assured, showy purebreds were appreciated. The profound beauty of so-called ordinary cats was overlooked.

Towards the end of a row of pampered, exotic creatures, I found a cage labeled OTHER. Curled up half- asleep in a cage underneath it was my beautiful, perfect feline.

"Mickey! Are you okay?"

The cat yawned, shook his head, and fixed me with the kindest gaze through his one eye.

"He recognizes me!"

Mickey stretched a paw through the chicken wire and patted my finger with the soft pads of his paw.

"I told you he'd be okay," Margaret said. "He likes it here."

"You're eating anyway, aren't you boy?" I said, examining his food bowl. "Drinking, too by the look of it. Don't worry. We'll get you out of here soon."

Mickey purred as if to say that would be very nice, but he wasn't in a great hurry.

"What happened to his eye?" Pam asked.

Ignoring her, I tore a triangle of newspaper off a trestle table and reached for the pencil in my pocket.

THIS IS A LUCKY CAT BECAUSE HE HAS EXTRA TOES, I scribbled, with my usual lack of concern about spelling. HE'S A POLLY DACKTLE AND STILL QUIET SHY. I'M GOING TO FIX HIS GLUEY EYE AS SOON AS HE LETS ME. HIS NAME IS MICKEY.

"Come see Scheherazade," Pam gushed.

While the girls drifted toward the Persian section, I threaded the note through the chicken wire on Mickey's cage. Pleased to have some entertainment, he clawed the paper and nibbled the edges.

Scheherazade was fluffy as a powder puff. She glowered out at the world through button green eyes. Long whiskers draped from her plump cheeks.

"She's beautiful!" I said, offering the cat the tip of my finger through the wire.

"Don't!" Pam yelled.

Scheherazade hissed and sunk a sharp claw into my flesh.

"Can't you read?" Pam said, pointing at the Do Not Touch sign above Scheherazade's cage.

"Let's go," I said, shaking my hand to ease the stabbing pain.

It was a relief to step outside into the cool night air. We crunched across the gravel toward the cavernous shed called the Queen's Hall.

"Wow!" Margaret said.

Just inside the entrance, the Electricity Department stand glittered like a spaceship. People fought for elbow room around a dazzling array of up-to-the-minute home lighting while a stereo pumped out Bert Kaempfert's "A Swingin' Safari."

A dreamy moon lamp presided over a table of excitable bubble lamps. Flying saucer lampshades hovered over cylindrical floor lights.

"It's straight out of *Seventeen* magazine," Margaret breathed.

Our tiny stationery store seldom stocked the hallowed American teenage magazine, *Seventeen*. On the rare occasions it appeared (at least six months out-of-date after a leisurely ship voyage from the US), it would be snapped up by older girls. My meager pocket money didn't stretch to *Seventeen*.

The music faded. Manager, and recently appointed chairman of the Electricity Department, Roy Lynch, mounted the rostrum. He took center stage in a semicircle of electric ovens and fancy bar heaters.

"Welcome, ladies and gentlemen," he boomed, shoving thick-rimmed spectacles up his nose. "'Specially to my lovely little daughter over there. Hello, Pammy!"

Pam pranced on her toes and waved back.

"We live in fun times," Roy went on. "And we're here to show you electricity is more fun than you ever dreamed of!"

He raised his hands to reveal shadows in the armpits of his drip-dry nylon shirt. Roy wanted people to cheer, but the onlookers shifted on their feet. Our townsfolk and dairy farmers were suspicious of frivolity.

"And to open our magnificent stand tonight," he continued, undaunted and rubbing his hand across a well-oiled comb-over. "We have a very special guest . . ."

The loudspeakers belted out Tom Jones singing "What's New Pussycat?" The crowd inhaled the smoky air in a single breath as last year's Miss Taranaki, Tina McFee, climbed the rostrum. Tina, the pharmacist's daughter and now a beauty queen, was practically world famous.

She patted the gleaming helmet of her flipped-up bob and waved to the crowd.

"What are those things on her eyelids?" I asked. "Caterpillars?"

Margaret, who was endlessly patient with my lack of worldliness, explained they were false eyelashes, and incredibly fashionable. Black-and-white flower drop earrings swung from Tina's ears. Her yellow miniskirt, no bigger than Dad's handkerchief, made her legs seem like pipe cleaners.

"How come her legs are orange?" I whispered to Margaret. "Did she dye them?"

"She's wearing pantyhose. They're all the rage overseas."

Tina blew a kiss to the rafters. The crowd erupted. Ron invited Tina to take his arm so he could guide her through his

maze of modern lighting and electrical appliances. He stopped
at every display, switching lights on and off to explain to Tina
and the audience exactly how many watts were involved.

My attention drifted to a gloomy corner in the distance.
Marooned on a modest plywood platform was a familiar
figure. With his hands clasped behind his back, discreetly
rocking back and forth on his feet, my father resembled a
beleaguered sea creature.

"Let's go see him," I said, dragging Margaret by the elbow
with Pam in our wake.

As we drew closer, a ruddy faced farmer approached the
Natural Gas stand. Dad, wearing his smartest jacket with silver buttons and three pens clipped like medals to the breast
pocket, looked hopeful. He smiled and offered his hand, but
the potential customer backed off and disappeared into the
crowd. My father's gentlemanly ways unnerved some people.

"Hello, girls," he said. "You've caught me at a quiet time."

It was dispiriting to watch the hordes file past his NAT-
URAL GAS—THE FUEL OF THE FUTURE stand without a second glance. I wanted to grab the prosperous-looking couple
in camel hair coats and drag them over to inspect Dad's meager assortment of gas ovens arranged in a U on the platform.

"Running low on funds, are we?" he asked, jangling coins
in his pocket.

My father could be a realist sometimes.

"My mum could do with a new oven," Margaret said, fixing him with a bright smile.

Dear Margaret had a heart wider than the sea. She was
feeling sorry for him.

"Could she now?" Dad said, creaking across the plywood.
"What sort of cooking arrangement does she currently
have?"

"A wood burner. It takes ages to heat up."

"Well, she might be interested in one of these," Dad said,
guiding Margaret toward a humble cooker at the modest end
of his display.

Like seasoned actors, Dad and Margaret assumed their parts and played them for all they were worth.

"Gas," Pam said, leaning against Dad's pride and joy, the new Beaufort split-level countertop burner with separate wall oven. "It stinks. And it goes out all the time."

"Is that so?" Dad turned to Pam, as if it was the first time he'd heard that news. "Well, once we change over to natural gas, the pressure will be strong and constant. And it will be a great deal cleaner."

Dad led us over to a showcase where a small blue flame rose steadily from a narrow pipe.

"See how clean that natural gas flame is?" he said. "It's much hotter than coal gas, which tends to burn in a yellowy color. It's counterintuitive when you think of it, because blue is usually regarded as cooler than—"

"Actually, Dad. I have run out of money."

"Oh," he said, emerging from a gas fueled reverie.

As he dug in his pocket and handed me two shillings, the loudspeaker crackled.

"Good evening, ladies and gentlemen," a disembodied woman's voice boomed across the hall. "The standard of entries in the Pet Competition was incredibly high this year. It's been a tough job for our judges, but I'm happy to say they've made up their minds . . ."

Pam grabbed my arm and forged into the crowd. I looked for Margaret, but she was ahead already, weaving around heavy winter coats and tweed skirts.

"I knew it!" Pam shouted, pointing at the blue ribbon on Scheherazade's cage.

"She's only best in the Persian section," Margaret pointed out. "There'd be two ribbons if she was Best in Show."

Scheherazade pouted through her chicken wire. There was no time to stop and congratulate her. I ran on to the OTHER section. Oblivious to the commotion, Mickey was curled up asleep in his cage. There were no ribbons tied to his wire. My note, however, had been replaced by an envelope with a see-through window on the front. I tore it open. A row of tightly formed words crept across a slip of yellow paper.

HIGHLY COMMENDED. GOOD MARKINGS. EXTRA TOES ARE LUCKY.

My heart floated like a balloon.

"Highly Commended!" I cried.

"That's not as good as *Very* Highly Commended," Pam said. "Let's go on the Ferris wheel."

Outside, icy air prickled our cheeks. Our breaths puffed tiny clouds into the night. The Ferris wheel spun garish colors against the sky. It rotated at manic speed. People were screaming.

"How about the Laughing Clowns?" I asked.

"Those people are crooks," Pam said. "They don't let anyone win. Who wants to waste money putting Ping-Pong balls down a clown's mouth?"

She had a point. I tugged a thread from the lining of my right pocket and massaged it into a tiny ball of wool.

"Or we could try the roller coaster," Pam said.

"No way!" I said, watching it loop through the fairgrounds like a demented centipede. The roller coaster rumbled to a halt. Two silhouettes stepped off and swaggered toward us. My brother shoved up the fraying cuffs of his leather jacket. The denim bomber jacket Shane was wearing was a better fit, but it was too flimsy for the night air.

"Hey," Jim said to me. "Got some cash?"

"Nah."

"Want a ride on the Ghost Train?" Shane asked. "I know a guy who works there. He'll let you on for free."

Pam bounced up and down like a pogo stick. I was tempted. The Ghost Train had more appeal than the Ferris wheel.

"Hey, Troy!" Shane called to a skinny guy standing outside the Ghost Train ticket booth. "Got a spare car for these ladies?"

Troy turned to appraise us. A skull tattoo leered out from his neck. Though he was probably not much older than seventeen, life had beaten the joy out of him.

I'd seen Ghost Train workers riding the back of peoples' cars and making spooky noises, putting effort into scaring them instead of just making them dizzy. But there were stories about people who worked in fairgrounds. Especially the ones who offered rides for nothing.

"No thanks," I said.

Troy shrugged and turned to a young couple lining up to buy tickets. Shane slid a cigarette from his pocket. His hands were raw with cold. Jim glowered at me. I hoped they weren't about to go inside to gawk at the Pet Competition.

The boys weren't interested in hanging around us. They turned and headed for the hotdog stand.

"Come on!" Pam called, joining the queue at the ticket booth for the Ferris wheel. "We'll have a cab all to ourselves."

They weren't cabs so much as wooden benches, each suspended by a flimsy arrangement of wires under a canvas canopy. The thing fluttered in the breeze, as if it was on the point of collapse.

Margaret took my hand and nudged me forward.

The wheel slowed and stopped occasionally so people could dismount cab by cab. A woman in a headscarf clutched her sobbing daughter's elbow. They staggered down the steps and vanished into the crowd. Two boys, aged about fourteen, strode past looking somber and pale. There wasn't a soul whose life had been improved by a ride on the Ferris wheel.

We climbed the steps. A man with a navy-blue cross tattooed on his cheekbone punched our tickets and lifted a bar so we could climb into our cab. I pulled my hood down over my eyes as far as it would go. Pam wanted to sit in the middle because she was cold. It was freezing. Rain fell in loud plops on our canopy.

Nightmarish music whined as the wheel creaked into action. After a sedate circuit or two, the operator accelerated the machine to a dizzying speed. Fairground and townsfolk melted into a nauseating blur as it hurtled through the night.

"I feel sick!" Pam whined.

"We *all* do!" I shouted back.

Pam went quiet. A line of sweat appeared above her eyebrows. She cowered into her coat and turned an actual shade of green, like Mum's chartreuse, except more yellowy.

"Get him to stop!" she moaned.

We waited for the machine to whirl past the tattooed man.

"Stop!" we cried.

He didn't hear us.

Our cab mounted the sky for another circuit. Poor Pam doubled up. We locked arms around her and shouted down at the man. As the cab lurched forward into the darkness, Pam opened her mouth. An arc of candy floss, popcorn, hamburger meat, carrots, corn, and unrecognizable goo spilled out of her throat. It splashed on the canopy of the car below us.

"Stop!" we yelled at the top of our voices. But the man was determined to give us full value for our money. When the wheel finally creaked to a halt, the three of us staggered off and parted ways.

"You could've stopped," I growled at the man.

He grunted and smiled at his next victims waiting in line.

Later in the evening, Dad helped me carry Mickey's carrier out to the carpark. "How did he do?" he asked, placing the box on the Zephyr's backseat.

"He got Highly Commended," I said, sliding in next to Mickey.

"Did he just?"

When we arrived home Mum was in the laundry running shiny, red fabric through her sewing machine. Fritz was in the kitchen, snoozing in front of the gas heater. Dad and I sneaked Mickey's box upstairs into my bedroom.

"Luckiest cat in the Winter Show, eh?" he said, pecking me on the cheek.

After Dad left and closed the door, I sat with the box on my knees and raised the lid high so the cat could jump out and run straight under the bed. Mickey was sure to resent me for subjecting him to so many indignities.

To my astonishment, he sat still and winked his eye at me.

"I'm not letting anyone take you away ever again," I said, lowering a tentative hand to his forehead. He dipped his head in acceptance and emitted a gentle purr as I ran my fingers over his soft, warm M.

I hardly dared believe it. He was beginning to trust me.

Sometime after midnight, I was woken by a soft thud on the eiderdown. Mickey nestled into the crease behind my knees. For the first time since I'd moved to my new bedroom, I did not feel alone.

Chapter Eleven

INSIDE THE CRACKS

From the moment I was born, I was comfortable in the cracks. It was only a matter of time before I ended up having fairies in my room and a cat for my soulmate.

Felines don't give a hiss about the materialistic obsessions that make people miserable. They live in the gaps, observing energies between themselves and other beings, offering affection when it suits them.

When a cat chooses to adopt you, he or she takes up residence in the conscious and unconscious corners of your mind. Whether in your presence or not, the cat's destiny and yours are forever intertwined.

A feline is never fully tamed. Maintaining its connection to the wild, it refuses to be bossed around or trained to sit like a dog. The cat is seldom open to bribery. When it offers trust, the gift is more precious than the first camellia of spring.

One thing was certain. Mickey couldn't continue hiding in my bedroom forever. The responsibility of changing his litter-box and stealing meat from the fridge was losing its novelty. Now he was beginning to trust me, I figured it was time to return the compliment.

Mickey sat on my bedside table. He fixed me with his eye and emitted a squeak.

"Today's going to be big for us both," I said, as he leaped off the table to devour the remains of last night's shepherd's pie.

Mickey's ears twitched. He was listening, but eating was taking priority.

"You're not going to like this part," I said, pouncing on him and bundling him into my cardigan.

Mickey writhed and twisted under my hold. Remembering Margaret's instructions about cat transportation, I held him in a relaxed, yet firm, grasp—and moved fast.

Sprinting downstairs, we rounded the dogleg under the stained-glass window and skidded to a halt.

"What've you got there?" Jim said, looking up from the wall telephone at the bottom of the stairs.

It was early for my brother to be up. His army cadet uniform offered scant protection from the morning frost. The woolen khaki shorts finished well above his knees and the bomber style jacket revealed most of his backside. The matching side cap looked like a folded paper dart.

"Nothing. Where are you going?"

"Parade Day," he said, examining my bulging stomach.

I was petrified Mickey's tail was dangling down. Though Jim knew about my cat, I wanted to delay their meeting for as long as possible, if not indefinitely. I didn't want him coming up with ideas that Mickey was an unwanted stray who could be used for experimental purposes.

I tried to swerve around my brother, but he stepped in my path.

"What are you hiding in there?" he asked.

"Jim!" Mum's voice echoed down the hall from the kitchen. "You've forgotten your lunchbox."

While my brother's attention was diverted, I darted sideways. Clutching Mickey to my belly, I scooted through the front door, and down the steps to the bottom lawn.

Early morning sun twinkled on frost-laden hydrangea leaves. Overnight, the grass had changed itself into a carpet of white frost that crunched under my school shoes. The air was crisp enough to cut with a cake knife.

Mickey wriggled out of my grasp and bounced across the lawn as if it was electrified.

"Don't worry. It'll melt soon."

The cat stood still beside the hydrangea hedge; his scruffy tail raised in a question mark as he gazed up at the sky. He seemed so small and vulnerable, a scrap of fur held together by little more than his determination to survive and my love for him. I longed to run after him and gather him up in my arms again. But something stopped me.

For the first time, I realized the hardest thing about loving someone deeply is the part about letting go. I couldn't keep Mickey prisoner forever. He needed to explore the world and try to make sense of it as much as I did.

A cold shaft ran through my heart as I struggled to accept this could be the last time I'd see that beautiful young cat. Mickey had every right to leave and make a life for himself. I couldn't force him to stay with me.

"Be a good boy."

Oblivious to my voice, the cat crouched in concentration. Every particle in his body was focused on a beguiling scent emanating from the bamboo.

"See you after school, Mickey?"

My chest imploded as the small gray tiger sprinted away. I watched his scraggy tail melt into the impenetrable cane columns of the bamboo forest.

The hands on the classroom clock moved at an agonizing pace. I stared out the window and watched frost melt on the playing fields while Mr. Jackson read the roll call.

He then gave us a spelling test, including the word *accommodation*, which seemed an unlikely combination of letters (even when spelled with one *m*).

Unsatisfied he'd inflicted enough punishment; Mr. Jackson told us to swap papers and mark each other's tests. I was chastened to discover the boy I sat next to, Ross, had scored 20 out of 20. Ross handed my test back with a sympathetic eyeroll (12 out of 20).

When we were allowed outside for lunch, the mountain

was radiant in a poncho of fresh snow. Seagulls swooped the playing fields while boys wrestled on the grass.

Margaret and I sat on a bench outside her classroom.

"Mickey's probably run away for good," I said, trying to work up enthusiasm for a honey sandwich.

"Don't worry," Margaret said. "He's used to living rough."

"But what if he's heading back to the gasworks to look for his family? The poisoner will get him."

Margaret assured me that would never happen.

After lunch, Mr. Jackson subjected us to Algebra.

When the long hand of the clock dragged around to three and the bell finally rang, I sprinted to the bike sheds, mounted my cycle, and pedaled so fast my calves nearly burst into flames. Turning the corner into our street, I prepared for the worst. *You're not going to cry; you're not going to cry . . .* My bike chain chattered. *He's just a cat. He's just a cat . . .*

The scruffy privet hedge drooped over the footpath outside our place. Our letter box, with its hand-painted 19, leaned drunkenly toward the front steps. The milkman left our bottles on the third step because it was slightly wider than the others. An unusual shape squatted there. I assumed Mum had forgotten to collect the milk.

Lungs puffing like bagpipes, I dismounted and trudged along the footpath. The bike chain made a faster, high-pitched noise.

Idiot, idiot. You should've kept him inside. Idiot, idiot . . .

As I neared our entrance, I squinted my eyes. The shape on the third step wasn't a milk bottle. It looked like one of Mrs. Gullery's statues. Mrs. Gullery at the end of the street had a garden bursting with concrete gnomes and creatures. She treated her concrete animals as beloved children. It seemed unlikely she'd abandoned one.

The sculpture raised its head and pricked its ears.

"Mickey!"

The cat sprang off the step and bounded toward me. My bike clattered to the ground. Happy tears streamed down my cheeks as I opened my arms.

Though pleased to see me, Mickey wasn't about to provide a Hollywood reunion. He stopped about three feet in front of me, turned, and trotted ahead. I picked my bike up off the ground and, like a humble acolyte, trailed after him. Tail aloft, the tiny tiger escorted me up the driveway and toward the basement.

When we reached the fishpond beside the basement archway, he dived into a clump of ferns. I lugged my school bag up the front steps and into the disheveled grandeur of our living room.

A wonky chandelier dangled over a low, Victorian table from Dad's side of the family. It'd been a full height table until Mum sawed the legs off and converted it to a modern coffee bench.

Above the dark brick fireplace (fitted with the inevitable gas heater) the remains of an eighteenth-century gold-plated dinner service roosted nervously on the mantelpiece. Like everything remotely classy we possessed, the plates were also from Dad's side (before they lost their money). The crockery bore chips and cracks from years of cohabiting with us.

Under the bay window, bookshelves glowed with vivid Penguin paperbacks. The lower shelf featured a somber collection— crimson encyclopedias, *Plutarch's Lives*, *The English Bible*, *Meditations of Marcus Aurelius*, *Shakespeare's Complete Works*, *The Drawings of Leonardo da Vinci*.

Crystal decanters winked from Dad's drinks cabinet across the room and told the bookshelf not to take itself so seriously. Dad's piano smiled from the corner. Above it, one of Vermeer's anemic women bent over her lute.

I wondered what became of the accomplished female musicians the Old Masters painted. Choices for those women would have been narrower than the corsets they were squeezed into. Their downturned eyes and blank expressions conveyed entrapment in an ancient cycle.

The black-and-white television, a rarity in our neighborhood, perched on spindly legs and fixed me with its lifeless twenty-four-inch eye. Every night at six o'clock, we sat on the lumpy brown sofa and watched men shoot each other in steamy jungles. The Vietnam sky was eerie silver, the men's blood, black.

Vietnam was not just America's war. It was New Zealand's war too. Our prime minister, Keith Holyoake, made sure of that after Vice President Hubert Humphrey flew in from America and told him about the domino effect. If we didn't stop the Commies in North Vietnam, they'd swarm down and get us too. Americans, New Zealanders, Australians, and Vietcong, they all had the same black blood on our television screen.

"Is that you, Geraldine?" Mum called.

I dumped my schoolbag on the piano seat and wandered into the kitchen.

"Never mind," Mum said, as if my arrival was an anticlimax. "Geraldine's lending me her earrings for the audition. She has quite a collection."

Unwashed plates slumped on the counter. A slab of bread lay in front of the circular blade on the slicer. More than half the loaf had gone since breakfast, a sure sign Jim was about.

Mum sat at the kitchen table, which in itself was another manifestation of her creativity. After we'd battered the old tabletop to bits, she resurfaced it with black, red, and white linoleum floor tiles. Though Nana withheld her opinion about the new look, I liked it.

Resplendent in her new red satin gown, Mum peered into a mirror propped against a stack of library books. Her hair was dyed blue-black and scraped into a bun.

"Fab outfit."

"Really?" she said, smothering her face with cold cream.

"Yeah," I said, like a Beatle. "The gold braid on the sleeves is groovy."

I'd last seen that braid on my old uniform before Brownies and I parted ways. After two weeks of darning socks and jumping over fake toadstools, I couldn't take the humiliation any longer.

Mum was oblivious to my new, up-to-the-minute use of English slang.

"Well, it's very Lady Thiang, don't you think?"

I loved it when she treated me as an adult with opinions worth hearing.

"Sure," I said, making a beeline for the pantry.

"You've heard of the famous Russian drama teacher, Stanislavski?" she called.

"Yep," I lied. The only Russian I knew of was Rasputin.

"I'm using the technique he invented. It's called The Method. The deeper I steep myself in character, the more convincing my performance will be."

I took a biscuit tin off the shelf and pried it open. It was a miracle that between learning her audition piece, sewing her costume, and taking vocal lessons, she'd managed to pump out another batch of ginger nut cookies. I stuffed one in my mouth and slid two more in my pocket.

"*Anna and the King of Siam,*" I said, taking a book from the table. "Is *The King and I* a true story?"

"Loosely. You sound like a dairy farmer, dear. If you can't round your vowels, we'll have to consider elocution lessons."

She had no idea how badly I'd been bullied for talking posh when I started school. No way was I putting myself through that again. Besides, I'd already had a run-in with a speech therapist when they tried to get rid of my lisp. Fortunately, Mum was too busy strutting about the Grand Palace of Siam to keep up the nagging.

"What happens if you get so deep into Lady Thiang you can't come out?" I asked, running a finger underneath the tabletop along the ledge where people left their used balls of chewing gum.

Mum leant into the mirror.

"I mean, how do you stop being Lady Thiang when the show's over?"

Her hand hovered over her forehead. A critical expression flickered across her face, as if she'd found a new wrinkle.

"Greasepaint's dreadful for the complexion," she replied. "It blocks the pores and leaves them permanently enlarged. Actors who forget to apply a cold cream base have *the most terrible* skin. Have you noticed?"

I tried to think of a thespian with pore damage, but none came to mind. Fredrich from *The Sound of Music*'s complexion was smoother than goat's milk.

The greasepaint sticks were wrapped in thick paper, like crayons. The paler tube had a 5 printed on the side, the darker one a 9. It was thicker and stickier than lipstick. Mum applied bold strokes to her cheeks and forehead. The waxy, oily smell evoked an alluring concoction of curtain calls, backstage dressing rooms, nervous actors, stardom, and devastating disappointment.

"What do you think?" she said, blending the colors with ferocious little circles on her skin.

"A bit orange," I said, sidling toward the fridge to see if there was something for Mickey's dinner.

"That's because it's daytime. It'll come to life under the stage lighting."

The fridge light flickered over a lump of gray ground beef.

"Curry again?" I asked, taking a handful of meat and sliding it into the pocket that wasn't loaded with cookies.

Other Mums served boring old mince with onions, carrots, and peas. I was proud of ours for exploring the exotic delights of curried mince cooked with bananas, raisins, and coconut.

"Are you quite sure you want to sign up for another term of dance classes?" she asked.

She might as well have asked if I wanted to breathe.

"I'm in the end of year concert, remember? You don't want me to give it up, do you?"

"Not entirely," she said, penciling a circle of vermillion around her lips. "Your talents might lie elsewhere, that's all. That poem you wrote for the school magazine had potential. Have you considered writing as a career?"

I slammed the fridge door. *Writing?* What was she trying to do, shape me in her own image so I'd avoid the millions of mistakes she'd made?

"It wasn't meant for the school magazine!" I said, hot with rage. "Mr. Jackson put it in there without asking me."

Distant yapping punctuated my fury. The high-pitched barks became louder, more insistent.

"That line you wrote, what was it?" Mum went on. "Ah yes, *Jasmine, with sweet-scented deception, strangles a rose.* That's quite good. Though perhaps *strangles* isn't strictly poetic . . ."

My mother's mouth dropped open. She clutched her throat, emitting an ear shattering shriek. Unable to speak, she pointed at the doorway to the living room.

A small gray blur burst into the kitchen. A slightly larger streak (also gray, but striped) was hot on its heels. Chasing them both, Fritz barked at the top of his lungs.

"Rat!" Mum screamed. She clambered onto the kitchen table, setting books and greasepaint sticks flying.

"Get it out of here!" she cried, gathering up the hem of her red satin gown and clutching it to her breast.

I had to do something. The last time a rat came inside, Mum had an asthma attack.

The rat had no interest in stopping for a reasoned conversation with me, however. It bolted straight into the pantry with Mickey in hot pursuit. I dashed over to the pantry door and closed cat and rat inside.

Fritz skidded to a halt. Mum, her eyes huge with terror,

crouched on top of the table. Every hurricane has its eye of serenity. For a split second we were suspended in time.

Fritz emitted a piercing bark and dived between my knees to burrow at the pantry door.

"Help ! Rat!" Mum wailed.

Jim emerged from the museum wielding a large metal bucket. He pushed me aside and charged into the pantry. I peered over my brother's shoulder into the shadows. Mickey had the rat backed up against a pile of newspapers. The rodent was almost Mickey's equal in size. Eyes narrowed, cheeks drawn to reveal pointed teeth, it was ready for a fight.

"Shut the door," Jim said.

I had to oblige.

Panic-stricken, I pressed my ear to the closed door to hear scuffling noises and the occasional thud.

"Got it!" my brother said pushing the door open and nearly knocking me over.

He swung the bucket in front of me. He'd flattened the top with layers of newspaper.

"Interesting species," he said, panting slightly. "Could be a rare native rat, but I need a closer look."

Jim disappeared into his museum, swinging the bucket like a trophy.

Mum sprang off the table and grabbed a broom from beside the fridge.

"Get that cat out of here!" she yelled, wielding the broom.

Mickey skedaddled out of the pantry, down the passageway and out the back door. To my horror, he left a trail of blood on the linoleum.

"Mickey!" I called, running after him. He was too fast. Before I could reach the clothesline, he'd scaled the monkey puzzle tree behind the incinerator. "Come down! *Please!*"

The feline was a tiny figure on one of the highest branches. Though he could hear me, he wouldn't—or couldn't—move.

I sat on the back step and waited for Mickey to come

down. Birds flew home to their nests. Darkness enveloped
the glen in its great velvet cape. Across the street a dog
howled. Mickey didn't budge, and neither did I, until Mary
called me inside for dinner.

"So *that's* why you had that stinky thing under your bed,"
Mum said, slapping curry onto my plate. "Who put you up
to this?"

Dad cleared his throat and loosened his cravat.

"I thought it would be good for Helen to broaden her
horizons," he said. "She needed something to think about
other than the eye surgery. You were concentrating on the
audition, so we decided it wouldn't do any harm to give the
little fellow a low profile for a while."

Mum shot him an exasperated look. Dad was being too
soft again.

"It's all very well for you," she said, her voice torn with
emotion. "But you know who'll end up feeding and looking
after it. As if I haven't got enough to deal with . . ."

It was true. Mum did everything. On top of compulsory
maternal duties such as feeding us, making our clothes,
washing them, hanging them outside to dry, and ironing
them; keeping the house presentable; taking us to the doctor;
teaching us to bodysurf at the beach; attending our school
concerts; hosting afternoon teas and birthday parties; wearing
corsets and high heels with pointy-toes; and never complaining about being uncomfortable, she was Dad's right-hand
man with house maintenance. She was forever daubing window frames with enamel paint, lugging bricks in a wheelbar-
row around the garden, or diving into impenetrable
undergrowth to haul out weeds.

And she loved us. Not in the clucky, cloying way other
mothers went about it. Mum read bedtime stories with different voices for Pooh Bear and Piglet. She made us feel we
were roaming the Hundred-Acre Wood with her, laughing at
Eeyore, Tigger, and the rest of A.A. Milne's menagerie.

Together we gloated over her library books of Impressionist and Expressionist painting. She took us to the local gallery where she pointed out the differences between genuine artists and Sunday painters. (*No imagination. Derivative. Appalling brush stroke.*) She taught us how to dive off a cliff into the Oakura River without breaking our necks. Flouting the pressure to be *just a housewife,* she encouraged us to ignore the judgment of fools, to refuse to conform simply to fit in. She was a wonderful mother who opened our eyes to the world's beauty. Through her we learned to see and appreciate the most precious aspects of being alive.

On top of all that, she needed to save something for herself—the vibrant woman she used to be. If she lost connection to that person, I felt sure she'd shatter like a porcelain plate. I understood how desperately she needed to cling to her individuality.

"You . . . know . . . I . . . just . . . can't!" Her breathing was shallow, her voice rasping.

"I'll look after him, Mum. Promise."

"It'll just be another disaster, like those white mice of yours," she said.

I had to agree. The mice were out of hand.

"You'd better find another home for that cat," she said, standing at the end of the table and worrying the eczema off the palms of her hands. "It can't come back inside the house. Otherwise, it'll have to go to Uncle Earl's farm."

A cloud of misery settled over the table.

"It's just a cat, Mum," Jim said, forming meditative circles in his rice with his fork.

For once my brother was on my side.

After dinner, I went outside. It was so dark I couldn't tell if Mickey was still up the tree. I called over and over for him. It was like asking the moon to land in our glen.

Tearful in bed, I prayed to God and the fairies to protect Mickey. God didn't reply, but the fairies did. They started shyly at first, a mere blush on the ceiling. I watched them gather strength and grow.

Warm bubbles of joy surged through me as they floated down the wall and surrounded me with shimmering reassurance.

The night air outside was icy. I loosened my window latch.

Chapter Twelve

THE FAIRY CONNECTION

It was silvery dark outside when my window glided open. I fumbled for the alarm clock on my dresser. Ten past seven on the dot.

"Thank you, thank you!"

Even though I had no idea where Mickey was, and how badly he might be injured, it was a relief to know I had non-physical beings on my side.

The fairies needed me to keep them secret. People's curiosity and disdain diminished their power. The only person who kept an open mind about magical beings was Dad. He said people should always have fairies at the bottom of their garden. When I'd told him about my bedroom guardians, however, he'd changed the subject.

I hurried downstairs in my pajamas and ran out the back door to the incinerator.

"Mickey!" I called up into the mist spiraling around the higher branches of the monkey puzzle tree.

Nothing. I examined the rough trunk for traces of blood. It was too dark to see anything. Shivering, I hugged my chest and wished I'd put something on my feet the way Mum was always telling me to.

The street was silent and lifeless under a wine biscuit moon. A tangerine streak formed over the horizon toward the port. Trees stood out against charcoal sky on the ridge above the glen.

As the streetlights flicked off, a yellow glow radiated from the Dooleys' shed. Shane slept there sometimes. He was probably the only other person awake this early on a Saturday morning.

The sky turned pewter. Sleepy ferns were bathed in emerald green light. The sun was on its way.

My chest filled with dread as the mist dissipated around the monkey puzzle tree. Mickey was no longer perched on the high branch, or any of the lower ones. At some stage during the night, he must've climbed or fallen down.

I ran my hands over the trunk's furrows and ridges. There was no sign of blood.

"Mickey!" My voice echoed across the valley.

A thrush emitted three golden notes. A host of sparrows replied with a chorus of chirping optimism. Blackbirds, bellbirds, finches, mynas, and fantails joined the choir, filling the air with jubilance. They sang as if waking to another day was the most surprising and miraculous thing that could happen.

Praying that Mickey was alive and feeling the same way, I ran along the side of the house and down the driveway to our front gate. Two large glass milk bottles sat on the third step. Their aluminum-foil tops gleamed in the dawn light. Our family had an unspoken agreement that whoever collected the milk had first dibs on the top milk. The glorious creamy stuff that settled in the highest third of the bottle was nectar.

I sensed a set of eyes gazing down at me from the cherry tree.

"Mickey?"

A pink-nosed possum blinked down at me. She flicked her tail, swung off the branch, and crashed through the rhododendrons.

As I gathered up the bottles, the shadow of the tower stretched like a menacing dagger down the path. The house, with its sloping eaves and myriad windowpanes, seemed taller, more sinister in the dark. Without sunlight, animals, and people, the place seemed aloof and disapproving, even haunted. The upright railings of the double verandas gleamed like teeth in a skull. No wonder some kids swore they'd never spend a night there.

I made my way, like a sleepwalker, up the two flights of steps to the front door and through to the kitchen.

As the fridge light flickered on, there was an alarming scream. It was so loud my ears hurt. I glanced over my shoulder to see where the noise was coming from. It was me.

Lying stiff and lifeless on the middle shelf next to a coil of sausages was a perfectly formed blue budgie. Resting on one side, its eyes half-closed, the bird seemed deep in thought. The yellow beak was partially open as if about to make a pronouncement. I maintained just enough calm to observe the blue-green stripe above its beak. The bird was male. Its black-and-white striped wings were neatly folded, the gray scaly claws curled around an imaginary twig.

"No need to fuss," Jim said, appearing in the shadows at my side.

"You killed it!"

"I didn't," he said, taking the milk bottles from my shaking hands and placing them between a half-eaten sponge-top pudding and a bowl of stewed rhubarb. "It died of natural causes."

The bird was exquisite. Though it showed no signs of violent death, I wasn't convinced.

"Whose is it?" I asked, trembling with shock. "I mean, was."

"Nobody you'd know."

"Mum will have a fit."

"Shane and I are working on it later tonight," Jim said, lifting the bird from the fridge shelf and cradling it in his hands.

"You mean *stuffing* it?" I said, repelled to the core.

"Taxidermy is a science. It's just as important to understand what's inside things as it is to know what's on the surface."

I was too scared to ask if he'd seen Mickey. Though he'd stood up for me the night before saying Mickey was just a cat, my brother was clearly capable of performing monstrosities in the name of science. Besides, if he sincerely believed Mickey was *just a cat*, he might regard my precious friend as a thing that could be subjected to any form of torture.

"Not when *you* do it!" I said, running out of the kitchen and upstairs to my bedroom.

Chapter Thirteen

BAMBOO
MAGIC

I pulled on my stretch bellbottoms and the pink-and-white Fair Isle sweater Mum knitted back when I was ten. Crimson chilblains itched around the edges of my toes. My school socks were ugly, but warmer than nylon ankle ones. I eased my headband on and flattened the folds against my scalp.

Dad emerged like a Shakespearean ghost in a plume of steam from the bathroom. Glowing from his cold morning shower, he hitched a pale blue towel around his waist.

"Have you seen Mickey?"

Startled, he tucked the towel in a firm knot over his stomach.

"You mean the little cat?" he said, running a distracted hand over his freshly shaven chin. "I'm sorry, dear. It was a dreadful mistake on my part. I should never have encouraged you. It was a ridiculous idea, when we have so many animals already."

My heart wilted. Adults and children were different species. Whenever there was a crisis, my parents ganged up and had whispered conversations behind their bedroom door. Mum had talked him over to her side.

Blinking back tears, I ran downstairs. Jim was in the kitchen pouring every last drop of top milk over his Weet-Bix. I was out of luck. There was an unspoken rule that nobody could open the second bottle till the first was finished. I tiptoed to the museum door and eased it open. A stench of formaldehyde hit the back of my throat.

A black-and-yellow African mask bared its wooden teeth. It leaned against a matching drum covered in animal skin. The baby alligator leered. I scoured bookshelves and window ledges. No sign of a deceased budgie. Jim was probably carrying it around in his pocket.

Cardboard cartons heaped in a tired-looking pile next to the window.

"Mickey?" I asked, lifting the flap of the top carton.

The front page of an old *Mad* magazine grinned goofily back at me. There was no room for a cat among the stash of dog-eared *Phantom* and *Batman* comics.

I closed the box. Everything in the room was drained of life. Through the wall in the kitchen, Jim's chair scraped the floor. I skedaddled before he could return to his macabre universe.

The countless number of hiding places in our house was proving to be a plus and a minus. I lifted a curled-up tuna salad sandwich from the fridge, stuffed it in my pocket and spent half the morning scouring the house from tower to Dad's darkroom in the basement.

"Why aren't you wearing your eye patch?" Mum asked, wafting past the darkroom door in her yellow Lady Thiang gown.

"It hurts."

"I'll loosen the elastic for you. What are you doing here, anyway? Has your father asked you to help him develop some film?"

Unable to summon a straightforward answer, I nodded.

"You're taking up photography? Marvelous!"

With a toss of her freshly permed curls, she drifted past the fishpond across the top lawn toward Geraldine's house. Dad was in his vegetable garden wearing Uncle Toby's gasmask from World War One. With a canister on his back and a malevolent-looking wand, he was spraying cauliflowers with

DDT. According to him, the chemical was by far the best way to deal with the white butterflies who chomped through his crop. We had the finest cauliflowers in town.

I beckoned him over. He flipped the mask up on his forehead, which was only slightly less scary than him wearing it on his face.

"Dad, any luck . . . ?"

"Your mother tells me you're interested in photography," he said. "I'm happy to teach you how to process a roll of film."

They had no right to talk about me behind my back. Dad slid the canister off his shoulders and, whistling a new romantic melody, wandered back toward the basement.

"What's that tune?" I asked.

"'Some Enchanted Evening.' It's about falling in love with a stranger across a crowded room."

"From *South Pacific?* Isn't that another Rogers and Hammerstein musical?"

"Exactly," Dad said, lowering his voice. "And in my opinion, it's far better than *The King and I.*"

He nodded at Mum and Geraldine engaged in intense conversation over the hedge.

"She'll need a cup of tea after this," he said under his breath. "I'll put this stuff away and fill the kettle."

Tempting as it was to follow him, I lingered to eavesdrop on Mum and Geraldine.

"Frankly, I don't care if I don't get the part," Mum said.

"It *is* a huge commitment," Geraldine said. "All those rehearsals."

"I *know*! And if you weren't so *busy* with your new job at the Intermediate School, you'd be perfect for it."

"Teaching domestic science is hardly rocket science," Geraldine said. "And you're so dramatic."

"But you are a natural mezzo," Mum argued.

"You'll carry it off magnificently," Geraldine said, distracted by her three adopted children, Deborah, Felix, and Portia, who were chasing each other through their cabbage patch.

"Really? You think so?" Mum said, straightening her spine and folding a strand of hair behind her ear.

"Absolutely. Children! Stop this minute! Go inside and take off those filthy shoes. Or it'll be the Naughty Seat."

The Naughty Seat was an old church pew installed in Geraldine's gloomy hallway. From what I could tell, Deborah, Felix, and Portia were angels, but Geraldine was always threatening punishment which involved sitting on the Naughty Seat for specified amounts of time.

Well-meaning idealists, Geraldine and her accountant husband, Kenneth, ensured their children were beautifully clothed and fed. But the little ones' lives seemed so controlled. They had no idea how to be genuinely naughty or make the raw animal noises that are second nature to children.

I felt sorry for those kids. Though every physical need was met, they didn't seem any happier than the three Dooley children, who were sprouting like weeds without books or piano lessons; or the Evans boy and his younger sister. Their Mum had a such bad heart, their granny had to live with them.

There had to be some way I could help the waifs of the glen.

"I probably won't audition tomorrow," Mum went on. "My throat's scratchy. The part should go to someone more talented."

"Well, I couldn't possibly," Geraldine said. "Not with three little children and the new job."

"You'll be a wonderful domestic science teacher," Mum said. "It's so important for girls to learn how to cook and sew."

Geraldine's lips set in a tight smile. Her gaze was focused on a clump of grass at Mum's feet. Dad hadn't got around to mowing the perimeter of the top lawn, which was sprouting like an English meadow. Maintaining a manicured lawn was essential to fulfilling one's role as a decent neighbor.

While Mum droned on about the thrill of taking housework to a professional level, I became aware of a distant figure waving from the bottom lawn.

I hurried down the steps and ran to join Mary where the grass transitioned into wilderness. My sister checked the surroundings, parted a stand of bamboos and guided me through a cane passageway. Above our heads, dry leaves shushed in the breeze.

"His paw's grazed, but he'll be okay," she said, scooping Mickey up from a bed of sweet-smelling bamboo leaves and handing him to me.

Mickey sank warm and soft into my arms and nuzzled my elbow.

"*He-len!*" Mum called from the top lawn. "Will you *please* clean up your room this minute? It smells *terrible!*"

"She's only saying that to make Geraldine think she cares about housework," I said.

"Better keep this one out of sight," Mary said, easing Mickey from my arms. "I'll take care of him. Off you go."

I hurried inside to remove the evidence from my room.

Chapter Fourteen

Log Cabin in the Shadows

With a river rock in my chest, I emptied Mickey's litter-box under the camellias. He couldn't stay in the bamboos much longer. He'd turn feral. I needed to create a new hideaway where I could continue feeding and caring for him under our roof.

Climbing over the woodpile behind the camellias, I plunged through an archway into the bowels of the basement. Watery light filtered through ventilation grilles. Chill wind whipped across my arms. Goosebumps shivered up my neck. If ghosts existed, they were here. A morose moan whistled from the darkness. Startled, I tumbled backward and grazed my knee on a plank of rough timber.

Dad's darkroom was quiet. He kept the door shut with a loop of worn rope hooked over a nail. I lifted it, crept inside, felt for the string above my head and yanked it. A lightbulb flickered to life over the grizzled workbench.

The darkroom was little more than a cave. When the door was closed, it was airless, sealed off from the world. It reeked of raw earth. The walls were unframed, and the floor covered in sacks. The original owner probably used it as a storage shed, but Dad fitted the workbench with a photographic en-larger and a small basin with a tap. Brightly colored develop-ing trays, bottles of chemicals, and gleaming coils of negative film transformed the place into a magician's den.

The sad round eyes of Uncle Toby's gas mask gazed down at me. Dad's brother Toby, a gentle and sensitive youth, had returned from World War One traumatized and unable to conform to peacetime society. Toby had complained of a mysterious stomachache for so many years his doctors decided the pain was imaginary. Convinced he must be insane, Toby had voluntarily committed himself to Porirua Lunatic Asylum, as it was then called. Fools and children referred to it as the *loony bin*.

Whenever I'm tempted to think humanity has learned nothing from its mistakes, I'm heartened by the extent to which attitudes about mental illness have improved. Those who suffered psychiatric disabilities in the mid-twentieth century were treated with ignorant cruelty both outside and within the institutions where they were incarcerated. I had yet to learn that one of our country's greatest writers, Janet Frame, had been rescued from undergoing a lobotomy when, days before the scheduled procedure, one of her doctors noticed she was about to receive a national literary award.

The gas mask stared at me with cavernous eyes as I lifted it off the hook. It was impossible to believe Uncle Toby was insane. When we were pen pals, he wrote exquisite letters about mist gathering around hills and jonquils blossoming in swamps. He even took interest in my dreary school career.

When Dad let me accompany him on a visit once, a guard unlocked a wall of heavy iron bars. Uncle Toby hunched in a chair next to the window of his tiny cell. He wore blue and white striped pajamas. It was three in the afternoon.

Not long after, Uncle Toby's brown leather suitcase was delivered to our front hallway. A sad collection of clothes was all that remained of Dad's brother. An autopsy later revealed a debilitating and painful stomach disorder. Nobody had taken time to listen to my uncle.

If he were still alive, I knew Uncle Toby would be first to champion Mickey. Toby, of all people, understood what it meant to escape death only to be marginalized and un-wanted.

A corner of the darkroom was devoted to masculine pur-suits. An ice axe and crampons were homages to manhood. The rusting springs of Dad's chest expander drooped from two wooden handles. One of my earliest memories was of him stretching the springs across his chest to build his torso muscles. He didn't use it much anymore. I couldn't blame Dad for needing to be manly. According to the back pages of Jim's comics, life was perilous for a narrow-chested man. The lightly built male never knew when a bully might kick sand in his face. His only solution was to emulate the famous Amer-ican body builder, Charles Atlas, and sprout muscles.

Dad was a wonderful photographer. Like a cat on the prowl, he was always watching, waiting to snare an image and preserve it for eternity. At the beach, or on family holi-days, The Single Lens Reflex camera was a permanent fix-ture around his neck. If the light was right (not too contrasty), and we were surfing down a river on our inflatable rafts or staring at plip-plop mud in Rotorua's volcanic region, he'd be there, watching—part of the scene, but not. Photography is the introvert's way of participating. Consciously control-ling his tremor, he'd raise the camera, swivel the lens, and press the shutter with a satisfying click.

If he was taking color slides, he'd send the yellow canister of exposed film away for processing. After six or more weeks of anxious waiting, the box of slides would arrive. Once din-ner was over and it was properly dark outside, Dad would lift the big old projector from its cupboard under the drinks tray and unfurl the huge pale screen teetering on its tripod. We'd settle on the sofa to relive the tensions and delights of our latest road trip in the Zephyr—at twice the size and in bril-liant color.

Mum would complain about her neck looking terrible in an unsettlingly sensual close-up of her doing the backstroke in a pool, while the rest of us searched for signs of favoritism, quietly counting the number of scenes we'd been excluded from.

Dad wasn't talkative. Most of what he needed to say was in his photos. He caught extroverts flinging their arms about mid-conversation, pompous city councilors sizing each other up, as well as the people who preferred to hover around the edges. We, his offspring, grew taller, more awkward year after year in front of his lens. There was more tenderness and devotion in those family photos than I was capable of understanding at the time.

Dad took slides of the Queen's visit, cousins' weddings, and funerals. When he flew off to Australia to discuss natural gas with people who understood what he was talking about, he came home with beguiling images of Sydney streets, tropical garden bars, and motels with swimming pools so blue they hurt my eyes. It was a world more glamorous than anything I'd imagined. Mum dragged on her cigarette and scoffed at the bikini-clad blonde lounging in the foreground on the Gold Coast. The tanned goddess wore big dark sunglasses and stared directly at the lens. I couldn't tell if she was flirting with the camera or with Dad.

While his color slides were ravishing, the black-and-white ones he brought to life in the dark room were edgy and artistic. I'd seen him take a roll of film out of his camera, develop the negatives, and transform one of them into a full-blown portrait of the mountain. Wizardry.

A row of A4-sized black-and-white prints dangled from a miniature clothesline. I tore down the one of me wearing my headband and a cheesy grin. Fritz, perky and cooperative for once, sat in my arms. It was a good photo of Fritz, but not of me. I ripped the photo in two and shoved it in the battered oil can under the counter.

I bent and picked up a burlap sack. It reeked. I gave it a shake. A plume of coal dust unfurled across the room.

The door hinge emitted a sinister creak. A triangle of

pearly light stretched across the floor. I stood still and swallowed hard.

"You're not keeping him in here?" my sister said, stepping into the shadows.

Alarm turned to delight, when I saw an impatient Mickey writhing in her arms. He regarded me with curiosity as I rested his damaged paw on my fingers. The gash was a dark line, slightly raised across the middle pad. It didn't look infected, but it was too early to tell.

"He can't stay in here," she said. "Dad keeps the door closed."

"I know," I said, collecting a couple of sacks. "I've got an idea."

With Mickey in her arms, Mary followed me out of the darkroom to a far corner of the basement archway, which formed a nook against the woodpile. It was discreet, almost invisible, and a perfect cat hideout. I arranged the sacks in a kind of nest.

"He'll need more than that," she said, taking offcuts from the timber pile with her free hand and shaping them into a rough shelter.

"Brilliant!" I said. "That'll keep the wind out. Mickey's cabin in the woods."

"Yes, but it could do with a roof."

Mary transferred Mickey into my arms and disappeared into the darkroom. When I stroked his soft gray fur, he stopped wriggling. The cat licked his front paw with his raspy tongue. I was concerned the wound was troubling him.

My sister returned with a piece of battered plywood imprinted with a faded blue logo, BUSHELLS TEA.

"It's a bit big," she said, lowering the board over the makeshift walls.

"Couldn't be better," I said, lowering Mickey onto his new front porch. "The overhang gives him a veranda."

The small gray tiger sniffed the sacks. He didn't mind the

smell of coal. Maybe it reminded him of his birthplace at the gasworks.

"I think he likes it," I said, as Mickey padded curiously into his cabin. "It's just the right size."

The cat curled himself into a ball and nestled in the shadows. I squeezed my hand through the doorway and rubbed his ear. Mickey approved of his new home.

I dug a dab of tuna salad out of my pocket, arranged it on a paint can lid, and placed it outside the entrance to the cabin.

Mary placed a cracked teacup full of water next to the paint can lid.

"He can drink from the fishpond too."

I was startled by the sound of soft regular thud of footsteps above our heads. Someone was up there, maybe following us. The dining room window scraped open. The stereo system screeched as a needle landed clumsily on a vinyl record. My shoulders sank with relief. It was just Dad treating the neighborhood to another of his musical extravaganzas.

"Shall We Dance?" the biggest hit from *The King and I*, boomed across the valley.

"Why can't we be a normal family?" Mary asked with a sigh.

"Never going to happen."

"I don't know why she's making me go to that audition with her tomorrow," Mary said. "Who wants to prance about on stage with everyone looking at you?"

"Swap you."

"Wish I could." I could tell by her tone she meant it.

Later that evening, after a feast of gray ground mutton and carrots on toast, I helped Mum clear the table. Devoid of makeup, her face was pale. There was a haunted beauty to her unadorned cheekbones and heavy eyelids. Her hair was in curlers tied back in a pale blue net. She was preparing for battle.

"Did you mean what you said to Geraldine?" I asked.

"About the importance of domestic science for girls?"

"No. The part about you not going to the audition to-morrow."

"Heavens no!" she said, flicking a tea towel over her shoulder. "Just a fit of nerves, dear. Ask any great artist. If you're not on edge, you'll never give your best performance."

"Do you think Elizabeth Taylor gets nervous?"

Mum rattled the dishwashing cage in the sink. I wondered who'd invented the idea of putting a yellow bar of Sunlight soap in a handheld wire prison. It was almost impossible to work up a decent lather.

"I wouldn't put Elizabeth Taylor in the same league as a great Shakespearean actress like Dame Sybil Thorndike," she said, studying a fly spot on the window.

"Did you ever get nervous doing journalism?"

"I tried to write the best sentence I was capable of at any given time," she replied, swishing the dishwashing cage in front of me.

I wiped a cup and placed it in the cupboard above the sugar bin.

"The most important thing is to find something you're good at and keep working at it," Mum said. "You mustn't neglect your talent. It's the best story in the Bible, the man who threw away his talents and regretted it."

I lifted the top plate from the pile of dishes draining over the counter. Mum had clearly sacrificed her talents at the altar of wifedom and motherhood.

"What would you rather have—another crack at journalism, or Lady Thiang?" I asked.

Mum tossed her head as if that was the stupidest question.

"The part, of course."

"You'll get it," I said, clattering forks into the cutlery drawer.

"Geraldine forgot to give me her earrings for the audition," she said with a warble of girlish anxiety. "Do you think she's changed her mind?"

"Why don't you give her a call?"

Mum plunged the dishwashing cage and rattled it vigorously in the sink.

"I'd rather the stage floor rose up and swallowed me."

Adults could be worse than children.

I put the last cup away, checked Mum wasn't looking, and stuffed my pocket with leftovers.

Later, I snuck a tin of Raleigh's medicated ointment from the bathroom cabinet and took it under the house.

To my delight, I found Mickey dozing on the sacks inside his cabin.

I dabbed his paw with ointment. He promptly licked it off.

Chapter Fifteen

ALL IN
THE SEEING

"Devils on Horseback," I said, trying to wrap a bacon strip around an uncooperative prune. "Who came up with that name?"

I stabbed the squishy mound with a wooden toothpick. The bacon unraveled. Prune juice squirted across the kitchen table and dribbled on the floor.

"Norman raiders covered their armor in bacon to scare their enemies," Aunt Lila said, appearing at my side. "These are a reminder."

"What of?"

"That men can be savages," my aunt said, enveloping a prune in a streak of bacon, and spearing it with graceful ease.

Mum was on a high from Sunday afternoon's audition. Everyone, including Eric the producer, agreed she was fabulous. She'd nailed all the high notes (despite the rehearsal piano being slightly off key). Her characterization of Lady Thiang was so impressive, David Carrington from the bridal fabric department of C. C. Ward's fell to his knees and kissed her feet in the middle of the rehearsal room.

In post-audition euphoria, Mum invited the world to a cocktail party at our place. Everyone who mattered was quick to say yes, including Dad's visiting American oilmen, Veronica from the local newspaper along with her suave German husband Wally, and the entire Operatic Society.

Even poor Geraldine agreed to attend. Aside from the fact she lived next door and there was no hope of hiding a party from her, Mum felt sorry for her. Apparently, Geraldine had decided to go along to the audition at the last minute and gone home afterwards feeling wretched. With her family and the new job, she'd had no time to prepare.

"How much longer do you think your mother's going to be preening herself upstairs?" Lila asked, tightening her apron in a firm bow behind her back.

As the older sister, Lila was one of the few people immune to Noeline's flamboyant ways. My aunt, as a rule, avoided social gatherings involving non-relatives. This time, however, she'd been forced to attend. She'd had to drive Nana into town for an afternoon hospital check-up. There'd been no choice but to stay the night. Jim had vacated his room to stay with a friend, so Nana could doze at leisure.

I pictured Mum rifling through the mountain of stilettos and homemade evening gowns in her wardrobe.

"She's trying out some new-fangled heated rollers," I said in her defense. "They come in a little box that warms up by itself and—"

"When does she wants these in the oven?"

A dozen bacon-clad devils oozed juice over the chopping board.

"Just before everyone gets here," I said. "A quarter to six, maybe. That gives us . . ."

The two black arrows on the kitchen wall clock slumped at a permanent six thirty. Dad had forgotten to change the battery.

"Never mind," Lila said, opening the fridge to retrieve a large block of cheese. "Bring that can of pineapple from the pantry."

My aunt and I stood side by side threading cheese and pineapple cubes onto toothpicks and stabbing them into grapefruits. The result was pleasingly Sputnik-ish.

"How's Mickey?" Lila asked, topping the cheese sticks with crimson cherries.

She listened without comment while I told her about the log cabin.

"Have you bathed his eye yet?"

I shook my head. Mickey and I were both on the waiting list for ocular procedures.

"Good evening, ladies!" Dad said, rubbing his hands together as he strode into the kitchen with Fritz trotting at his heels.

Dressed in his maroon-and-mustard paisley cravat, hair slicked back like a seal, Dad was in full party-host mode. The introvert in me understood the price he was paying to be jolly and solicitous.

"Can I interest you in a sherry?" he asked, sliding the plumpest cheese stick into his mouth.

I could hardly believe my ears—*ladies*? He was inviting *me* to have a *grown-up* drink? The amber liquid trembled in the two crystal glasses as Dad passed them to us with a solicitous bow.

As I raised the glass to my lips, pride percolated through my veins. I was the sort of *lady* who drank *sherry* . . .

My tongue sizzled. A blaze flickered in the back of my throat. I repressed a cough.

"Too dry for you?" Dad asked. "I have a sweeter one in the decanter."

"No, thanks. It's . . . delicious."

"Excellent," he said, glowing with pleasure. "Now to move the speakers."

He shifted the giant speakers from the dining room and set them up in the living room. The stereo system crackled to life.

"Put on something good, Dad! Not one of your string quartets."

As the warm, optimistic staccato of Herb Alpert's trumpet playing *Tijuana Taxi* echoed through the kitchen, Fritz yelped and skedaddled into the museum.

Free from the critical gaze of adults, my aunt closed her eyes. She tossed her head back and swallowed her sherry in a single gulp. As she rested her hand on the tap and considered the darkening valley through the kitchen window, her lips curved in an enigmatic smile. Transported to some half-forgotten world, she swayed her hips in time with the music.

I took the opportunity to sidle up to the sink and flick the contents of my glass down the drain.

"Everything all right in here?" Mum said, tapping across the linoleum in her six-inch stilettos.

My aunt jumped like someone woken from a dream and turned her attention to the cheese sticks.

"You look like a movie star, Mum!" I said, admiring her low-necked green velvet gown, marcasite earrings and matching watch.

She drew a lace handkerchief from her décolletage and dabbed her crimson lips.

"Is there a runner in this stocking?" she asked, flicking up her calf to teeter on one heel.

"No, Mum."

She had an uncomfortable relationship with compliments.

"Pass those cheese sticks around, will you?" she said, sinking the handkerchief back in her bosom. "Eric's at the door."

Babbles of excitement wafted from the living room on clouds of cigarette smoke, perfume, and mothballed fox furs.

"Here they come," Lila said, in a tone a swimmer might use to warn of an approaching shoal of stinging jellyfish.

People tend to adapt their behavior to suit the size and shape of their surroundings. Our province offered ample space for personalities to expand and become larger than life.

I straightened my headband and shuttled two plates of cheese sticks into the throng of local celebrities. Veronica from the newspaper office threw her head back and laughed like a man. Her gold lamé dress sparkled with nonchalant splendor. I nudged a shy cheese stick at her chest.

"No thanks, darling," she said, flourishing her long cigarette holder with a caterpillar of ash dangling from the end.

Veronica's husband, Wally, balanced a cigar between uneven teeth and squinted through thick black spectacles at my offering. He bowed curtly and raised a hand in polite refusal. Wally emanated mystery. After he'd been released from a British prisoner of war camp, it was said he'd changed his name from Werner to Wally and sailed the world to take up a job in our post office.

Wally's jacket sported leather elbow patches, a suspiciously intellectual fashion accessory. His refined accent and passion for classical music were enough to make him a spy, according to some kids and a few of the more narrow-minded adults in town. Personally, I found it hard to imagine Wally steaming envelopes in a back room of the post office to share vital dairy-farming secrets with enemy powers. From what I'd seen, he was more interested in pottery and philosophy.

I was pathetically grateful when a pink-faced Texas oil man assailed my plate of sputniks.

"Why thank you, young lady," he said, oozing caramel-coated charm.

He took a cheese laden toothpick in each hand. A blush radiated up my neck as he slid them into his mouth, one after the other, and returned the empty toothpicks to my plate. Americans exuded prosperity. Their skin was shinier, and their clothes smelt new. Their mothers didn't make rag rugs out of third-hand cardigans.

"Have you found oil yet?" I asked by way of small talk.

"We need to do some more testing analysis, but I think . . ."

I pretended to understand, but Dad's oil people spoke a foreign language. Savoring the twang of his accent and wafts of his peppermint breath was enough for me.

The artistic types swarmed like sandflies when they saw my cheese sticks. The town's foremost part-time theatrical producer, Eric, towered over them like a giant praying mantis. Though he wasn't handsome and too introverted to be charming, Eric had extraordinary power. He could snap off aspiring performers' wings and let them die in their day jobs. Alternatively, if he liked the look of a humble bank teller, he could transform them into a star to twinkle their incredible talent all over the province.

I smiled at Eric, but I was an outer asteroid to his sun. Surrounded by a tightening solar system of aspiring artistes, he bathed in their fawning desperation. Mum suffered the same affliction. They all ached to escape their life's drudgery to inhabit a vivid, exciting world—if for just a few weeks.

"We all know who'll be King of Siam," said Christine, a secretary/dance soloist with a beehive to rival the Tower of Babel.

Eyeballs swiveled to Bruce the South Taranaki dairy farmer, who was resting an elbow on the piano lid as if it was an old friend. Good-looking in a ruddy, square-chinned way, Bruce had the finest baritone voice under the mountain. Not even Gordon MacRae from the movie of *Oklahoma!* could surpass his "Oh, What a Beautiful Mornin'." Bruce raised his beer glass and winked.

David Carrington shouldered himself into Eric's orbit.

"Any update on the doomed lover, Lun Tha?" he asked, batting his enviable eyelashes.

Eric sucked his pipe and picked a thread from the hem of his fair isle vest.

"Ben Sheen should get that part," Christine said.

"Why, because he's your cousin?" David snapped, folding up the cuffs of his purple psychedelic shirt.

Eric scratched one of his protruding ears. Victim to the type of freckles that flake in sunlight, he spent most of his days at a desk in the accounts department of the abattoirs just out of town.

Though he didn't talk much, Eric's manner could be hypnotic. Eyes flickering like flames, he'd turn up the edges of his mouth and mesmerize a person. Dissolving into his gaze, they would sense him devouring all their beauty and promise.

"Who are you casting for Anna?" asked Susan Knight, the soprano. Susan had shone in *Oklahoma!* before slipping past the wrong side of forty, according to Mum.

"I bet it's Stephanie Fields," David said.

Eric studied the ice cubes in the bottom of his glass and rattled them as if casting a spell. The group inhaled a single breath in anticipation of the great man's reply.

Mum knew all about Stephanie Fields. Having played Katisha to Stephanie's Yum Yum in *The Mikado*, she was still bruised from Stephanie's talent for upstaging.

"We'll announce the cast list tomorrow," Eric said.

The artistes exhaled disappointment and consumed another round of cheese sticks.

I scanned the room for outsiders who might welcome some calorie intake. Over in the bay window, Geraldine and my sister were engaged in somber conversation.

"I couldn't sing a note," Mary said. "Then Eric asked me to walk across the room and bow to an invisible king."

My chest jarred. I'd bow to a sewage pipe if Eric asked me.

"I know," Geraldine said, accepting the last cheese stick and examining it as only a domestic science teacher could. "Auditions can be very challenging."

I collected a couple of overloaded ashtrays, piled them on the empty plate and hurried back to the kitchen.

"It's a zoo in there," I said, shaking cigarette butts and broken toothpicks into the trash bin.

The stereo cleared its throat. High-pitched vocals of "The

Lion Sleeps Tonight" were greeted with raucous cheers. Voices, already raised, shouted to be heard over the glorious music, impelling them to laugh and drink even more.

David's unsettling falsetto reverberated through the kitchen as he trilled the song's chorus.

I peeked through the door to see him and other theatrical types launching into whimsical versions of the twist, even though the music was wrong for it.

"Do you think they're having fun?" I asked my aunt.

"No idea," she said, assembling cocktail sausages on a plate.

I had yet to appreciate the nuances of adult enjoyment. My beloved aunt was one of the few who seemed immune to the excesses of drinking, smoking, and flirting. We were allies in that regard.

"Why don't we visit that young cat of yours?" she said, sliding the devils into the oven, untying her apron, and folding it over the back of a chair.

"I've got an idea," I said, lifting a small red cocktail sausage from a platter.

With Mum focused on entertaining, Jim away, and Fritz in the museum, I figured it was safe to collect Mickey from the basement. A less resilient cat might have run away from the sounds of a noisy party above his head. When I went outside and down the front steps, however, Mickey was waiting for me beside the fishpond. He bounded through the shadows and into my arms, as if to say, *what took you so long?*

When we reached my bedroom, Mickey sprang onto the floor, sprinted across the room and leaped on to my bedspread.

"He's never seen one of these before," I said, offering him a cocktail sausage.

The cat's ears pricked forward. He was quick to understand the meaty cylinder meant food.

"He is beautiful," Lila said, watching him demolish the cocktail sausage. "But that eye should have opened by now."

I'd grown so accustomed to Mickey having one eye, it hadn't occurred he needed to look any different. Lila slid a white handkerchief from her cardigan pocket and moistened it under the bathroom tap. I scooped Mickey off the bed and tucked his paws close to his body while my aunt dabbed his closed eye. The cat understood we had his interests at heart. He flattened his ears but tolerated the discomfort while Lila, with the steady skill of a country woman, gently massaged the lid.

"It looks clean," she said, as the eyelid appeared to soften under her fingers and became malleable.

I watched in awe as the eyelid that had been sealed shut ever since I'd known Mickey began to open. Mickey shook his head in disbelief as the slit peeled apart to reveal a gleaming, green-and-gold flecked orb to match his other perfect eye.

"He really is beautiful now." Lila said as Mickey wriggled out of my grasp and bounded across the bedspread.

Downstairs, the stereo system lowered to a background murmur. Lila and I stepped out onto the landing and peered over the balustrade. An expectant burble from the guests was followed by a flourish of piano chords and cheers.

Dad avoided playing piano in public these days. He claimed to have lost his touch since slicing a nerve in his wrist while fixing the downstairs toilet. Either someone had oiled him with whiskey or he felt obliged as a host.

His opening bars faded while Mum launched into the first lines of *Moon River* in her rich velvet voice. I could hear his long fingers caressing the keyboard, weaving around her melodic line, soothing her performance anxiety, smoothing over the occasional imperfection in tone. He urged the tempo forward, enabling her to reach the end of a phrase before her breath waned. Toward the end, they rallied to the crescendo in triumph.

At the final chord, the two performers would be flushed with exertion, exchanging breathless astonishment. Together they had created something magnificent, ephemeral.

A bubble of silence hung in the air. The party goers understood they'd witnessed something special.

"Bravo!" Geraldine called, breaking the spell.

Encores and cheers rumbled up the stairwell.

"I'd better find out how those devils are getting on," Lila said, disappearing downstairs.

I sat alone in the shadows on the top stair, resting my chin in my hand as my parents launched into their version of "Bewitched, Bothered and Bewildered." A shared love of music had brought them together. Their first meeting had been over sheet music, when Dad accompanied her on the piano at an afternoon tea party in her hometown, Hawera. A person could be forgiven for assuming my parents would produce a tribe of Mozarts, but Jim hated his violin, Mary couldn't tolerate flute lessons, and my fingers refused to work a keyboard.

A small tiger padded across the landing, tail aloft, and snuggled against my knee. *Never mind*, he seemed to say. *You'll find something.*

"How does it feel to have two good eyes?" I asked, massaging a spot behind his ear. Mickey leaned into my fingers and purred the deep, warm growl of a happy feline.

Applause rumbled up the stairwell. My parents had wowed them. I didn't mind belonging to a family of misfits.

Downstairs, the stereo grumbled to life again. The ululating chorus of "The Lion Sleeps Tonight" grew louder, more primal.

Our house could have a strange effect on visitors of all ages. Perhaps the fairies had something to do with it. Or maybe the unconventional architecture encouraged people to shed their inhibitions.

We were so familiar with the phenomenon that we barely mentioned it to each other. Some visitors would change their personality the instant they stepped over the brass threshold. Previously shy adults would go berserk and slide down bannisters. Wild extroverts sank into pits of gloom, glowering out at the sea from the top veranda as if contemplating self-annihilation.

The guests reached a tribal frenzy. Walls shook in time with their rhythmic footsteps. A conga line meandered down the hall.

Listening to the merriment, I hummed along, gathering Mickey to my chest and swaying side to side.

Our reverie was interrupted by the ear-splitting screech of the needle being torn off the record player. I winced. In a household with hardly any rules, somebody had just broken one we all took seriously (along with don't thump the piano keys): Never scratch a record.

The music stopped. A man's voice cut through the burble of confusion. He spoke in clear, measured tones, but I couldn't make out the words. A woman's voice—my mother's— responded loudly, in words jagged with emotion.

The front door slammed. A woman's footsteps hurried across the veranda and down the front steps.

A wintry silence spread across the foyer and sent a chill up the stairs.

"Knock me over with a feather boa constrictor!" David Carrington shrieked.

A hush settled over the entrance hall. Artists and oil men made excuses and asked where to find their coats. They stampeded out to the veranda, down the front steps into the safety of their vehicles.

A shroud of misery descended over a house that minutes

earlier had been brimming with laughter and music. Clutching Mickey, I crept down to the half-landing under the stained-glass window. Through a haze of cigarette smoke, I detected the shape of Eric hovering like a reluctant executioner over my mother.

"I'm sorry, Noeline," he said. "You struggled with those high notes. Geraldine's a true mezzo."

Chapter Sixteen

LIVING IN THE MEOW

Mickey stayed with me that night. With everyone consumed by their own dramas, I was confident no one would notice him curled like a sculpture on top of my pale green eiderdown.

"Trust me," I said, screwing the window latch shut (it was too cold for fairies). "I'll take care of you."

Mickey blinked back at me. I was amazed how beautiful he was with two gleaming eyes beaming from under the M. He could have stepped out of the pages of National Geographic. It seemed incredible that such a wild, dignified animal could have chosen me to look after him.

We'll take care of each other, my friend, a voice whispered in a tone both wise and kind.

Mickey yawned and stretched his mitten feet.

"Mickey! Did you just say something?"

The cat blinked. My heart raced with excitement.

"You spoke to me . . . with your thoughts! Why did you take so long?"

I've been talking to you since we first met. You just weren't ready to listen.

The cat twitched his long pale whiskers.

"Well, I can hear you now."

Good, Mickey said, licking his front paw. *People need cats to show them how to be better humans.*

"Cats teach people?"

We certainly do.

"What can you teach me?"

Have you noticed we cats meow only at humans? We hardly ever bother meowing at other cats.

"Why is that?"

People are slow learners. We send you the message over and over, but you never seem to hear.

"What message?"

"Meow."

"Meow?" I said, confused.

We felines have trouble getting our mouths around some of your human consonants. When we meow, we're really saying "now." It's our way of reminding people to live in the present the way cats do.

Goosebumps shivered down my arms. I reached for Mickey, but he sprang off the eiderdown and hid under the bed. I leant over the edge of the mattress and peered into the darkness.

"Come back!" I called to the silhouette crouched behind my school shoes.

He refused to move.

"Mickey! Talk to me."

"Meow," he replied softly.

The cat fell silent. After a while, I pulled the bedcovers up to my chin and sank into a deep, silent pool of sleep.

Around midnight, I was woken by gentle footsteps padding over my chest. I pretended to be asleep as Mickey crept over the bedding and pawed at the sheet around my neck.

Purring like a tractor, he kneaded the bed linen until I surrendered and lifted the covers. I couldn't stop smiling as Mickey crawled into the warmth and nestled into the crease behind my knees. Maybe he was just a cat after all.

Next morning, the house was icy quiet like the mountain after a fresh snowfall. I hauled the cat out from his warm, sleepy nest and patted his M.

"Was that you talking to me last night?" I asked.

Mickey shook his whiskers and jumped off the bed. He landed with a soft thud on the rag rug.

"I get it," I said, pulling a red sweater over my pajamas. "You're just a cat."

Mickey fixed me with his shimmering gaze. I felt a tingling warmth at the back of my mind.

Be kind to yourself and others, he said. *"Meow."*

I had no idea how to be kind to myself. It was easier to think of being nice to Mum and Dad, especially after their disastrous cocktail party.

The banner of Mickey's tail guided me outside, down the front steps to the letter box. A blackbird carved a line across pearly sky as we collected the milk and newspaper.

Back inside, the kitchen was a demolition site of dirty glasses, plates, and overflowing ashtrays. I skidded on a left-over horseback devil. Mickey pounced and unraveled the bacon with his claws.

I swiveled a knob under the stove top. The familiar, sickly smell of gas swam in my sinuses. I clicked the hand-held lighter, but it refused to spark. The gassy smell became more intense. I struck a match. The stove top ring burst to life. While the kettle simmered, I placed two cups and saucers on a tray with a milk jug. Mickey meowed and wove figure eights around my ankles.

"You want to go outside?" I said, opening the back door for him.

The cat squeaked a polite thankyou and sprang down the steps.

Upstairs, Mum and Dad lay next to each other, lifeless, like a medieval king and queen in a crypt.

"Sorry, I slopped it," I said, tiptoeing around Mum's cock-tail dress and stilettos, scattered like crime scene evidence across the seagrass matting.

Dad's eyebrows drooped like macramé wall hangings as I lowered the tray on his bedside table.

"Never mind," he said, hoisting himself up on one elbow. "I do that all the time."

Mum emitted a groan. Rivulets of mascara cascaded down her waxen face.

"Look what Helen's brought us," he said.

Mum forced herself to consciousness. Dad plumped a pillow, propped her up against the bedstead, and passed her a cup of trembling tea.

Still wearing her pink satin petticoat from the night before, she drained the liquid and placed the cup on top of her pile of library books. Balancing the saucer on her chest, she lit a cigarette and watched the smoke spiral toward the ceiling.

"Geraldine planned this from the start," she said. "I should have known when she refused to lend me those earrings."

The blue horses in the Franz Marc print above their bed bent their necks in sympathy.

"People live as they can," Dad said.

"Why must you always be so tolerant?" Mum said, dragging on her cigarette. "And fancy Eric releasing the cast list at our party. The nerve of it."

"It wasn't his fault," Dad said. "The paper fell out of his pocket on his way to the bathroom. That boy from the shop, David, picked it up and read it out to everyone."

"Humiliating," Mum said, rolling over to stub the cigarette to death in her saucer. She pulled the maroon candlewick bedspread over her head.

"At least Mary landed a part," Dad said.

"Consolation prize," Mum muttered from under the bedcovers.

A lance of envy speared my chest. Mary was to be a royal child?

"Bet she turned it down," I said.

"Of course not," Dad replied. "It'll do wonders for her self-confidence."

I glowered at his pink long johns hanging from a hook behind the bedroom door. My parents didn't understand that the only reason I did Creative Dancing, dyed my hair, wore the stupid headband, had hardly any friends, put up with being at the bottom of the clever class, and kept looking after Margaret's white mice was lack of confidence.

"You're not upset, are you?" Dad asked.

"No. My hair's the wrong color, anyway."

"Well, if humiliation's a competition," Dad said. "You'll never guess who's been crowned King of Siam."

"Bruce the dairy farmer?"

"That's what everyone thought, including Bruce. Eric changed his mind at the last minute," Dad said. "It's going to be King Roy."

"*No way*! Not Pam's dad? Electricity Department Roy?"

My father nodded.

"He didn't even audition, did he?"

"Roy's been busy with appliance sales since the Winter Show," Dad said in a tone laced with irony. "Eric made a concession and gave him a private audition after work last Tuesday. Turns out Roy and Stephanie Fields have chemistry on stage."

Dishes clattered down in the kitchen. Aunt Lila would be fully dressed, hangover-free, and muttering to herself about having to clean up after another of Noeline's disasters.

"I'd better help out," Dad said, rolling out of bed.

My father had always been old. He was forty-eight when I was born. As he shuffled across the room in his green striped pajamas, he seemed fragile, a mere strand of moss on the slope of an eternal mountain. He slid his tartan dressing gown off the hook next to the long johns and made his way downstairs.

"Are you okay, Mum?" I asked the mound under the bed-covers.

Mum's body formed peaks and troughs under the blankets, as if she was willing herself to sink into the foothills of an alpine range. She stayed in bed like that, silent and unmoving, for the rest of the weekend.

When I arrived home from school on Monday, Mickey was waiting for me beside the letter box. He ran ahead of me up the driveway and led me to the closed door of Mum and Dad's bedroom. Despite Mum's rejection, he seemed to care a lot about her.

I dumped my school bag on the landing chair and tapped on the mottled green glass of their bedroom door. No answer.

Mickey sat down, curled his tail around his back legs, and blinked up at me.

"You want me to go in?"

The cat sat and waited. I turned the handle as quietly as its arthritic innards would allow. The door creaked open. Mickey waited on the landing while I tiptoed in.

Mum was sitting up in bed, a red cardigan draped over her petticoat straps. A library book, *Greatest Women Singers of the World*, was splayed across her lap.

"Kathleen Ferrier was the finest contralto who ever lived," she said. "Her voice was very similar to mine. Except she had better opportunities growing up in Britain, and—"

She didn't finish the sentence, but I knew how it went. Kathleen Ferrier had been smart enough to annul her marriage and avoid the perils of childbirth.

"Isn't she beautiful?" Mum said, flattening the pages to show a black-and-white photo spread. "Kathleen was only forty-one when she died."

Only? The woman was ancient.

"Throat cancer . . ." Mum's voice tailed off as if she'd known Kathleen personally. "Tragic."

The door moved. A gray paw appeared.

"Would you like a cup of tea?" I asked, waving my hanky to shoo the intruder away.

Mum was oblivious, thank goodness.

"Pass me the cortisone ointment, will you?" she said, raising her hands in a gesture of surrender.

My throat tightened. Her palms were raw as steaks. As she peeled flakes of semi-translucent skin off her palms, a four-legged shadow crept across the floor and slithered under the bed.

"They look awful," I said, taking the silver tube off the mantelpiece.

"I'm seeing the color man on Wednesday. He says I need more yellow."

The color man was a genius, according to Mum. He healed people using vibrations emitted by different colors. He wasn't doing much for Mum's eczema. She wore gloves whenever she went out.

"All great women artists have terrible lives," she said, working the cream into her palms. "Poor Maria Callas. Isn't she striking? Her voice was magnificent, until she fell in love with that rich fool, Onassis. She lost sixty pounds just to please him. The quality of her tone was never the same."

A coil of dust lingered in a beam of sunlight over the bed. I prayed Mickey would stay put—and silent.

"Would you like coffee?" I asked. "I'll make you a French press."

Mum let the book slide off her knees. She took another off the pile beside her.

"And we mustn't forget Virginia Wolfe, hearing voices and drowning herself in a river. Or the poet Sylvia Plath. Tremendous talent. But being an artist and running around after all

those children was too much for her. She was only thirty
when she put her head in the oven."

Sylvia's oven ran on coal gas and was therefore, in a remote way, connected to Dad. Suicide by gas oven was popular, particularly with women.

I kicked my shoes off and took a quick look under the bed.
Mickey sat still as a stuffed animal, directly under Mum. I lay
on the bedspread next to Mum and latched an arm across
her stomach.

This was all my fault. If I hadn't been born at the tail end
of our family, a *late baby*, she could have claimed her freedom
years ago. Instead of fretting over missing out on a stupid
part in a lousy musical, she'd be strutting the stage in Covent
Garden, or cutting a dash in a newspaper office. She might
even have an important-sounding job, like features editor.

"It'd be such a peaceful way to go," she added.

The narrow face of her fox stole leered out from the
wardrobe.

"Or would you rather have some of that instant coffee?" I
asked.

"I'd just kneel down and put my head in the oven," she
said, dreamily. "Except the bottom of the oven would be
hard. I'd need a cushion to rest my head on."

I glanced around the room for candidates. Three new-ish
cushions hunched together in a drunken row on the window
seat. They were covered in an abstract pattern, and probably
too fresh and clean to go in the oven.

Mum's sadness seeped into the walls. It rose over the roof
and saturated the house in gloom. I snuggled into the soft
part under her ribs the way I used to when I was little. The
squeaks and gurgles of her digestive system reminded me of
a time when life was warm and simple.

Did she really want to die? Every opera and play was lit-
tered with the corpses of dead women. I'd seen enough to

know difficult women were doomed. *Difficult* meant intelligent, adventurous, and unwilling to bow to male expectations. It seemed the only way men knew how to handle intimidating women was by killing them off.

Overwhelmed with guilt, I resolved to do everything possible to make Mum's life tolerable. If I disappeared, she'd be free to piece herself together without having to worry about me. I'd get out of school and leave home as soon as possible. Maybe I'd marry a farmer. According to Mary, the best way to meet one we weren't related to would be at Saturday night dances in the Queens Hall. But I wasn't allowed to go along with her yet.

"What's that sound?" Mum said.

It was Mickey licking himself in steady strokes under the bed.

"Can't hear anything," I said.

I sprang off the bed and opened the French doors in hope the blackbirds and sparrows would out-squawk Mickey's self-grooming session.

"Can't she give it a rest?" Mum groaned, closing her eyes and raising a hand to her forehead.

Far below, from the kitchen window of the house next door, Geraldine's powerful mezzo rose through the trees. The king of Siam was getting more wonderful every day.

Chapter Seventeen

BRANCH BY BRANCH

Everyone needs a tree. Dad had the two majestic kauris he called The Lovers on the top lawn. Their great lichen-covered trunks stood side by side, roots and branches enmeshed. Mum adored the flame tree at the bottom of the steps next to the Taylors' hedge. The flame tree was every bit as dramatic and breathtaking as she was. Every spring, in an act of astonishing bravado, its leafless branches ignited in a blaze of scarlet flowers.

Deep down I knew Mum wouldn't be fully alive and in tune with her spirit until the flame tree blossomed again. Nevertheless, there were signs she was inching her way out of despair. She was out of bed and dressed, at least.

The tree behind the letter box was too small and unremarkable to have a name. Its soft emerald leaves rippled on the breeze. Branches spread out horizontally from a slim, mottled trunk.

Let's climb, Mickey said, grasping the trunk with his capable claws and scaling it like a mountaineer.

"Wait a minute!" I called after the stripey tail. "I'm scared of heights."

You're only as scared as you think you are.

I drew a deep breath of early spring air.

"Why do you always talk in riddles?" I asked. "The last time I climbed a tree I fell down in front of my cousins and nearly broke my arm."

Which part of you suffered more damage—the arm or your pride?

I had to admit he was right. My cousins' ridicule had been more painful than the arm.

The stripy tiger scrambled further up the trunk into the lofty canopy.

See how easy it is? he said, smiling down from a woody elbow.

I grabbed a lower branch, found foothold against the trunk, and swung into the tree. Above me, Mickey scrambled higher and higher, daring me to catch up.

Come see the view!

"I can't!" I said, damp with sweat. "What if I fall?"

Don't worry about future tumbles, or the times you lost your footing in the past. Be here with me now. Take it slowly, one branch at a time.

Soothed and reassured, I allowed my body to move into conscious slow motion, considering the feel of each woody limb before trusting it with my weight. Leaves shimmered in the sunlight and nodded encouragement. I sensed life coursing through the branches.

The tree has given permission for us to be here. There's nothing to fear.

Glowing with newfound confidence, I straddled the branch below him and savored a leafy aroma spiked with sea salt.

"We climbed a tree!" I called to the letter box.

Camouflaged amongst the leaves, Mickey and I drifted into other worlds. Our leafy fortress became a castle, a sailing ship, a giant seagull floating through the sky.

The tree offered a vantage point from which we were largely invisible. We saw Mary whiz past on her bike, on her way to rehearsals. Her huge smile and glowing cheeks belied all the reluctance she had expressed about Eric choosing her to be a Royal Child.

Mum, on the other hand, was still smarting after her humiliation, though she claimed she'd never wanted the part in the first place. She'd lately thrown herself into a frenzy of baking, sewing, and rug making.

Across the street, Shane Dooley, cigarette drooping from his lips, slouched along the gutter, kicking stones with his worn-out winkle pickers, the pointed-toed boots that were all the rage in the British rock scene. Shane hadn't been around our place for a while. I wondered if he'd given up taxidermy or had a disagreement with Jim.

On the path up to his house, Mrs. D was on her knees, trowel in hand, worshipping at the altar of her fuchsias. Next door to her, Mrs. Finkle, the widow who claimed to have been a diplomat's wife before the war, sat motionless in her window. With her white hair and bun, she looked like Aunt Myrtle's cameo brooch. Mrs. Gibson, resplendent in white gloves and a meringue of a hat, headed home from some stuffy afternoon tea party.

"Hey!"

The high-pitched shout was startling. Someone had seen us. I grabbed a branch to steady myself. The little Evans boy—the one whose mother had a bad heart—stood at the letter box gaping up at me.

"You got a cat?"

"He's not a cat. He's a tiger"

The boy put his head to one side. His face was long and thoughtful, his hair bright as orange cordial. With his checked shirt tucked into belted shorts, he was dressed like a miniature bank manager.

"Did you have an accident?" he asked.

"No. Why?"

"That bandage thing on your hair."

"It's a headband."

Mickey slid down from the heavens to nestle on a branch next to my shoulder. I tickled the sinewy depths under his furry chin.

"Where's your sister?" I asked.

"At home."

"How come?"

"Granny says we have to stay home and look after Mum's heart."

The responsibility of caring for his mother's vital organ gave the boy the air of a middle-aged man. We exchanged names. Danny was six years old.

"That's not a tiger," he said.

"Yes, he is. He's magic."

"Prove it."

"He grows ten times his size and takes me for rides on his back," I said.

"Liar."

"Doesn't your granny need you at home?"

"I'm running away."

My heart expanded.

"Where to?"

"Dunno," he said, squinting up at a cloud.

With a jolt of recognition, I realized the boy and I had a lot in common. Largely invisible to others, we were both floating through an incomprehensible world that we were desperate to escape. The only available refuge was inside our heads.

"You got a television set?"

I nodded, wary.

"How big?"

"Twenty-two-inch."

"Can I come over and watch it?"

"No."

Mickey's spine arched under my hand.

"You'd better go home. Your granny will be worried."

As Danny turned on his pale grasshopper legs, I felt a pang of guilt. Or regret at the possibility I'd turned down a chance to befriend a kindred soul.

Either way, I could have been nicer to the kid.

He picked up a stone from the side of the road and hurled it at the letter box. It missed.

"That's not a magic tiger!" he yelled.

"Yes, it is."

"I hate you!"

I climbed down from the tree, picked a lemon from its glossy neighbor, and went upstairs to the bathroom. I squeezed the juice over a comb and ran it through my hair. Lemon juice didn't seem to work any better than peroxide.

Chapter Eighteen

CAT IN THE ETHER

As I revisit those days with Mickey, it doesn't seem strange that he communicated with me. In recent years, on countless occasions, I've seen our three granddaughters, Annie, Stella, and Alice, tune into animals at a level most adults are incapable of.

It's not until the loss of innocence (or, more accurately, the gaining of stupidity), that people's minds become so steeped in the material world, they forget the ability to tap into the inner lives of other beings.

People often tell me about telepathic connections they had with pets when they were young. The relationship can be empathic and profound from both sides. Some credit their pets with saving their lives, both physically and emotionally.

Early next morning, I dressed, raided the kitchen, and hurried down to the basement. Mickey blinked up at me from his cabin.

"Do you think I was mean to that boy?"

The cat blinked into the milky light and gave no answer.

"So, I *was* mean! What can I do?"

I ran my fingertips over his barred forehead.

A soft heart is stronger than a hard one.

Mickey dipped his head into my hand. I massaged the soft spot behind his ear. Though his ribs didn't stick out so much anymore, he was no fireside feline. The texture of his coat remained stubbornly dull. He was wary and furtive around people, especially adults. Like a thief, he could melt into the background, dragging his low hook of a tail, and vanish. His reticence made the tenuous bond between us more precious.

"I'm going away for a few days," I said. "Don't worry. Mary's promised to feed you when she gets home from rehearsals. Stay away from Fritz, and whatever happens, don't run away, okay?"

A wintry draft wafted from the basement. I flipped up the hood of my duffle coat, fastened the top toggle, and placed three paint-can lids on the dirt floor.

Seven nights was too long. How would I survive without Mickey?

"Here you go," I said, sliding a soggy paper bag from my pocket.

Mickey's ears pricked forward. I slipped the ground meat onto my palm, divided it into three portions, and arranged them on the lids. I'd seen him drinking from the fishpond a couple of times, but I topped his saucer up with water from the outside tap just in case.

The cat assailed the largest pile of mincemeat as if he hadn't eaten for a year. I knew how he felt. I was starving too. Mum had shown me a horrible note from Dr. Hughes decreeing NIL BY MOUTH from midnight. That hadn't stopped me sneaking a Neenish Tart for breakfast. Rules were made for breaking.

Mickey and I had been through our ups and downs. I still felt terrible about letting him out of the tower window onto the roof of the top veranda on the day of the flying mice. It was a miracle he'd survived the fall onto Mum's camellias. And I should never have let Margaret talk me into entering him in the Cat Competition at the Winter Show.

Yet he'd forgiven me time and again. From those fragile foundations a powerful bond was forming between us. Mickey didn't care how big my bones were. He had no opinion about my headband or how soon I should get married. Uncritical and loving, Mickey's voice had taken up residence inside my head. He was teaching me to slow down and take responsibility, not just for him but for myself. Through doing my best to care for my four-legged ward, I was beginning to understand who I was.

Watching him lick around the edges of the paint can lid, I tried to pinpoint the moment he'd started to trust me. Most likely, it was that afternoon Aunt Lila wiped his eyelid open and gave him sight in both eyes.

"It didn't hurt, did it?"

Mickey was too engrossed with his food to answer.

I thought of Dr. Hughes up at the hospital in his green gown polishing his scalpels. If there was a God, the surgeon would have caught a tropical virus overnight and stayed in bed. Or he might've fallen downstairs and be in traction. Alternatively, God might have arranged for him to tire of slicing into people and hang up his stethoscope . . .

"Helen!" Mum called from the veranda above us. "Time to go."

I wiped my mouth with the back of my hand while Mickey demolished the second pile of meat.

"I'll be thinking of you every single minute," I said, stroking the curve of his spine. "Just don't go inside the house, okay?"

Dad needed the car to entertain a bunch of Australian gas men, so Mum and I walked up the hill to the hospital. She wore the green tweed suit and white gloves reserved for serious occasions.

"The Australians have found natural gas in the Bass Sea off their coastline," Mum said. "I think your father's a little jealous."

The mountain glistened against cobalt sky. A coating of sugar snow sprinkled across the ranges. On a normal day, the sight would have sent my spirits sailing up over the wild coastline, across my cousins' dairy farms to the shimmering white peak. But as I trudged across Churchill Heights, carrying my hospital bag stuffed with a new pink dressing gown, pjs and a toothbrush, nothing could dissolve the lump in my chest.

"Cheer up," Mum said. "They'll give you ice cream when you wake up."

That was a cruel bribe. When I woke up from having my tonsils and adenoids out, the sad little plate of melted ice cream floating in a pool of green jelly had no flavor.

The hospital smelled of floor polish, disinfectant, and fear. A nurse escorted us into a little gray room with four narrow beds that people had probably died in.

The nurse pulled a screen around a bed in the right-hand corner and told me to put my belongings in the locker beside it. A hospital gown lay folded on top of the sheets. I shed my duffle coat and bell bottoms and picked up the gown. The fabric felt like cardboard, and there was hardly any of it.

"You've put it on the wrong way," the nurse said, peering around the edge of the screen. "The opening goes at the back."

Mum helped me turn the gown around. She tied the strings in a tender bow at the back of my neck and beamed at me.

The nurse raised her clipboard and asked questions while Mum settled in a chair beside the bed.

"Have you eaten anything since midnight?" the nurse asked.

"No," I lied.

"Bowels?"

"What?"

"Say pardon, dear," Mum said, lifting a powder compact from her handbag and dabbing her nose.

"Have you had a bowel movement?"

"*What's she talking about?*" I whispered to Mum.

"She wants to know if you've *been to the toilet!*" Mum stage whispered back.

Adults had no business asking about my private functions.

"Of *course* I have!"

Mum twisted her wrist to take a surreptitious look at her marcasite watch.

"You can go," I said.

I knew she'd apologize for her insensitive behavior and insist on staying.

"Really?" she said in a bright, hopeful tone. "Are you sure you'll be all right, dear?"

I nodded glumly.

"Right," Mum said, brushing my forehead with her lips. "Hospitals are such dreary places. I'll drop by later when it's visiting hour."

"Visitors can only be here for an *hour?*"

"Well, you know the doctors and nurses are going to be very busy looking after you. We mustn't get in their way."

She snapped her handbag shut and, with a movie star swing of the hips, left the room.

A mournful, unshaven orderly appeared and motioned at me to climb onto his trolley. He wheeled me through a rabbit warren of corridors. We sped under fluorescent lights, a clock, and past a sign that read ONCOLOGY. The word had an ominous ring to it, like *octopus*.

The operating room doors swung open to reveal Dr. Hughes in a green cap and strange, elongated spectacles with magnifying lenses several inches away from his face.

"Your mother tells me you're experiencing light flashes on your bedroom walls at night," he said.

The fairies. How did she know about them? Dad must have betrayed me. Again.

"It's just the milk truck. Headlights flashing on the wallpaper. That's all."

"I can't decide whether to operate on one eye or both of them," the surgeon said. "Could we run through those tests again?"

It seemed late in the day for him to be changing his mind. I followed his finger left and right, up and down.

"You can do both if you like," I said. If he operated on both eyes, I'd get more time off school.

"We'll see how it goes," he said.

Frankly, I'd stopped caring. It was a relief to hand over re-sponsibility for my sight and everything else in my stupid life to so-called adults, even though they were all nut cases. I was sick of trying to make a go of things. The sooner Dr. Hughes's sidekick slapped his black rubber mask over my face and knocked me out, the better.

"Here we go, sweetheart," the anesthetist said, lowering the mask. "Take a few deep breaths."

The gas hissed. It smelt colder, harsher, different from Dad's.

"Now, let's count down from ten . . . nine . . . eight . . ."

I thought of that boy Danny and how he'd looked so lost. Did he really hate me?

"Seven . . . six . . ."

And what did Mickey mean about softening my heart? Life was so complicated, I thought it'd be a lot easier if I didn't wake up. All my problems would dissolve into a cloud with the fairies, and we'd float away together.

"Five . . . four . . ."

There was only one reason to come back.

"Three . . ."

Mickey.

Chapter Nineteen

PAW MEDICINE

Lying on my back, I tried to lift my head. Nothing happened.

A sharp pain stabbed my left eye. I raised a hand to explore my face. Only one side was bandaged. A thick wad of gauze was taped down with bandages. Disappointment mingled with relief. If Dr. Hughes had operated on both eyes, I might have scored more time off school, but it would have been twice the agony.

I opened my right eye. Gray walls spiraled into focus.

"How are you, dear?" Mum said, resting her white-gloved hand on mine. We were back in the ugly room with the screen around the bed.

"Is it visiting hour?"

"You're green about the gills. Would you like a bucket?"

What was she thinking? I was hardly likely to leap out of bed and mop the floor.

As I opened my mouth to decline the offer, a nauseating ache rose from my stomach. It gushed to the back of my throat and spouted a hideous mess over the sheets. Foul-smelling slime dripped off the bed onto the brown linoleum floor. Floating on the sea of goo were unmistakable chunks of Neenish Tart.

"Poor thing!" Mum said, snapping her handbag open and raising a snowy handkerchief to her nose. "Wait there."

She disappeared behind the screen. The nurse was far from thrilled. She summoned an orderly to mop the floor.

"Are you sure you didn't eat anything this morning?" the nurse said, briskly changing the sheets around me.

"Absolutely."

The nurse made a *harrumphing* noise only I could hear. She folded the screen back like a piano accordion to reveal a roommate. The old woman's gray hair spread like vines across her pillow. Both her eyes were covered with black patches. If the ancient one had heard—or smelled—anything, she wasn't letting on. Or perhaps she was unconscious.

The last two times I'd been in hospital, they'd put me in a long row of beds in the Children's Ward. The other kids were annoying, but they were cheerful most of the time.

Eight days dragged. Mum and Dad took turns showing up for visiting hour. One day, Dad brought in a toy cat knitted in black-and-white wool.

"Mrs. Dooley made it for you," he said, placing it on the cotton blanket.

"Really? How does she know I'm in the hospital?"

"Nobody keeps a secret in this town."

The toy was a goofy thing with leather buttons for eyes. I was way too old for it, but I loved it. The black-and-white splotches on its coat reminded me of the Friesian cows our cousins milked twice daily. I christened it Moo.

"How's Mickey?" I asked, clutching Moo to my chest. "Is Mary remembering to feed him?"

Dad nodded vaguely and smiled at the chart attached to the bars at the end of my bed.

"Dad! You're not listening!"

"Nothing to worry about," he said, running a hand over my forehead.

His gaze drifted to a patch of sunlight on the wall above my head. I could tell something was wrong.

"Is Mum okay?"

"She doesn't go down the front path any more in case she bumps into Geraldine," he said. "But the Color Man seems to be working."

He wasn't telling the full story. Something else was troubling him.

"How's the gasworks?"

"Oh, fine," he said in the offhand manner he used when he wanted a subject closed.

"Tell the truth, Dad."

He crossed his legs. His brown shoes gleamed with polish.

"The Winter Show was a flop for us. Roy gazumped us with his UFO lights and beauty queens. Everyone wants electricity now. Nobody's buying gas appliances. To top it off, we've had some serious leaks lately."

"I thought you were going to pipe natural gas from the sea."

"We don't have anything like the Bass Coast fields in Australia. Our American friends have discovered plenty of oil off our coast, but very little gas."

"You're always saying gas is the fuel of the future."

"I'm afraid I was letting my imagination get away from me," Dad said with a wistful smile. "To be honest, we may have to close the gasworks down."

Dad crossed his arms and sighed.

I could live without the condescending tone of our farming cousins asking, "How's the gas, Bill?" Gentleman to the core, our father always responded graciously.

But I couldn't imagine him without the smell of coal saturated into his tweed jacket. Gas ran in his veins.

Back when coal gas was the powerhouse of nineteenth-century industry, his father had designed and managed several gasworks throughout New Zealand and Australia. His brothers and uncle worked in gas too. Dad could remember gas streetlights in his hometown of Masterton, and even a gas-powered cinema.

The great Victorian monolith of the gasometer, the piles of coke, the heat, and demonic flames from the retorts, they were all part of him.

Further back, his forebears owned a candle-making business in London, UK. They lived in a mansion with nineteen servants on the river Thames, before inadvertently losing their money. Dad and his family had no talent for finances. The newspaper ran a story saying Dad earned less than the stokers who worked for him, but he didn't care about money. He was more interested in improving people's living standards by providing energy, using the most technologically advanced methods available. Now those dreams seemed to be dead in the water.

If the gasworks closed down, the whole town would run on electricity. Worst of all would be the smug grin on Roy's face.

"What will you do for a job?"

Dad interlaced his fingers in his lap. "Oh, I don't know. I've always fancied myself as a truck driver. What do you think?"

The image of my father in his cravat steering a milk tanker across languid green countryside was surreal.

My eye throbbed. I tucked Moo into my elbow.

"Do you think . . ."

I was about to ask if he could bring Mickey into hospital. Instead, I dropped into a chasm of sleep.

Chapter Twenty

THE
VISITOR

The drive home from hospital was excruciating. My left eye rolled about like a ball wrapped in barbed wire every time Mum went over a bump. I clutched the gauze dressing as she zoomed up our driveway and parked under the house.

I couldn't wait to see Mickey again.

"Straight to bed, young lady," she said, yanking the handbrake.

"Can I visit the goldfish?" I asked, desperate to check up on him without her knowing.

"Why on Earth?"

"I want to see if . . . they've grown."

"Don't be long," Mum said, sliding a cigarette packet from her handbag.

I hurried past the darkroom to Mickey's cabin. The little house was empty. Three upturned paint-can lids lay on rumpled sacks. There was no sign of him. My eyeball throbbed.

"How are they?" Mum asked as I opened the passenger door.

"Who?"

"The fish, of course," she said, exhaling a plume of cigarette smoke.

"Oh," I said, trembling inside my duffle coat. "Orange. I mean, they're more orange than last time. Where's Mary?"

"Dress rehearsal. She'll home after dinner."

Upstairs in my bedroom a bunch of Czar Japonica Camellias sprouted from a dainty crystal vase on the dresser. Yellow stamens glowed outrageous optimism against fleshy crimson petals.

"Thanks Mum," I said, settling Moo on my pillow. "They're beautiful."

"I thought you'd like them. Isn't it miraculous the way they bloom before all the other flowers have even thought about it?"

The seasonal rhythms of our garden had a powerful effect on Mum's well-being.

"Is the flame tree flowering?" I asked.

Of all our plants and trees, the flame tree at the bottom of the front steps was her totem. Like her, the flame tree was prone to extremes. Its branches were either bare and bereft or blazing with glorious scarlet flowers.

"Heavens no! Not after a winter like the one we've just had. Now, have a little rest," she said, tucking my blankets in. "I'll bring you sponge cake later."

A shimmer of warmth filled my chest and radiated through my arms and legs. She knew sponge cake was my favorite. I finally had Mum where I wanted her, baking and coddling like a normal mother. She kissed my unbandaged cheek and closed the door.

I woke to the sound of Dad's heavy footsteps mounting the stairs. He stopped outside my closed door and paused to blow his nose. Mum's stilettos clicked across the landing toward him.

"She's still obsessed with that cat," she said in a whisper that could fill an auditorium. "It's not doing her any good."

I clutched Moo to my chest and held my breath while Dad assembled his thoughts.

"It could help her recovery," he said.

"You can't be serious," Mum said. "She needs to rest and catch up with her schoolwork."

"But a pet—"

"We're awash with animals!" Mum said, struggling to keep her voice down. "Why can't she spend more time with Fritz, or her wretched mice? Or the goldfish, for heaven's sake?"

My father cleared his throat.

"I haven't seen the cat around lately," he said, clearing his throat. "Have you?"

My body turned to ice. What had happened to Mickey?

"Why do you always think if you ignore something it'll go away?" she said under her breath.

The door handle rattled to reveal my parents, radiant with fake smiles. Mum lowered a tray of tea and sponge cake onto my knees. I checked the cream to make sure it wasn't the sour-tasting stuff straight from a farm. It wasn't. Dad kissed my forehead. Much as I appreciated their efforts, they weren't the ones I needed to see.

"What's this?" Dad asked, taking a handkerchief from his pocket to dab the tear rolling down my cheek.

"Poor dear," Mum said. "She's tired."

Later, evening shadows flickered across the wallpaper, making the forest seem alive. The clatter of after dinner dishwashing echoed up the stairwell. I needed Mickey more than ever. He wouldn't have abandoned me, not by choice. Someone—or something—must have forced him to run away.

As I lay sobbing into Moo, my door creaked open to reveal a stately silhouette. My sister stood tall and composed in a soft glow of colors filtering through the big stained-glass window. A regal vision, she wore a full-length stage costume of purple brocade with a gold flap down the front. A small gold hat glinted against her dark hair. Her gentle face radiated affection and concern.

"Did Mum make it for you?"

Mary nodded. It was big-hearted of Mum to create such a magnificent outfit considering how she felt about *The King and I*.

The gold flap of her costume bulged and writhed. Mary stumbled and raised a furtive finger to her lips. She was hiding something under there. Cradling the weight with her free hand, she hobbled toward me and released a stripey gray tiger onto the bed cover.

"Mickey!" I cried, gathering him into my arms and smothering with kisses.

Purring loudly, the cat strode across the eiderdown and dipped his *M* in the palm of my hand. He looked up at me, raised a gentle paw and patted the bandage.

"He hasn't lost weight," I said. "You remembered to feed him."

"Most of the time," Mary said, adjusting her little gold hat.

"Thank you, *thank you!* I'm so happy to see you, boy."

The cat narrowed his eyes at Moo. He batted the toy to make sure it wasn't alive. Satisfied it wasn't, Mickey nestled between my sheets and rested his head on my pillow.

"We can't stay here long," Mary said, peeling the cat from his nook. "I'd better take him down to his cabin."

"No! Do you have to?"

"I'll bring him back tomorrow," she said, secreting him under her flap.

"Promise?" I called after her.

Alone in the dark, I waited for the fairies. I was pretty sure they knew Mum had told Dr. Hughes about them. Nonphysical beings could be sensitive at the best of times. I hoped they hadn't taken offense. I rolled painfully onto my side to loosen the window latch.

Early next morning, when pearly light played across my forested walls, I woke to find the window firmly shut. My eye pulsed under the bandage. According to the alarm clock, it was 7:15. The fairies had abandoned me.

Chapter Twenty-one

WATER
MONSTER

My heart lifted at the sound of paws skittering up the stairs. Mickey leaped on my bed and snuggled under the blankets.

"Meow," he said.

I meowed back.

"How did you get inside, boy?"

Mickey gazed deeply into my good eye.

Heal well, my friend, he said.

"It's so good to hear your voice again!"

Purring ecstatically, he unraveled his tongue and sandpapered my right cheek. Curved into the shape of each other's bodies, Mickey and I basked in the joy of being reunited.

Around breakfast time, the cat's ears flattened. His limbs stiffened. Mickey's hearing was sharper than mine. He sprang off the covers and hid under the bed.

The door handle rattled, and Mum swept into my room.

"Your cheeks are pinker today," she said, balancing a tray on my knees. My mouth moistened at the feast she'd prepared. Weet-Bix topped with tinned peaches, buttered toast, and orange juice. "How did you sleep?"

"It's getting itchy," I said, picking at the plaster on my cheek.

"That's a good sign," she said, offering an aspirin tablet from the folds of an embroidered table napkin.

Even through one eye I could tell she looked stunning in her new pink jacket based on the one Jackie Kennedy wore to the assassination. Coco Channel would never have guessed a provincial New Zealand housewife could run up such a creation.

"What's this?" she asked, taking a book from the pile beside my bed.

"Mr. Jackson gave me a ton of homework. I'm not doing it."

Nervous Mickey might make a noise, I searched for an excuse to make her to leave.

"Henry the Fifth is a wonderful play!" she said.

"It's just a boring old writer droning on about some dead king."

"That couldn't be further from the truth," Mum said, perching on the side of the bed and thumbing through the pages.

To my alarm, the mattress began to quiver. Mickey was sharpening his claws on the bottom. I coughed and rattled the ice cubes in my orange juice. I needn't have worried. Mum was oblivious, floating on a theatrical cloud.

"Imagine you're a young hooligan who spends most of your time at the pub with your rough friends, but you're really a prince," she said.

I thought of Shane Dooley. Compared to his friends astride their Triumph motorbikes outside Woolworths on Friday nights, he had a regal air that set him apart.

"Then one day, your father dies and you have to grow up all of a sudden and become king."

In such a situation, Shane would have to shave off his sideburns, buy a rayon suit, and get a job in a bank.

Mum had a genius for making Shakespeare seem a half-decent writer. She slid a cigarette packet from one pocket, a box of matches from another. As the match flared to life, a sharp whiff of fireworks tingled my nostrils.

"When Henry decides to take his kingly duties seriously, he dumps most of his friends and invades France."

"Why would he do that?"

"Because his ancestors came from France, he believes France belongs to England."

Mum kicked off her shoes. Her nylons crackled as she swung her legs up on the bed. She inhaled deeply and waved her cigarette like a baton.

"Once more unto the breach, dear friends, once more."

She spoke in a man's voice, fearless and royal. I was alarmed to notice regular thumping sounds from underneath the bed. Mum was so consumed by Henry's persona, she was deaf to the unmistakable sound of Mickey scratching behind his ear.

"What's a breach?" I asked.

The tip of her cigarette glowed red.

"Henry and his soldiers have managed to break through part of Harfleur's city wall. That's the breach. The French are fighting back, which is understandable. It's their town."

Cigarette smoke circled and enclosed us in the battle scene. I could hear the horses, the soldiers shouting, the rumble of masonry falling.

"Henry's men are dying all over the place," Mum said, narrowing her eyes in the haze. "He's urging the ones who are still standing to go back to the breach and have another crack at it. He's giving them courage, telling them he'll be alongside them. He's even calling the troops his dear friends. That's unheard of for a king."

"Shouldn't they just turn around and go back to England?"

"That's the last thing Henry wants. Listen to this: 'Or close the wall up with our English dead.'"

A thrill fluttered down my spine. No English teacher could make Shakespeare so real and exciting. The old-fashioned language flowed like a mountain stream from her lips. The words were beautiful, understandable. I was beginning to appreciate I had the most wonderful mother a girl could wish for.

Mickey was silent, probably asleep.

"What happens next?"

"Well," she said, closing the book with the authority of a star who knows her audience is hooked. "Why don't we start from the beginning tomorrow?"

She stood and ran her hand through my hair.

"Is Dad really going to lose his job?"

Mum stopped to peel a flake from her palm.

"Who told you that?"

"He said he'll have to be a truck driver."

"Don't worry. Even if the gasworks burns to the ground, we . . . Well, *I* actually have something up my sleeve."

Mum could be relied on to find creative solutions to the most unsolvable problems.

"I probably shouldn't tell you this, but remember how your grandfather, my father, owned three farms?"

I nodded. As a fourth generation New Zealander, Mum was proud of her pioneering heritage. She loved telling stories of courageous forebears who escaped persecution and poverty in Scotland to carve out new lives for themselves on the other side of the world. There was never any mention of who might have owned the land before her ancestors burned down the forests to plow their farms.

"When Nana dies, she'll pass the properties on to her eight surviving children," she said.

"Will we be rich?"

"Not technically," she said with a rueful smile. "But we'll be comfortable."

Mickey crept under the covers and curled into the gap behind my knees that night. We were soon fighting a battle alongside each other in the flaming ruins of an old castle. Masonry tumbled off parapets and landed with ground-shaking smashes at our feet. Mickey bounded ahead into the rubble.

"Come back from the breach!" I screamed.

The bed jolted me awake. It was rocking violently. The walls creaked in a sharp, brisk rhythm. A low, rumbling sound rose from deep under the earth. I gripped Mickey in panic. He dug his claws into my forearms.

When I cried out he slipped from my grasp. He puffed his tail out and in a shaft of moonlight flew like a witch's cat across the room. I lunged, caught him mid-air, and wrestled him onto the bed. The shaking grew stronger, so powerful I thought the house was about to collapse and tumble onto the street.

My bedroom door opened to reveal a triangle of yellow light.

"Don't be frightened," Dad said, steadying himself against the door frame.

He swaggered across the room like a sailor at sea and sat on the edge of my swaying bed.

"It's just the old *taniwha* shaking his tail. He'll move on soon."

I knew from Maori legends that a taniwha was a great water monster, who could be good or evil depending on his mood.

"An earthquake?"

"We're feeling it more because we're upstairs. If we were down on the ground, we wouldn't be rocking around so much. This old house has been through worse. It's nearly done now. Listen . . ."

He stroked my forehead as the rumbling subsided. The squeaking walls grew quieter until they stopped altogether. At last, the room resumed its solid, unmoving status.

"Now snuggle down with your friend," Dad said, rubbing Mickey's ear. "Sleep well, you two."

Chapter Twenty-two

THE SECRET
LIFE OF CATS

Through the dreary days of recovery, Mickey was a constant source of comfort and entertainment. He knew to stay away from the bandaged side of my face. In the late afternoons when I was tired or in pain, he would nestle gently into my right shoulder and fold his tail in an elegant curve around his haunches. I could feel the tender vibrations from his purrs relaxing my muscles from the neck down. Warmth and healing resonated through my body.

You are loved, he hummed.

I ran my hand over his soft spine.

"Oh, Mickey. I love you too."

After a few days, the pain in my left eye wasn't so sharp. Boredom set in. Mickey decided to liven things up by declaring war on Moo. He chomped one of the toy's leather eyes and flicked it across the room.

"Poor Moo!" I laughed as Mickey lay on his back beside the dresser, snaring the toy between his teeth and kicking it with his hind legs.

Victorious, he jumped back on the bed and pressed Moo into my hand as if it was a present. Mickey put his head to one side and fixed me with a quizzical gaze.

"You mean it's my turn?"

I tossed the toy across the room. Mickey pounced and brought Moo, whose right front paw was unraveling, back to me.

Whenever we heard Mum's footsteps echoing up the stairs,

he dived under the mattress and hid till the coast was clear. It was a miracle he never got caught. I occasionally wondered if Mum was pretending not to notice his presence.

At night, he became a mystery cat. Once satisfied I was asleep, he'd leap off the bed and trot downstairs. According to Mary, he escaped through the scullery window with the broken latch Dad was thinking about fixing.

I had no idea what Mickey got up to in the hours between midnight and dawn. Occasionally, my dreams were interrupted with discordant yowls from outside.

Though I scoured the forest wallpaper for fairies every night after Mickey had gone, they refused to visit. Maybe Mum and Dr. Hughes had been right, and they were an optical illusion. If I'd known the operation was going to obliterate them, I would not have been so keen to have it. In my bones, I felt they hadn't disappeared forever. Fairies were as real as earthquakes, taniwhas, and talking cats.

The morning of my post-operative check-up, Mickey somehow knew not to sneak up the stairs to see me after breakfast. While Mum fussed over her makeup, I squeezed into my bellbottoms and duffle coat to ferry a gray meatball down to the basement. To my disappointment, Mickey's cabin was vacant. I left the lonely meatball on a paint can lid outside his front door and headed back upstairs.

Dr. Hughes's office was on the ground floor of a pretty, full-sized doll's house. Mum and I stepped over the gleaming brass threshold into the waiting room. The carpet had the same paisley pattern as ours, except the colors were rich and warm, not faded and threadbare.

An old man rested his gnarled hands over the top of a walking stick in a corner by the window. His dark glasses were impenetrable. A little kid with tape across one lens of his glasses sat cross-legged on the floor and played with a small lead fire engine while his mother clicked her knitting needles.

Suspended in time and space, the wood-lined room was an oasis of reassurance between surgeries past and future.

I picked up a battered copy of *Life* magazine. WHAT REALLY KILLED MARILYN? the headline shouted over a photo of Marilyn Monroe pouting from the cover. Even though she was dead, Marilyn wasn't on Mum's list of tragic heroines. Mum had an aversion to blondes, and Marilyn was too lowbrow for her taste.

I slid Marilyn aside in favor of a vibrant red mushroom cloud glowing from the cover of the magazine beneath her.

"Is the world really going to end?" I asked.

"Ssshhh!" Mum said, raising a gloved finger to her lips.

The old man creaked forward on his stick. The woman stopped knitting mid-row. Her son continued to work on a large, immovable object lodged near his sinuses.

"Are we all going to fry in a nuclear explosion?"

"No, dear!" Mum said in her reassuring stage voice. "Of course not!"

"The Russians and Americans are going to blow each other up, right?"

The woman put her knitting down and beckoned her son. She pulled him onto her lap and stroked his hair.

"We were a bit worried when Mr. Khrushchev and Mr. Kennedy started arguing over Cuba," Mum said. "But things have settled down."

"Have they destroyed their nuclear bombs?"

"Not exactly."

"*What?* They're *keeping* all that stuff? Why are they doing that?"

"Well, if Russia wants to blow America up, they'll think twice because they know America will blow *them* up a few minutes later. "

"What's wrong with them?"

"It's their way of keeping world peace, dear."

Henry the Fifth bashing a hole in a wall had nothing on the Russians and Americans.

"What's wrong with people?"

"It's men, dear," Mum said. "They can't help themselves. If women were in charge, the world would be a very different place."

The old man wheezed disapproval.

A receptionist ushered us into the surgery. I climbed into the big black chair and watched the chart of alphabet letters swim in ever decreasing lines while he fiddled with a box of lenses.

"Just look at those hands of yours!" Mum gushed.

She worshipped any man with a university degree, especially one with medical qualifications.

The short, bald surgeon looked up like a startled pixie.

"You perform such miracles with them," she said, breathing heavy perfume over us both.

Mum had an ability to reduce a certain type of introverted, studious man to a gelatinous blob.

"This town's lucky to have a great man like you," she added. "We should name a street after you."

Dr. Hughes removed his spectacles and unfurled like a sunflower under the blaze of Mum's flattery.

"You're too kind, Mrs. Blackman," he replied, forcing his attention back to the box of lenses.

"So, tell me, Mrs. Blackman," he said, taking a lens from his box and holding it up to the light. "What did you do before you were married?"

The room fizzed with electricity. Mum loved that question. It was a hundred times better than the usual *Did you do anything before you were married?*

"Well, I started out as a classically trained singer," she said, straightening her shoulders so her breasts jutted forward. "I won a scholarship that would have taken me to

Great Britain, but The War came along. While the men were away fighting, I was offered work as a journalist, a general reporter, so . . ."

She reveled in the opportunity to explain she'd been more than just a country girl with a dowry chest. Much more. Dr. Hughes was mesmerized.

I coughed.

The surgeon dragged himself out of the vortex of Mum's glittering past, replaced his spectacles, and approached my chair.

"You'll probably have double vision for a while," he said peeling plaster strips away from the gauze patch.

Two Dr. Hugheses appeared, followed by two Mums and a matching pair of alphabet posters.

"And now," he said, raising two steel pincers. "Let's remove those stitches."

Though I'd felt the stitches digging into my eyeball, it hadn't occurred they'd have to be taken out. The doctor dug into my eyeball.

"I think we can say the operation was a success," Dr. Hughes told Mum. "She can return to school next week."

Next *week?* Mum and I had only just started on *Richard III.* King Richard was such a wounded, complicated character, I was falling in love with him. We needed at least another month to get through the play.

Dr. Hughes fitted a plastic skin-toned eyepatch for me to wear till the muscles grew stronger. I looked like a second-rate pirate. At least I was able to wear my headband again.

On the way home, we stopped off at C. C. Ward's to buy fabric for my mud puddle costume.

"Let's see," David Carrington said, running his hands over a row of fabric bolts. "Sunlight on a mud puddle. That must be gold!"

My pulse raced as he unraveled a roll of shimmering Lurex over the glass countertop.

"Congratulations on getting the part," Mum said, taking a piece of folded paper from her handbag.

"Why thank you," David said. "But Lun Tha is just a secondary character."

"Yes, but 'We Kiss in a Shadow' is a beautiful duet."

David blushed and told Mum how much everyone was missing her at rehearsals.

"Geraldine's good, of course," he added. "But not magnificent the way you were in *The Mikado.*"

Mum ignored his flattery.

"According to this note," she said, "the fabric must be beige."

"Beige?" David and I recoiled in simultaneous horror.

Mrs. Harris's pattern for my costume consisted of a one-piece bathing suit with legs holes cut high to make mine look slimmer and longer. David took a roll of flesh-colored fabric from under the counter and sliced through it with a pair of giant scissors.

"We need two yards of satin for the cape," Mum added.

"Can it be sparkly?" I asked, hopeful.

"Dark brown," she said, examining her instructions. "It's a mud puddle."

I wasn't looking forward to The Magical Fairy Garden Dance Spectacular.

Mum was on edge because Nana and Lila were coming over for dinner, along with Great Aunt Myrtle and her new *boy*friend.

David folded the pieces of fabric and encased them in brown paper, which he secured with a tightly knotted string bow.

"Break a leg," he said, sliding the parcel across the counter to me.

"He doesn't want to you literally break a leg," Mum clucked as we headed out into the sunlight. "It's a theatrical saying meaning . . ."

"I know what it means," I said, trailing after her down the street to the butcher shop.

A pair of naked bird corpses lay side by side in the butcher's window. Mum admired their pearly, goose-bumped skin.

"They're iridescent," she said. "So expensive!"

Dad was still recovering from the time Mum had persuaded him to behead one of our laying hens. Everyone was trying to forget the ghoulish spectacle of a bird running around headless, spurting blood from its neck. Dad gave up execution after that, leaving Mum to order chicken meat for special occasions only.

In a rare extravagant mood, Mum asked the butcher to take the smaller bird from the window. She handled the parceled-up chicken with the tenderness of a nurse carrying a newborn child.

My eye was stinging by the time we reached Mr. Wainwright, the grocer.

"How's the family?" he asked, adjusting the pencil behind his ear.

According to some, Mr. Wainwright's business was doomed because of the concrete barn of a supermarket taking shape across the road from him.

"Very well, thank you," Mum said (which I thought was stretching it. She still refused to mention anything to do with Geraldine and Lady Thiang).

She asked for half a pound of rice. I ogled the candy jars behind the counter while he went out back to scoop rice from a sack.

"They've put the doors on across the road," Mr. Wainwright said, gloomily measuring the rice on his scale. "People say they open automatically."

"How can doors do that?" Mum asked.

"Sensors, or something. I hear it'll be ready to open next month."

"Don't you worry, Mr. Wainwright!" Mum said with startling vehemence. "Nobody's going to shop in a place like that. Who in their right mind is going to buy meat, dry goods, and vegetables all from the same place? Especially when they have a fine grocery store like yours close by, and a butcher up the road."

Reassured, the grocer slid the rice into a brown paper bag.

"Rice pudding tonight, is it?"

"Just my point," Mum said. "No supermarket's going to take an interest the way you do. A supermarket doesn't care if a person's making rice pudding or pavlova."

"Fancy a pound of broken biscuits?" Mr. Wainwright pointed at a large tin on the floor next to the counter. "They're excellent for lemon slice."

"No, thank you. But I would like custard powder."

"You'll have to find that for yourself," he said, nodding proudly toward a row of shelves squeezed in behind the store window. "We're moving with the times."

"You mean I take it from there and bring it to you?" Mum asked, as if he'd presented her with an algebraic equation.

"We're changing to the supermarket layout," he said, scratching his auburn wig. "People seem to like choosing goods for themselves. Though it does encourage shoplifting."

My eye throbbed under the pirate patch. I needed to find out if Mickey had eaten his meatball.

"What are you having for the main course, to go with the rice pudding?" Mr. Wainwright asked, taking the pencil from behind his ear and scribbling numbers on a notepad.

A warm tear blistered from my good eye. Poor Mickey was never going to be a pampered cat who knew the taste of chicken.

Chapter Twenty-three

BIRD ON
THE WING

The meatball lay untouched on top of the paint can lid outside Mickey's cabin. It wasn't like him to ignore his food. I climbed over the woodpile and called into the depths of the basement. My voice echoed back.

Perplexed, I wandered up the back steps to the kitchen.

"They're here already!" Mum said. "Hurry! Put the kettle on."

Mum switched to manic hostess mode, rattling biscuit tins and assembling her best china on the tea trolley.

"Here," she said, thrusting a plate of homemade cookies me. "Help your sister entertain them, will you?"

Afternoon sun filtered through the windowpanes to form golden mosaics on the living room carpet. Nana acknowledged me with a kindly nod from Dad's armchair. Great Aunt Myrtle and her new *boy*friend, Jack, snuggled up to each other on the sofa underneath Monet's waterlilies. Mary sat at the piano and thumbed through a book of sheet music.

"Mary, dear, why don't you let everyone hear your song from *The King and I?*" Mum said, flourishing an orange teapot shaped like a dragon.

Blood drained from my sister's face.

"I've got homework."

"It can wait," Mum said, lifting the piano lid and hammering out an introductory chord.

My sister reluctantly began the song "Getting to Know You."

"Sing out!" Mum boomed. "Project your voice to the proscenium arch at the back of the theater! Remember to breathe from your diaphragm."

Mary took a deep breath and started over.

Under normal circumstances, I'd have begged to join in, or at least provide accompaniment on the ukulele. My eye was pulsating, though. I needed to lie down somewhere quiet.

"Bravo!" Jack cheered before the song was finished.

"Oh, Jack, you fool!" Great Aunt Myrtle laughed, slapping his knee.

The old woman's face was carved in deep, generous lines and her brown eyes blazed with vitality. Having sidestepped the cycle of relentless childbirths, she'd always lived in bold adventurous strokes, with a fashion sense to match.

Whether riding a camel across an Egyptian desert or visiting distant cousins in Argentina, she'd invariably attracted male admirers. It was a habit she had no intention of stopping now.

Mum rolled her eyes and lowered the piano lid. Myrtle was immune to her disapproval. From the senior woman's perspective, Mum was a child who had no right to sneer at her for taking up with a new man friend at the age of 88.

Jack, crimson with admiration (or possibly a heart condition), beamed at his new love interest through picket fence teeth.

"Are they soft?" she asked, adjusting a vibrant scarf over her purple blazer as she examined my plate of cookies.

I assured her they were.

Back in the kitchen, Jim and Lila were engaged in an intense exchange over the table.

"You know I don't believe in it," Jim said, hitching up the sleeve of his leather jacket and uncurling his hand. Lila examined his palm.

A good fortune teller is an asset to any family. Though

Lila's personality descriptions could be a little insulting at times, and her predictions vague, nobody forgot a reading from her. Some scoffed. Others were spooked by her accuracy. My aunt was impervious to their reactions. She insisted her information came from a higher dimension, and she personally had little to do with what was said. Nobody could force Lila into giving a reading. She only did it when *they* had something to say through her. Though Jim feigned reluctance, he knew he'd be crazy to turn down the opportunity.

"This is a creative hand. You have artistic fingers. See how long they are?"

As Lila spoke, Fritz trotted across the lino floor. I hadn't seen him in ages. No wonder Mickey was hiding. The dog sniffed my ankle, licked crumbs from under the table, and flopped in front of the gas heater. His tan fur gleamed with health. The white blaze down his chest shone like a vicar's collar. Despite his lack of interest in behaving like a family pet, he was a handsome little dog.

"Creativity won't be much use in the gas industry," Jim snorted.

Fritz rested his head on his front paw and drifted to sleep. Lila closed her eyes and inhaled. Her wrinkles softened as her face lengthened and her eyes sank into their sockets. The timid maiden aunt took on the persona of an ancient deity.

"Your dream is to run a gasworks like your father?" her voice was suddenly deeper. The tone was loud, authoritative.

The fridge stopped gurgling. Fritz twitched an ear. Jim ran his free hand through his hair. He was growing it long on top in an Elvis style, like Shane's.

"That's what they want me to do," he said at last. "They say I have to find manly work."

The pantry door squeaked. It was such a discreet sound, nobody else heard it. I watched, mortified, as a stripey gray paw with extra toes slid down the gap and nudged the door open.

"Do not strive to please others this way," Lila said in her strange voice. "You have a good intellect, a strong mind. A little too strong, at times . . ."

Fritz, immersed in an exciting dream, curled his lips and twitched his legs in pursuit of an imaginary feline. I prayed he wouldn't wake up and see the paw. A bubble of laughter floated from the living room.

"I had two men fighting over me," Aunt Myrtle crowed. "Joe, who mows my lawns. He's only eighty-four. Jack's a bit older, but he does a wonderful Irish jig. The numbskulls forced me to choose between them. It took less than a minute to make up my mind. Do you know why?"

Reluctant eavesdroppers, we waited for the answer. The benign snuffle of Nana's snores assured us of her position on the subject. Having given birth nine times, she wasn't interested in anything that whiffed of romance.

"No, why?" Mum asked in dutiful response.

"I say jigging's far more interesting than a tidy lawn!" Great Aunt Myrtle cackled.

Mum rattled the tea trolley back into the kitchen.

"Disgusting!" she muttered, clattering the cups into the sink. "Imagine those old bones grinding together. They'll kill each other."

Jack the Jigger shuffled in her wake.

"Is this the way to . . . ?" he asked, feigning boyish innocence.

Mum indicated the door that led to the bathroom. Unabashed, The Jigger shuffled past us all to tend to his prostate while Aunt Lila continued Jim's reading.

I held my breath as a cheese nose and whiskers emerged from the gap in the pantry door. A pair of eyes gleamed like suns and locked with mine. My lips formed a silent *"No!"*.

"You're not up to this nonsense again, are you Lila?" Mum said.

Lila didn't seem to hear. Mum leaned against the counter

and gazed through the kitchen window as if the solution to all her worries was somewhere out there.

"You have a fierce, creative spirit," Lila went on. "I see a career in the arts."

My brother's face lit up.

"Really?" Jim said. "I can give up math and science?"

Mum took a butter knife from the countertop and wiped its dull surface with a tea towel. Her spine was straight and tense.

"A scientific calling is not for you," Lila said.

"That's a relief," Jim said.

Lila nodded and drew a breath from the depths of her being.

"You have the vibrational energy of a playwright or an actor . . ."

The idea of Jim writing plays and performing on stage sounded wonderful to me. Mum spun furiously on her heel.

"Acting's not a real job," Mum said, pointing the butter knife at her sister. "Our son needs a solid career so he can support a wife and family someday."

A thundercloud settled over the kitchen. Mickey's eyes flashed from the pantry's shadows.

"You're driving me crazy!" Jim yelled, scraping his chair back. "*All* of you. I can't wait to get away from this place."

Jim stormed out of the kitchen and slammed the museum door. Mum stood open-mouthed, butter knife in hand. The fridge emitted a loud burp.

"Afternoon, ladies," Jack the Jigger said, adjusting his trouser buttons.

The old man sucked his teeth, nodded at Mum, and shuffled back to the living room.

"Is that chicken?" Aunt Lila said after a long silence.

Our attention turned to the pearly corpse poised on the countertop. Mum's shoulders sank. She slid the butter knife into a drawer.

"Yes, actually," she said, flicking a stray curl behind her ear. "I thought it would be a nice way to celebrate having everyone here." Re-assuming her hostess duties seemed to calm her.

"Scrawny looking thing," Lila said, resuming her role of older sister. "Not much to go round. Have you got any sausages? We'll need something else to fill out our plates."

Mum's mouth set in a grim line.

"There'll be plenty of potatoes. Besides . . ."

Mum was having one of those thoughts that was going to lift her mood.

"It won't be long before everyone's eating chicken all the time. Have you seen those huge sheds Mr. Burmaster's building out near the airport? He's putting hundreds of cages in there, rows and rows. He says it'll make chicken a lot cheaper. People will be having it twice a week."

Lila buttoned her cardigan in response to another of Noeline's fanciful notions.

"How will that many chickens breathe inside a shed?" I asked. "Will it have windows?"

"Probably not. Ventilation fans, I suppose."

"What if one chicken gets sick and spreads the bug to all the other chickens?"

Mum opened the fridge door and peered inside as if the answer to my question was resting on the cool glass shelves.

"Peel the potatoes, will you, dear?" she said.

I longed to go upstairs to bed, but with Mum under pressure, I had no choice.

As I stepped toward the utensil drawer under the window, a miniature tiger glided through the air with the grace and single mindedness of a small war plane. I watched helpless as the cat landed artfully on the counter and sank his teeth into the chicken's right wing.

Mum emitted a long scream. Fritz, suddenly awake, backed her up with a series of volcanic barks.

With the wing and attached chicken firmly wedged between his jaws, Mickey sailed off the counter onto the floor. Fritz lunged. Hisses and growls echoed across the kitchen as the animals wrestled for ownership of the precious bird.

"Let it go, Mickey!" I cried. But nobody heard over the yapping and yowling.

I grabbed the tea towel and tried to throw it over the battle scene to calm things down. It missed.

Mum dived into the tangle of paws and claws. She grabbed the chicken in both hands and shook it free from the rivals.

"Shoo!" she shouted at Mickey.

Fritz scooted under the table and whimpered, while Mickey skedaddled, brandishing a triumphant chicken wing between his teeth.

"Don't you ever let that cat in here again!" Mum panted.

"I didn't! I won't!" I said, running for the door.

I tried to keep pace with Mickey as he scooted around the outside of the house, but he was too fast. Crestfallen, I watched his stripy tail vanish into the basement.

Chapter Twenty-four

TEARS AND HEALING

Lila coaxed Jim out of his museum to join us at the dining room table later that evening. Mum was still annoyed with her sister. Dad was doing his Easter Island monument impersonation. Jim was furious with all of us.

As Lila had predicted, there wasn't enough chicken to go round. We loaded our plates with potatoes, pumpkin, and peas, and smothered them in gravy.

Great Aunt Myrtle invigorated the atmosphere with tales of her adventures in the Sudan.

"Mother disapproved of me gallivanting around the world," Aunt Myrtle said. "We were supposed to stay home and marry well. She encouraged us to be artistic. A girl who could wield a paintbrush or tickle the piano keys had a better chance of marrying well."

"What sort of man did she have in mind for you?" I asked.

"You know, dear. One with a decent-sized farm."

Dad raised his table napkin and dabbed his lips. He'd entered marriage as a penniless gasworks manager. A vegetable patch was the closest he'd ever had to a farm. The only reason he'd been able to afford that (along with our house) was the *little windfall* from a deceased relative of Mum's.

I scraped remnants of rice pudding from my bowl and asked to be excused. I bolted upstairs, collapsed on the landing armchair, pulled off my eyepatch, and sobbed through my one good eye.

As I sank deeper into self-pity, I became aware of a presence at the top of the stairs.

"Don't be ashamed of your tears," Aunt Lila said, settling herself on the chair's arm. "They open the heart to healing."

"It's not fair! Mum lets Fritz inside whenever he wants. She hates Mickey. He's just a reject. He's going to get eaten by wild animals under the house."

Aunt Lila seemed to be listening with her whole body.

"Your Mum doesn't hate Mickey."

"Yes, she does!"

Lila was silent. I hoped she was going to tell my fortune.

"Noeline has the soul of an artist," she said softly. "You know how upset she is about losing that part in *The King and I*. She's putting on a brave face because she's proud. She doesn't want people feeling sorry for her."

There was truth in her words.

"It takes courage to be human," Aunt Lila continued. "Every day, people wake to a new chapter in their lives. They like to think they're in charge of the plotline, but it doesn't work that way very often. Others say or do mean things. Bad things happen. That's when you have to dig deep within and find a way to keep going."

"How?"

Lila stroked my hair.

"Forgiveness," she said.

"That's impossible."

"Parents are never perfect, but you can be sure they're doing their best. Just when you think you can't forgive anymore, you find yourself having to forgive again. And again. It's the only way to be truly free and at peace. Forgive and let go . . ."

Her voice trailed off as if she was remembering a monumental sacrifice in her own past—one she was still living with.

"Noeline might never learn to love Mickey, or even like him," she went on. "It's not her fault. She's going through a tough time. And we all know she's . . . highly strung."

Wind whistled through the crack in the stained-glass.

"Mickey talks to me," I said quietly.

Though it felt risky making the confession, I thought Lila, of all people, was most likely to understand.

"Ah, he's one of those cats, is he?" She nodded, her smile illuminating her face.

"I thought so. We must take special care of him in that case."

Sharing my secret with another human made me light with relief.

"How would you like to bring Mickey for a holiday at a place where he's welcome inside and out someday?"

My cat. The words rang like bells.

"I don't think a place like that exists," I said.

An enigmatic smile rippled across my aunt's lips.

"Let's see what we can do," she said.

"That would be amazing!" I said, latching my arms around Lila's neck to inhale a combination of lavender and lawn-mowing petrol.

Laughing with gratitude, I buried my face in the soft wrinkles of her neck. For the first time in ages, my eye stopped throbbing.

Chapter Twenty-five

THIEF IN THE GLEN

"How much longer do you have to wear that thing?" Mrs. Harris asked.

"This?" I said, tugging my head band.

I hadn't been able to focus on anything much since I'd seen Mickey's tail disappear under the house. He'd have run out of chicken by now. I'd called for him and even tried telepathy.

"Not that," Mrs. Harris said. "*That.*"

The dance class girls swiveled their heads in unison to zoom their attention in on me. Margaret sent a silent signal across the room, indicating my eyepatch.

"Oh, you mean this? Just till the muscles get stronger. I can take it off now if you like, except my eye's still a bit red."

Mrs. Harris retreated to the tape-recording machine.

"No, keep it on," she said. "Just make sure you're not wearing it for The Magical Fairy Garden Spectacular."

"It'll be fine by then. I don't have much of a part, anyway."

The tape-recording machine squealed as Mrs. Harris rewound it to the start of our dance.

"The mud puddle is a great dramatic role," she said.

"All I have to do is let Pam dry me up," I muttered.

"Take your place in the middle of the floor," Mrs. Harris boomed. "Curl yourself up in a ball. Not like that. A *graceful* ball. Tuck your legs away. Hide your face. That's better. Now where's Pam?"

Pam pranced forward with theatrically dainty steps.

"Pam, my little Sun Goddess," Mrs. Harris said. "You represent the dawn of creation, and your costume will reflect that. When the music starts, I want you to rise slowly from the horizon. Mud Puddle will sense you coming. She'll rise from her gloomy swamp and try to engulf you. But you'll beat her back with your magnificent golden rays and destroy her in the end."

Pam repressed a smile.

"I'm not used to being choreographed," I said, mainly to myself.

"That's my point, dear," Mrs. Harris said. "You gallop about like an old horse. The dance is a *visual* medium. You need to move your body in a way that's attractive, so people actually want to *watch*."

I flopped about in my finest imitation of a mud puddle while Pam flashed across the hall in glamorous leaps. When the final chords struck and she reduced me to dried-up flakes of dirt, I was relieved. All I wanted was to go home and find Mickey.

The best thing about cycling home was once Margaret and I rode across the flat, most of it was downhill, apart from the last stretch.

"I'm giving up creative dance!" I yelled over my shoulder.

The wind whipped straight off the mountain to carve out caves inside my ears.

"Don't!" Margaret said, pedaling to keep up with me. "Please don't."

"Why not?"

"I won't have anyone to stand next to."

"I don't want to be a moronic mud puddle!"

"How do you think I feel about being a stupid pixie?" she said, leveling her handlebars with mine.

Margaret's cheeks were red as lollipops. Her long brown hair trailed behind her. Her twisted spine was barely visible under the tartan scarf tucked into her camel hair coat. She looked so beautiful and outdoorsy; she could've been a model in an English country magazine.

"What's wrong?" Margaret asked.

"Mickey's missing."

"I thought you were hiding him under the house?"

"I was, but he came inside last night and stole a chicken wing. Mum says if she sees him again, he's going to a farm."

"A real one?"

"She's gone nuts. And if Jim and Shane catch Mickey, they'll stuff him and put him in the museum."

Margaret and I pedaled in silence as we passed under the rustling silver leaves of the giant Pohutukawa tree. Threads of cloud stretched above the mountain's pristine cone.

"I'll help you find him," she said.

Margaret's unassuming loyalty dismantled my internal barricades.

"I can't come over now, though," she added. "Mum wants me home for tea."

A sad, sweet bitter smell hit my nostrils. The sharp-edged perfume of hope mingled with despair was unmistakable.

"Can you smell something?" I asked as we squeezed our brakes to dismount at the STOP sign.

"You're always smelling gas," Margaret said.

"Must be a leak around here. We should report it. Someone could die."

Margaret smiled up at the Presbyterian Church, its steeple rising stern and stony into charcoal clouds. The new Methodist church sat on the opposite corner, its sleek, modern roof suggesting God could be trendy as well as judgmental.

Our bicycle wheels clicked faster till they made a satisfying whir. Icy wind combed my hair. My nose started to run.

As we reached the bottom of the hill, the road eased to gentle undulations. Margaret turned right at the Catholic church and peeled off to her surrealistic home life.

My heart shooshed in my ears as I pedaled up the last lit-

tle hill and turned into Bracken Street. The front steps beside
our letter box were empty. I checked our tree in hope of seeing Mickey draped over one of the branches. Not a whisker.

Closing my eyes, I pictured Mickey's soft gray fur, his
glowing eyes, and the way he purred when I massaged the *M*
on his forehead. Summoning every fiber of my being, I sent
him a message: "Mickey, can you hear me? I miss you so
much. Please, please come back home."

I imagined my thoughts stretching like tendrils across the
valley, over rivers and hills into the vast unknown, searching
for a connection with my beloved feline. But as seconds
turned to minutes, a boulder settled in my chest. There was
no response, no flicker of recognition, no sign that Mickey
had received my message.

Children's voices reverberated across the glen. Neighborhood kids were making the most of the evening light before
their Mums called them inside for dinner.

The Evans boy, Danny, and his curly-haired sister were
staring down a drain outside their house. Across the street,
Geraldine's three hovered like impeccably dressed ghosts at
the top of their path. They watched in silent envy as the wild
Dooley children cartwheeled through long grass next to their
garage.

"Have you seen my cat?" I called Danny.

"Your tiger? Did he go back to the jungle?"

"No, but if you see him . . ."

"Why have you got that thing on your eye? Are you a pirate?"

"Sure," I called over my shoulder as I pushed my bike up
our driveway. "Better watch out or I'll kidnap you."

Heart pounding, I clattered my bike onto the floor under
the house. I strode past Dad's darkroom.

A gloomy shadow hovered over the far corner of the archway. I scoured the darkness for the familiar outline of the
plywood roof.

"Mickey?" I called in a trembly voice.

A ghostly wind moaned. The cold permeated my bones.

I stumbled forward and steadied myself on the woodpile. To my horror, Mickey's cabin had disappeared. Someone had dismantled it and removed every piece of timber, as well as the sacks and paint can lids.

A tall, male figure emerged from the darkroom.

"Did you do this?" I raged at my brother.

"No!"

"You took Mickey away and now you've torn down his house!" I said, raising my fists.

"Hang on a minute," Jim said, grabbing my wrists before I could punch him. "I didn't touch your cat."

"What are you doing here anyway?"

"Looking for my leather jacket," Jim said. "I thought I left it on my bike."

"When did you last have it?"

"Couple of days ago."

"I haven't seen it."

His concern was legitimate. A leather jacket—even a battered second hand one—was the ultimate status symbol for boys his age. Not just because Elvis wore one. A leather jacket implied the owner might own a silvery stallion fueled with freedom, danger, and sex appeal—a motorbike.

"It's just a jacket," Jim shrugged. "Rick Gibson reckons someone's pinched his motorbike too."

My breath caught in the back of my throat. Every boy in the street coveted Rick's motorbike.

"There's a robber in the neighborhood?"

"Dunno," he said. "Mum wants Dad to call the cops."

Chapter Twenty-six

WHERE HUMANS DON'T BELONG

The glen had always been a magical place tucked away from the world. It was hard to believe a robber might be interested in anything about us or our possessions. Now three things were missing—Jim's leather jacket, Rick's motorbike, and Mickey—the possibility of a thief was likely. Adding to the confusion was the destruction of Mickey's bungalow.

Multiple scenarios swam inside my head. Had the robber zipped Mickey up in Jim's leather jacket and roared off on the motorbike? Surely somebody would have seen or heard something.

Alternatively, and more chilling, Mum could have packed Mickey off with Great Aunt Myrtle and the Jigger to live close to the mountain on some cousin's farm.

Next morning, Dad clomped into the kitchen wearing his mountaineering boots. The old canvas backpack, ice axe, and crampons were propped up against the hearth under miniature prints of Hogarth's London. His hand-knitted balaclava lay on the table next to the Weet-Bix packet.

"Have you called the police yet?" Mum asked.

Dad poured a creamy cascade of milk over his cereal.

"I think we all need to calm down," he said, smothering his Weet-Bix slabs in brown sugar.

"But there's a *criminal* in the neighborhood!" Mum said, sliding a tray of burned toast out from under the broiler.

"We don't that know for certain," Dad said, taking a blotchy banana from the fruit bowl. "They might have been passing through."

"Why can't you take this seriously?" Mum said, smacking butter on her blackened toast. "Just because you're having the day off to go wandering up the mountain."

"George and I planned this weeks ago. The weather forecast couldn't be better. No wind, and the mountain's perfectly clear."

"It's all very well for you two boys tripping off in your big boots," Mum said. "But there's a thief in our street. Authorities should be informed."

"I'm sure that's happening already," Dad sighed, peeling the banana and rolling it in a saucer of white sugar.

Knowing I disapproved of his sugary excesses, he flashed me a benevolent smile before swallowing half the banana in a single gulp.

"Well, I don't have a sweet tooth, so I can't see any harm in having a fresh banana for breakfast."

Dad's so-called lack of sweet tooth was legendary. A master chef of home-made confectionary, he could boil up fudge and coconut slice to die for. As for boxed chocolates, he'd perfected a technique we called the *Dad Reach*. Presented with an array of Cadbury's Roses, he could extend his hand in a way that gave the illusion he was lifting a single chocolate from the box, when two or more were concealed his palm.

"If you don't call the police, I will," Mum said, tightening the belt of her dressing gown.

"I think we should let the dust settle," Dad replied, devouring the second half of the banana.

Mum slid a packet of filter tips from her dressing gown pocket.

"How can you be so relaxed?" she said, tapping a cigarette furiously on top of the packet.

"An old leather jacket's hardly a diamond necklace. And Jim may well find the thing under his bed. Let's give it a day or so."

Dad's attention drifted toward the barometer on the wall next to the pantry.

"Have you seen how low the snow is today?" I asked.

I'd been up since dawn, scouring Mickey's favorite hiding places—under my bed, the chair on the landing, and outside, the monkey puzzle tree and bamboos. The unmistakable chill of an overnight snow dump lay heavy on the air.

"Don't worry. The mountain's my second home."

Much as I understood Mt Taranaki's hypnotic allure, I was aware there were parts of the world humans didn't belong in. I'd learned that from the fairies. Like the mountain, they held a mystic fascination, but only a fool would relinquish earth-bound reality and follow them to the boundaries of existence. Their unseen energies were part of the place we'd come from before we were born, and where our souls returned after we'd finished with this physical life.

Whenever Dad came home from one of his mountain adventures, he'd be flushed with triumph, as if he'd conquered something. He didn't seem to understand it was the other way around. With each ascent, the mountain increased its power over him.

"Are you climbing to the top today?"

"Heavens no. Early spring's the worst time to attempt a summit. The ice will be melting," he said. "George and I thought we'd have a crack at Fantham's Peak today."

Our father often lectured people about the dangers of Fantham's Peak, also known as *Panitahi*. Perched like a pimple on the side of the main volcano, it resembled a harmless mini mountain. Like everything else above the snow line, the innocuous looking peak was much steeper than it looked. Climbers who underestimated its perils risked landing up in hospital. Or worse.

Fantham's Peak held a special place in Aunt Lila's heart because it was named after the first European woman to climb it. Aged nineteen and in her physical prime in 1887,

Fanny Fantham hoped to reach the main mountain's summit. To her lasting disappointment, she was persuaded to
turn back because of the impropriety of an unchaperoned
woman embarking on such an expedition in the company of
men. My aunt viewed the story as another example of a
woman undermined simply to keep men feeling pleased with
themselves.

"How come you're taking crampons?"

"Precautionary measure," Dad said, lifting the oilskin
parka from the back of his chair.

He swung the backpack over his shoulder, swept the ice
pick and crampons off the floor, and strode toward the back
door.

"Don't forget your balaclava!" Mum called after him.

Dad clomped back across the linoleum, retrieved the
headwear without a word, and left.

"Did you two have a fight last night?" I asked.

Mum stood at the kitchen window and shook her head as
the car retreated down the driveway.

"Every time I gave birth, he'd take off up that mountain,"
she sighed. "After you were born, he went away for two
weeks. Can you imagine what that was like for me? Everyone
makes a fuss over Edmund Hillary for climbing Everest, but
I couldn't care less. Mountaineers are selfish people."

As Mum sank into a haze of not so pleasant memories, I
tiptoed outside, ran down the front steps and up the path to
Geraldine's house. Rows of cabbages and spinach stood at
attention in her back garden. There wasn't a weed in sight.

A blackbird's melody penetrated the ice-clear morning. A
morose child stared from a bedroom window. The door
creaked open.

"Your mother's not upset with me, is she?" Geraldine asked.
"I left a bag of grapefruit on your doorstep. She hasn't said a
word."

"She's fine."

"Thank heavens!" Geraldine said, shaking flour off her hands. "I was worried she'd taken offense."

"About you getting the part? She was a bit surprised . . ."

"But she's over it now?" Geraldine's tone was hopeful.

"I think so."

"I knew it! She's a trouper. I hope she has tickets for opening night."

I glanced up at the flame tree's naked branches twisting against baby blue sky.

"Have they caught the robber yet?" Geraldine asked.

"Not that I've heard."

A silver sheath glinted from the hat stand in the hallway. I shifted weight to peer over Geraldine's shoulder without seeming nosy. A full-length gown hung in sequined glory from a coat hanger. It shimmered like a creature fresh from the depths of the ocean. A red sash draped diagonally across the torso, and it had a Chinese collar.

Geraldine's Lady Thiang costume eclipsed Mum's audition outfit by a thousand suns. The red sash and Chinese collar were master strokes. Geraldine's gown was crafted to caress all her womanly curves. Regal *and* sexy.

"I've got a pretty good idea who the thief is," Geraldine said, tilting her head toward the Dooley place.

Her suspicion had a sleety edge. Sure, the Dooleys had the shabbiest house in the street, but that didn't make them criminals. Mr. Dooley's work was irregular. He drank beer from half gallon jars and rode home drunk on his pushbike on Friday nights, but that didn't make him a . . .

"Why would Mr. Dooley want a motorbike?"

"Not the father," Geraldine said, running an imaginary comb across her forehead in a passable imitation of Shane.

"Maybe it's not a real robber," I said, flustered. "There must've been an emergency, and someone had to borrow Rick's motorbike in a hurry."

"One thing's certain," Geraldine said, brushing down the front of her gingham apron. "We'll be locking our doors from now on."

It was impossible to imagine everyone carrying around keys all the time. She was overreacting.

"I was just wondering if you've seen my—"

"That's a strange eye patch they gave you. Is it comfortable?"

"It's okay, I was just—"

"I hear your surgery went well," Geraldine said.

There were no secrets in the glen.

"Have you seen my cat?"

Geraldine's gaze drifted to her vegetable patch.

"You mean a real one?"

"Yes, he's gray with dark brown stripes and green-gold eyes that have flecks in them and—"

Geraldine checked her watch.

"Girls!" she called over her shoulder. "Five more minutes on the Naughty Seat. Don't move a muscle!"

"They've been raucous today," Geraldine sighed. "I've had to shut Felix in his bedroom."

"When will you let him out?"

"Oh, about lunch time."

It occurred to me that kids need to be wild and free. Geraldine bit her lip and glowered. With a prickle of embarrassment, I realized I'd just expressed my thoughts aloud.

"So you think we should let them grow up like animals?" she said frostily. "What sort of cat is it anyway?"

"A gray striped one with extra toes. He's called Mickey."

Geraldine hadn't seen any cats.

"Can we come and play at your place?" a plaintive voice echoed down the hallway.

Geraldine glanced at her watch.

"Sure!" I called back, almost by accident.

To my surprise, Geraldine didn't object.

"Send them over after lunch, if you like," I added.

"Thank you. I'll keep an eye out for your cat, Ricky."

"Mickey."

The exchange seemed fair enough.

"I'd better go."

The Gibson house was a tidy white cube with yellow trims around the windows. Only rude, entitled people knocked on front doors. I climbed the Gibsons' back steps, past three concrete gnomes, and tapped on their bubble glass door.

Mrs. Gibson had forgotten to pencil in her eyebrows, which made her look more startled than ever. Pipe smoke hovered across the ceiling, signaling Mr. Gibson was home from work. Mrs. Gibson was pale and twitchy as a rabbit. Maybe they were waiting for the police. It didn't seem wise to mention the robber.

Mrs. Gibson hadn't seen a cat of any description. She handed me a Macintosh toffee in a yellow wrapper. I took it and left.

As I wandered through their garden back to the street, an ominous cloud cast an eerie shadow over the glen. It stretched out in the shape of a huge, sinister feline with sharp, pointed ears. Elongated front paws clawed the air. A long slender tail formed a menacing curve. The shape was so vividly cat-like, it was almost as if the cloud had sprung to life.

The cloud cat glared down at me through two deep voids of eyes and filled the glen with foreboding.

I shivered and pulled up the hood of my duffle coat.

"Are you trying to warn me about something, Mickey?" I called.

Solemn and silent, the cloud drifted toward the sea.

Brutus the Alsatian bared his teeth from the top of the Adams's steps. I hurried past to the Evans's house, smiling through a row of white fretwork around its balcony. From the clump of ferns beside their gate came an unmistakable meow

"Mickey!" I cried, heart leaping into the space where my tonsils used to be.

To my disappointment, a black-and-white cat slithered out from under the ferns. He shot me a haughty stare and stalked off down the street.

Old Granny Evans, silver hair set in curlers, welcomed me with a radiant smile. A tiny woman in a powder blue dressing gown, she had a deeply lined face that could melt with tenderness. Her lolly jars were always full. Her expression softened when I told her about Mickey.

"I had a cat of my own when I was a girl," she said. "Fluffy meant the world to me. I wouldn't have survived without him."

We didn't mention the robber. Maybe she hadn't heard about him. More likely, Granny had witnessed greater disasters in her time than a missing motorbike and a worn-out leather jacket.

Danny and his little sister Linda wafted to Granny's side.

"Hello, Pirate Lady."

"Don't be cheeky," Granny said.

"Can we see your castle?" Linda asked.

The child's green eyes widened under her mop of auburn curls. She clutched a plastic doll as if her life depended on it.

"The Taylor kids are coming over after lunch," I said. "Send these two over as well, if you like."

"Are you sure? That'll be five little ones to chase after."

"No problem. We'll play on the top lawn."

I omitted to add that five extra people would be a great addition to my search-and-rescue mission. If Mickey was anywhere around our house, one of us would be sure to spot him.

"Well, that's good of you, dear, but I don't think you'll be playing outside," the old woman said. "Have you seen the mountain?"

"But the forecast's good."

"They don't always get it right in the newspaper," Granny said. "Didn't you see that cloud? The cold front's getting worse. Days like this, people get themselves killed up there. I hope nobody's been fool enough to climb today."

A chill ran through my torso, down my legs and into my feet. I wriggled my toes but felt nothing. Dad and his stupid mountain.

Chapter Twenty-seven

BEER AND LEATHER

A coil of smoke rose from the Dooleys' chimney. Tiny clouds puffed from my mouth as I climbed the uneven path past fuchsia bushes. When I reached the top where the path flattened, I paused in the shade of the house and glanced over my shoulder in case Mum was watching from our kitchen window across the gulley. Though she hadn't specifically banned me from going there, she didn't encourage me to visit.

"Hello, stranger!" Mrs. D said, flinging her back door open before I had a chance to knock.

I loved her chaotic kitchen, redolent of stale beer and tobacco. A lazy fly circled the naked lightbulb above the table. Rumors about the Dooleys ran wild. Mrs. Dooley was Mr. Dooley's second wife. She loved her three kids, two girls and a boy, with the ferocity of a lioness.

A short, big-hearted woman with wild brown curls and a curvaceous figure, Mrs. Dooley embraced life with untamed enthusiasm. Though our friendship was clandestine, I valued it.

The Dooley household was opposite to ours in countless ways. Books were scarce, and there were no neurotic pretensions. It was a judgment-free zone. They had no time for Impressionist art prints or etchings by Hogarth. Three china ducks of diminishing size flew brazenly across the living room wall next to a color photo of the mountain set in a mirror.

Her pride and joy were the large portraits of each of her children, Stacey, Donna, and Martin taken on their second birthdays in the photographic studio on Devon Street. It was the sort of organized thinking my parents would never get around to.

Even though Mrs. D was an old woman of thirty-one, I appreciated the way she spoke to me as her peer. I could relax and be myself with her. She occasionally drank too much beer and took her teeth out, which she thought hilarious. If I reacted in any way, she'd pick the teeth up and snap them at me. Once, she got carried away, clicking the teeth like castanets and chasing me down the path past the fuchsias. I stayed away for a while after that. My confusion and annoyance soon melted, however, and I was drawn back.

The house was saturated in acceptance and love, most of which emanated from Mrs. D. Her kids spent a lot of time playing in the outdoor playhouse their dad had knocked together out of old packing cases. The playhouse was dark inside and reeked of sawdust, but it was a symbol of love. I'd always wanted Dad to build me a playhouse.

"I made too much fairy bread for Donna's birthday last week," Mrs. D said, rubbing her red, calloused hands on her apron. "Have as much as you like."

She laughed as I demolished the plate of white triangles covered in brightly colored sprinkles. Though curled at the edges, the fairy bread was delicious.

"Hungry, eh?" she said, taking her usual spot at the table in front of a packet of loose tobacco, an orange sheath of Zig-Zag rolling papers, and a paua shell ashtray. "Your dad took off early today."

"He's climbing Fantham's Peak."

"In this weather?" she said, glancing up at the brooding sky.

"He'll be okay," I said, wiping my mouth and shedding a shower of sprinkles over my lap. "Have you seen my cat?"

"You've got a cat, eh?" she said, placing a wad of tobacco on a rectangle of paper and rolling it into shape between her thumbs and index fingers. "What's the name?"

"Mickey. I love him so much. He needs me."

"Missing, eh? That's no good," she said, twisting the cigarette paper at both ends. "What color is he?"

She placed the cigarette between her lips, struck a match, and listened while I gave her a full description. The smoke had a more brazen edge than Mum's Matinees. Mrs. Dooley's eyes narrowed as she inhaled to the pit of her lungs.

"Want one?" she asked, nudging the tobacco packet toward me.

The offer was incredibly flattering. Much as I appreciated her treating me as an adult, I explained I wasn't ready to take up smoking yet.

Mrs. D tapped ash into the paua shell and called the kids in from the playhouse. Mute as the china ducks, they lined up against the kitchen counter. Dark-haired Stacey, about eight years old, held the youngest one, Martin, in a firm grip. Donna, the middle one, with wispy fair hair, shot me a cheeky grin. From what I could tell, they were all wearing hand-me-downs.

The three of them shook their heads when Mrs. Dooley asked if they'd seen Mickey. I invited them over to play with the other kids at my place later. The girls giggled, which I took to mean yes, and the little boy didn't care one way or the other.

"Nearly lunch time," Mrs. Dooley said, lifting a half gallon flagon off the floor and placing it on the table in front of her. "Want a beer?"

She wasn't offended when I said no, which was another reason we were friends.

"Squash for you then," she said, pouring neon orange fluid from a jug into a schooner.

As I raised the glass to my lips, the back door opened to reveal the silhouettes of two young men.

"You boys finished chopping that wood?"

They shifted uncomfortably.

"I cut myself," Shane said, raising a dripping forefinger.

Mrs. Dooley, cigarette drooping from her lips, examined the wound.

"It's just a scratch," she said twisting a tea towel around his hand. "Hold it up till it stops bleeding. Get a Band-Aid from the bathroom. You've met Helen, haven't you?"

Shane leaned against the door frame and nursed his hand inside the tea towel. His face was flushed from the exertion of wielding the axe and the shock of the accident. He studied the floor. A curtain of hair draped over his forehead. He was pretending he didn't know me.

"Sure, Mrs. D, we know her," the other boy said in a fake friendly voice.

My mouth formed a silent *O* as my cheeks started to fry. Troy from the Ghost Train at the Winter Show was an official bad boy. He was a Friday night regular with the motorbike gang outside Woolworths. Troy's gang had dangerous allure for a boy like Shane looking for somewhere to belong beyond the glen. I hoped Troy wasn't tempting him to join.

"C'mon, let's go," Shane said, turning toward the wood-shed.

Too late. I'd already seen what Shane was wearing—Jim's leather jacket.

Chapter Twenty-eight

DING DONG DELL

My throat was sore from shouting "Puss! Puss!" into bushes and trees. The plants shook their branches with derision and said nothing. Nausea swirled in my stomach. There wasn't a trace of small gray tiger in our entire neighborhood. I was beginning to try and come to terms with the probability Mickey was either kidnapped, lost—or worse.

There was no one like Mickey. He didn't make barbed remarks about my weight. He didn't care if I changed schools so I could get away from the bullies in the clever class. My darling cat never said anything rude about my headband, which, by the way, was incredibly fashionable in Carnaby Street, London (a fact people in our town were too ignorant to know).

Mickey and I were mountaineers, held together by a fragile rope of trust and telepathic connection. If one of us lost footing, we'd both tumble into the abyss.

The sweet natured cat had been with me just a few weeks. It was a miracle I'd survived a full twelve years without him before that. Mickey had expanded my heart and changed me for the better. The unwanted cat with extra toes was teaching me life doesn't mean much till you love someone—or something—beyond yourself.

I ached at the thought of never seeing those soft, kind eyes again, and how, at certain angles, sunlight filtered through his ears to make them semitransparent. I'd put those moments in a treasure chest of memories, but there was something I couldn't live without—the pure unwavering beam of Mickey's love.

Ghostly mist enveloped our valley. The mountain was up to its old tricks, retreating behind cloud so dense you couldn't cut it with a hacksaw.

At lunch, I couldn't eat. I sculpted the baked beans on my plate into the shape of a cat.

"Don't worry about your father," Mum said.

"They'll be well up Fantham's Peak by now," I said, shoving a forkful of beans in my mouth. They had no taste.

"Yes, but you know how experienced Dad is. They'll have turned back when the cloud closed in," Mum said, bustling into the pantry. "Gosh, these shelves are dirty. It's about time I painted them again."

According to her theory, covering surfaces in paint was far more time effective than going to the bother of cleaning them.

"That's what he says other people should do, but he thinks he's different," I said, scraping my baked beans into the pedal bin while she wasn't looking.

"What do you mean?"

"He thinks the mountain's part of him."

"Nonsense, dear," Mum said, pale as Casper the Friendly Ghost. "They'll have headed down to the carpark back at the start of the track. I bet they're having sandwiches in the Zephyr right now. Did you see how many spoons of sugar he put in that thermos flask? Rinse the dishes, will you? I'm having a bath."

Mum always took a bath when she was worried.

It was a good thing she'd moved with the times and started using dishwashing liquid. It made better bubbles than Sunlight soap in a cage. I squirted a green blob in the sink and watched the foam rise.

My industriousness was interrupted by a tap on back door. I ignored it. The second knock was more assertive. Mary was at dress rehearsals and Jim was out, so I had no choice but to answer it.

My heart sank at the sight of eager young faces beaming up at me from the doorstep. The neighborhood kids, all eight of them, had taken me at my word. I was tempted to send them home, but something made me hesitate.

"Why have you got that thing over your eye?" Donna asked.

I'd already identified her as a cheeky one.

"I had surgery."

"Are you blind?"

"No. Did any of you see a gray striped cat?"

A sea of kids waved their heads from side to side. It was almost impossible to sort them out as individuals.

The simplest way to identify which family they were from was their clothing. Geraldine's three wore outfits straight out of an Enid Blyton storybook. Deborah's pleated skirt and tortoise shell glasses gave her the air of a young academic. Portia's gingham dress, smocked to perfection, was a perfect match for her brown pigtails. Felix wore gray woolen shorts with a V-necked navy top. All three had glossy, rigorously trimmed hair.

By contrast, the two Dooley girls' nylon frocks seemed flimsy. Stacey's hair needed a good combing, while Donna's was hitched in messy ribbons. Martin sported a spectacularly snotty nose. They were all barefoot.

Danny was also technically underdressed. In those days, boys were expected to wear shorts year-round until they reached manhood, but his turquoise shorts were miniscule. No doubt Granny had forced him into the long-sleeved shirt and lace-up shoes to compensate for his exposed, goosebumped legs. Little Linda, clinging to her doll, wore a pink pinafore with a matching cardigan and bow in her hair.

The silence was weighted with expectancy from their side, wariness from mine.

"Can we watch television?" Donna asked.

So, that was it. The only reason they wanted to come over was to gawp at our TV.

"No."

The older ones hung their heads, disappointed to the point of disillusionment.

"Can we look over your house?" Danny asked.

"All right. But you'll need name tags."

I expected them to turn on their heels. Instead, they seemed intrigued. They waited, patient as cattle, while I scribbled names on scraps of paper and pinned them to their skinny little chests.

Once classified as official guests, they trooped up the back steps, through the kitchen into the living room.

The television set stood on sloping skinny black legs with gleaming brass feet. A pair of antennae rose from its mahogany top. The kids gathered around the twenty-three-inch gray eye of the lifeless alien.

"Switch it on," Danny said.

"There's no point. The programs don't start till five o'clock."

"Liar."

I was developing warped respect for him.

"Make it work," Donna begged. "Please, please!"

I reached for the knob embedded in a fabric panel beside the screen. A roar of static blasted the room. The kids pulled faces and clapped hands over their ears. I reached for the volume knob and turned it down. Like pilgrims in front of an oracle, they stood mesmerized as the snowy, pulsating screen settled to a hazy black-and-white circle.

"What's that?" Felix asked.

Geraldine's three had been predictably silent and well-mannered till this point.

"Test pattern," I said, swiveling the antennae.

"Like an exam?" Deborah asked.

I pictured Deborah working in a law office someday.

"It helps people adjust their sets before the programs start," I said.

The kids were silent. I took a handkerchief from my pocket and handed it to Martin, who, after a brief inspection, dropped it on the floor.

"Can we go up into the tower?" Stacey asked. I was pleased to hear from her, at last. She'd been silent as a sphynx.

"On one condition. You have to keep looking for my cat. Anyone who sees him will win a prize."

"What sort of prize?" they asked in unison.

Kids. So materialistic.

"A . . . magic one."

Mystified and goggle-eyed, they followed me upstairs.

"Is this a witch's house?" Portia, asked.

"Yes," I said, escorting them past the stained-glass window halfway up the stairs.

"Is she a good witch?" her sister, Donna asked.

"Sometimes."

My guests exchanged glances.

"No need to be scared," I said, riding a surge of psychological power. "Providing she's in a good mood. Who wants to be first up the ladder?"

The two bigger boys pushed forward. I climbed up and opened the trap door to help them and the older girls off the top of the ladder. The gaps between the rungs were too deep for the younger ones. I climbed back down and stood below them to guide their ankles so they could ascend without losing their footing. It was hardest for Linda, the shortest. She handed me her doll to look after while I helped her up the ladder. Her pluck was impressive.

Once inside the tower, they all wanted to hold a white mouse. Tail-less was particularly popular. None of them was interested in helping me clean out the cage.

"I want to scribble up there, too," Donna said, pointing at the Beatle portraits on the wallpaper.

"That's not a good idea."

"What's the meanest thing anyone's ever said to you?" Danny asked.

He was clearly the philosopher of the group. I thought for a bit.

"Well, once my brother made up a song. It went *I'm Helen the Melon from Bracken Street, with the great big nose and the dirty feet.*"

"Did it make you cry?"

"Not anymore. I quite like it now."

"I want to watch television," Portia said.

The kids emitted a collective groan when I told them it was time to go home. I escorted them back down the ladder, closing the trapdoor after us so Jim wouldn't suspect there'd been trespassers in his territory.

I herded them through the living room toward the front door.

"What is it?" Linda asked, pointing at Dad's old Bechstein.

"A piano," I said, wondering who was in charge of the teasing now. "Know this song?"

The children watched as I lifted the lid and picked out a primitive "Spoonful of Sugar" from the movie *Mary Poppins*.

Seven small heads nodded along in time. I coaxed them through the tune, line by line. My piano playing was atrocious as usual, but they didn't care.

The eighth head, Felix, was not enthralled. Refusing to sing, he stared wistfully at the television set.

"What time is it?" he asked.

"Meow o'clock."

"Meow?" the boy said, dumbfounded.

"That's right! It's my favorite time."

"Can we play outside?"

"It's cold out there," I said in a Julie Andrews voice. "Does everyone have a woolly sweater?"

The D girls looked at each other and giggled.

"Why don't you go home and put on warmer clothes?" I asked.

"We're not cold," Donna said.

I slid into my duffle coat and took them down to the bottom lawn for a game of hide-and-seek. The older kids made a beeline for the bamboos, while the younger ones huddled under damp hydrangeas. I told them they could hide anywhere, providing it was outside.

Danny pretended to cover his eyes and count to twenty while the others charged up the front steps to the top lawn. I trailed behind, watching them scatter like birds into bushes and garden beds.

Mist solidified into rain. Wild-eyed, wet hair flattened against their faces, the kids were so elated and free I didn't have the heart to send them home. I pulled my hood up and sheltered in the archway next to the fishpond.

A mournful sound echoed from the depths of the basement behind me. I figured one of the younger Dooleys had wandered under the house and stood on a nail. People were forever giving themselves tetanus from rusty nails. I scanned the garden and counted eight heads all trying to hide badly enough to get caught.

Piteous and discordant, the yowl became a wail. Somebody—or something—needed help.

A sour earthy sensation hit the back of my throat as I clambered over the wood stacks and crept toward the darkest recess of the basement. I closed my mouth against the dust and waited for my good eye to adjust. The space was dense, formless, infinite.

Following the source of the cries, I crawled toward the old well in the far corner underneath the kitchen. A stack of dusty boards crisscrossed the menacing abyss. Dad had warned us to stay away from there. He had hardly any rules compared to other fathers. I decided a warning was as good as a rule under the circumstances and turned to go back.

A meow—a definite cat sound—jolted me with such force, my head collided with a floor beam. I dropped to my knees and crept back toward the well. As I reached the edge of the well, I felt a presence at my shoulder, and a waft of Juicy Fruit on the breeze. Shane.

"What are you doing here?" I asked.

"I just came over to give Jim something, then I heard that noise. Your cat. I think it's down there."

I fell on my stomach and leant over the edge of the hole.

"Mickey!" I yelled.

An unmistakable meow reverberated from the bowels of the Earth.

"It's him! How did he get down there?"

"Dunno. I just followed the sound."

"Can we get him out?"

"Depends," Shane said. "I could try to climb down there. How deep is it?"

"I don't know. It's from before the days people had piped water."

"Is water still down there?"

"Dad says it's dried up, but it's deep. Mickey will never get out."

My ribs convulsed with sobs.

"Wait here," Shane said.

He returned with a rope looped around the handle of a large wicker basket from Dad's darkroom.

"This might work," he said, lowering the basket into the well.

"Mickey!" I called. "Jump in!"

We heard scuffling from the depths of the well, then silence.

"I think he's in," Shane said, hauling the basket up.

It was empty.

"He doesn't know what to do!" I cried.

"Give him time."

It felt strange and dangerous to be lying in the dark next to Shane. I caught a glimpse of his chiseled silhouette against the watery light of an air vent. He smelt warm and leathery with a hint of Old Spice.

"Take your coat off," he said.

I hesitated.

"If he recognizes your scent, he might jump in."

I peeled the coat off and stuffed it in the basket. Goose-bumps shivered up my arms as Shane lowered the capsule for a second time.

Scrunching up my good eye, I peered down into the vortex and willed every cell in my body to tune into the tele-pathic connection Mickey and I shared.

"C'mon, boy!" I called in a softer, coaxing voice. "Hop in the basket. You can do it. We'll be together again. You can have chicken every day. Here kitty, kitty . . ."

Shane's shoulders shifted. The tension on the rope changed. With a few brisk heaves, the basket emerged and toppled on its side.

Mickey sprang into my arms. He was so tense and fright-ened he dug his claws into my bare skin. Shane handed me the coat. I bundled the cat up in it and carried him out to the dimly lit basement.

"Thanks!" I called over my shoulder to Shane. "We couldn't have done it without you."

Shane lowered his head and shoved his hands in his pockets. As I stumbled forward to give him a hug, a jolt of confusion brought me to a halt. Back in the depths of the basement, I hadn't noticed his clothes, but now it was clear as Dad's crystal decanter. He was still wearing Jim's leather jacket.

The silence between us was shattered by Mum's voice booming from the veranda above our heads.

"Help!" she wailed. "The place is seething with children!"

Shane slid the jacket off his shoulders and shook his arms out of the sleeves.

"Here," he said, thrusting the garment at me.

"Did you steal it?" I asked, running my fingers over its tarnished zipper.

Shane hesitated beside the basement arch. His lips curved in a secret smile.

"I just borrowed it without asking."

Watching him disappear down the driveway, I savored the aroma of aged leather mingled with a hint of motor oil, musk, and a trace of campfire smoke. The once black leather had faded to dull charcoal gray etched with countless creases and scars.

I couldn't help smiling back.

Chapter Twenty-nine

WALKING INTO A TSUNAMI

Dad didn't return that night. Mum called George's wife Mabel on the wall telephone at the bottom of the stairs. I watched her twist the crimson cord around her hand. Mabel hadn't heard from George, either.

Mum telephoned the secretary of the Alpine Club, Ian Frogget. He'd heard nothing, aside from warnings about the dismal conditions. Ian said nobody in their right mind would be up there in weather like this. If there was no news by lunchtime tomorrow, he promised to send out a search party.

From a twenty-first-century perspective, it's almost impossible to step into a time when people couldn't communicate with each other at the tap of a screen. My parents' generation, and those before, were well practiced in the hollow art of waiting. The war years had taught them to accept week-old news, heavily curated by authorities, through crackling radios. Parents had no idea if their sons were dead or alive on foreign battle fields.

To save their sanity, they invented ways to endure the chasm of not knowing and dreading the worst. Some took to their gardens and thrust their spades into the soil, others turned to prayer. Mum retreated to the bath with an ashtray and a stack of library books. She roosted in there for hours, willing her worries to evaporate into the steam and the stories of Somerset Maugham. I snuck Mickey up to my bedroom. Clutching his warm soft fur to my chest, I prayed to the god of the mountain to release Dad and bring him home.

I'll never leave you again, Mickey purred.

Jim and Mary shut themselves in their rooms. It was not a night for fairies. Or sleep, for any of us.

We woke to a morning clear and blue as a bridesmaid's gown. The mountain glistened in a fresh coat of snow. Untouchable and god-like, it feigned innocence of inflicting pain and suffering on any type of creature.

With Mum still lingering in bed, I figured it was safe to carry Mickey down to the basement. He demolished bacon scraps from my dressing gown pocket while I gathered a few chunks of wood.

Mickey perched on an upturned paint can while I laid out foundations for a new cabin.

"You'll always have a home with me, Mickey. Even if Dad never comes back."

Mickey's ears flattened. He always heard things before I could. The whirr of a car's engine grew louder as it revved up the driveway. I listened breathless as the vehicle stopped outside the kitchen and backed into the space under the house.

"Dad!" I cried, running to the driver's side, and opening the door before he even pulled the handbrake. "What happened? We were so worried!"

"No need for any of that nonsense," he said, climbing out and wrapping woolly arms around me. "You should've seen the blizzard. It was like walking into a tsunami. Marvelous."

"Didn't you turn back?"

"Heavens no. By the time the weather changed it was too late for that. We pushed on to the summit. There's a hut up there, you know. Syme Hut. They call it The Refrigerator. I've got chilblains to prove it. Still, we were better off in there than out in that snow."

I squeezed Dad's waist tight and pressed my head against his chest.

"I'm so glad you're home!"

"You should have been up there this morning," he said,

stroking my hair. "The air was so clear, we could see right across to Mount Ruapehu in the center of the island. New Plymouth was a little toy village at our feet with whole coastline curving out into the sea. The horizon was so blue we could hardly tell where the sea ended and the sky began. As I stood there, I looked down on my life with its foolishness and regrets. And, you know, I've never felt such love for you all."

Mum, Mary, and Jim ran down the side of the house. They smothered Dad with kisses and tears.

The house breathed a sigh of relief as we escorted Dad upstairs for a hot shower and a change of clothes. Sitting on the edge of our seats over lunch, we kids listened spellbound to his stories of heroism in the snow. Scott of the Antarctic had nothing on Dad and George. Mum stood silent at the sink and flicked a tea towel at a passing fly. Happy as she was to have her husband home, she made it clear her opinion of mountaineers hadn't changed.

After dinner that evening, Mickey and I met in the shadows under the clothesline. The monkey puzzle tree formed a towering, enigmatic silhouette against a star-sprinkled sky. A smoky, acrid scent wafted from the incinerator. It was glowing with bright flames. Mickey and I were drawn to the heat.

"I'm so happy Dad's home, aren't you?"

Mickey rubbed his nose against my leg in agreement.

The eyepatch was itching again. I eased it off and turned it in my hand. The elastic was frayed, the plastic cover battered.

"Know what? I don't need this thing anymore."

Mickey emitted a squeak of encouragement as I hurled the eyepatch into the fiery abyss. Like participants in a religious rite, we stood in silence to watch the plastic melt and curl into blackened wisps. I felt a surge of liberation as silvery particles of ash floated above the flames.

"Nothing bad is ever going to happen again," I said.

We should have known it would take more than an incinerator ceremony to make our troubles go up in smoke.

Chapter Thirty

THE GOBLIN'S CAVE

Mum was furious with Dad for getting stranded up the mountain. She burnt his mountaineering books and hurled his climbing gear over the woodpile under the house. Instead of protesting, he just smiled like a naughty boy—which annoyed her even more.

She knew there was no point trying to make him promise never to go up there again. That would only make the yearning in him stronger.

Fortunately, my parents were hopeless at sustaining grudges. As the icy atmosphere in our house thawed, I was free to focus on building Mickey's new cabin.

It was smaller than the original, there was no *balcony,* and since the plywood had disappeared, I'd had to use sacking for the roof. Mickey didn't seem to mind snuggling into a space barely wider than his body. His new dwelling blended into the basement surroundings so well, it was barely noticeable. It felt cozier, somehow, safer.

Upstairs, household tensions were running high on the opening night of *The King and I.* Mum stood in front of the mirror and arranged her fox fur stole across her shoulders.

Glassy eyes glowered from the fox's pointed little face. Pin-like teeth lined the perpetually gaping mouth. The sad old tail and dangly legs with their dried-up paws were tragic. It stank of mothballs.

Nevertheless, Mum insisted on draping it around her shoulders. The decrepit animal pelt was a declaration that, despite her scars of rejection, she was still queen of musical theater in our town.

"You look like Audrey Hepburn," I said, as her eczema-ravaged hands disappeared into black elbow-length gloves.

"Nonsense, dear," she replied, clicking a marcasite watch around her wrist outside the glove. I admired how the watch sparkled against the dark fabric.

"Is that a new dress?"

"Frock, remember, dear. Or gown. Not a dress."

Mum was obsessed with Nancy Mitford's U and Non-U guide to the British Upper classes. U stood for Upper Class. According to Nancy, refined people called dresses *frocks*. Unfortunately for Mum, nobody else in town knew about the Mitford system. Respectable housewives blanched when she gushed about the joys of a stupendous frock.

"This little thing?" she said, twirling coquettishly on her black patent-leather stilettos. "I ran it up with a remnant from C. C. Ward's sale."

"I don't remember seeing it in the shop," I said, admiring the galaxy of glitter set in plush dark brocade.

"Friends in high places," Mum replied, attaching dangly silver earrings to her lobes. "David set it aside for me."

Her hair was dyed darker than usual and set in rigid waves folding back from the forehead in the style favored by Queen Elizabeth II. Mum raised her crystal atomizer. Of all her possessions, it was the thing I coveted most. The elegant orb was worthy of a Russian princess. I adored the tiny rubber hose and squishy ball covered in finely woven fabric. My favorite part was the jaunty sage green tassel. Mum aimed the atomizer at her cleavage and squeezed the nozzle. A floral haze of Chanel 22 encompassed us.

"Where's your eye patch?"

"Burnt it," I said, recalling the jubilation of standing be-

side the incinerator with Mickey and watching the horrid accessory melt in flames.

"You did what?"

"The muscles are strong enough. I don't need it anymore."

I ran my hands over my new crimson dress and flattened
the skirt against the petticoat. The velvet was soft and sensual
as cat's fur. Mum had spent ages bent over her Singer machine creating my new dress . . . er, frock. The white lace collar was a masterstroke. It was her way of making me feel
better for not being in the show.

"Are you sure about the headband?" she said, mascara
stick poised over her lashes.

"It's all the rage in . . ."

"Yes, I know, but orange clashes with your new frock,
don't you think?"

I ran downstairs and dived into the safety of my duffle
coat.

Dad always insisted on arriving at the opera house thirty
minutes before a performance. Jim and I bundled into the
back seat of the Zephyr. Showered and polished up, we made
a half-respectable family. Mum glided onto the front seat
and adjusted the rear-view mirror to apply finishing touches
to her lipstick.

"Is that your leather jacket?" she asked, turning to Jim.

He pretended not to hear.

"I asked you a question."

"Yeah."

"It's not stolen after all?" Mum said, incredulous.

"I found it under some camping gear."

"That pile of rubbish in your museum? That's the first
place you should have looked."

"I did, but it wasn't there first time. I swear. I found it
there yesterday with the sleeping bags."

Mum and Dad exchanged glances. I suppressed a smirk. I'd gone to a lot of trouble to leave the jacket in a place where my brother could *find* it.

"Do you know anything about this, Helen?" Mum asked.

I squirmed in the shadows of the back seat.

"Why would I?"

"Just as well we didn't call the police." Dad turned the ignition key.

"We haven't heard the last of this," Mum said, adjusting her stole. "Rick's motorbike is still missing."

The opera house foyer glowed like the entrance to a goblin's cave. My cheeks flushed as we stepped inside the portal between our dreary lives and a world of music and song where things always worked out fine, and every stray cat found a home.

Dad made a beeline for the luridly lit Nibble Nook in the corner while Mum chatted with Pauline, the program seller. In her younger days, Pauline starred as Josepha the landlady in a famous production of *The White Horse Inn*. Her amateur theatrical career had since dwindled from cameo role to chorus back row, to props manager, and now this.

"Everyone's so disappointed you're not in the show," Pauline said, handing Mum a program.

I studied the crimson carpet swirls and hoped Eric was regretting his stupid decision. Nobody could match Mum.

"But I hear your daughter has talent," Pauline added.

My ears blazed until I realized Pauline was referring to Mary, not me.

"Nice jacket," Pauline said, turning her attention to Jim. "Are you a dramatic soul like the rest of your family?"

My brother became unusually animated.

"Our school has a theater group," he said. "They're doing *The Yeomen of the Guard*. Have you heard of it?"

"Gilbert and Sullivan," Pauline said, nodding.

"They're putting it on later this year," Jim said, his handsome face bisected by a stripe of neon red light from the Nibble Nook. "I'd love to get into production—"

"But actually, he's more interested in science," Mum interrupted. "Aren't you, dear?"

My brother retreated inside his leather armor.

Dad, his smile wider than the foyer itself, strode toward us.

"Have you got the tickets?" Mum asked.

"What do you think?" he said, sliding a large block of Cadbury's Fruit and Nut into his jacket pocket.

My parents approached the purchase of theater tickets with the obsessiveness of Marie and Pierre Curie collating radioactive material. They bought tickets weeks, often months, in advance. Finances permitting, they preferred the front row of the dress circle, slightly to one side. This allowed uninterrupted view of the director's and choreographer's art. Actors nearly always played to the circle.

If Mum and Dad opted for downstairs and a closer view of the performers, they favored a position two thirds back from the stage and near the center. These seats were passable, providing they weren't so far back they were condemned to the acoustic graveyard under the dress circle.

Occasionally, if there was no choice, we'd sit on the wooden planks up in the tier above the dress circle, known as *the gods*. I didn't mind the gods or the people in them. They were hardcore supporters, so desperate to see a show they were willing to subject their backsides to hours of discomfort.

The greatest curse, no matter what level of the theater we were in, was the damnation of sitting behind a pillar. Nothing was worse than being forced to crane your neck around either side of a pole to see the stage.

Exhilaration coursed through my veins as we climbed the stairs to the dress circle door. When Grant, a bank teller by day, escorted us to the front row, slightly to the right side of the stage, I could hardly breathe. Apart from those set aside for newspaper critics, they were the best seats in the house.

I stroked the worn brown velvet along the top of the rail-
ing while the fire curtain trundled up and down to assure
everyone it was operational. Excited townsfolk trickled down
the aisles. Flushed from the night air, they nodded to each
other, removed their hats, and folded their coats over their
seat backs. Every tier of the opera house was packed and
bubbling with anticipation. The air swooned with a concoction of tobacco, Minties, beer, perfume, mothballs, and an
infusion of ever-present cow dung combined with dust and
disinfectant.

Dad chuckled as he opened the program at a page of Roy
resplendent in his King of Siam costume.

"Never thought I'd see Roy in pantaloons," he said.

He flipped quickly to the next page to spare Mum the
agony of seeing Geraldine's headshot. In full makeup and
costume Geraldine looked sultry as Marlene Dietrich. He
was too slow. Mum saw the photo. She didn't say anything
but rested her elbow on the balcony rail and gazed down at
the orchestra pit, where violins squawked in protest at being
tuned.

Mum's high cheekbones and strong chin were in striking
profile. She was thinking of Geraldine leaning into her dressing room mirror, applying streaks of greasepaint to her face.

My thoughts turned to Mary. I'd have glued my toenails to
the opera house chandelier and swung upside down to be in
the backstage frazzle she was part of right now. If only it
could have been me standing in the wings in that glorious
costume with the little gold hat shaped like a beehive.

Dad pressed a rectangle of chocolate into my palm. A
semi-circle of light appeared on the curtain above the orchestra pit. The audience fell silent, then exploded into applause as Marjorie Bourke, the music teacher from Girls'
High, ascended the conductor's podium. She bowed and
raised her baton.

Spasms of delight rippled down my spine as the brass section poured golden chords through the theater. They floated us through a Rogers and Hammerstein version of a royal palace in nineteenth-century Thailand. The percussion instruments melted into strings of sweeping romance. Tears trickled down my chin onto my lace collar.

The King and I transported us to another world where people had the same yearnings and disappointments as we did, yet the costumes, singing and music made theirs more powerful and real.

Ron made a pretty good King of Siam, especially when toward the end he lay on the royal bed, closed his eyes, and let his arm go limp and drop to the floor to show everyone he was dead. In her starring role as Anna the English teacher, Stephanie Fields preened her way through every number. David from C. C. Ward's was a convincing soon-to-be-executed forbidden lover Lun Tha. Although I wasn't sure this production's Tuptim (Carol Jury from Woolworth's stationery counter) would have been his choice in real life.

When Mary appeared toward the end of the procession of royal children, the tangled knot of jealousy inside me dissolved. As one of the tallest children, she was magnificent. She nudged the younger ones along with all the tenderness and dignity she possessed in real life.

For Mum's sake, part of me was hoping Geraldine would forget her lines or trip over her gown. When our neighbor stepped on stage, however, she took charge of the auditorium. She wasn't Geraldine anymore, but a dignified queen with a singing voice rich as gold on the roof of the royal palace.

When we drove home afterwards, the inside of the Zephyr was silent.

There was no point arguing or telling lies to make Mum feel better.

Geraldine was . . . wonderful.

Chapter Thirty-one

ROYAL COMMAND

As I pedaled around the corner into the glen, Mickey scampered toward me, his tail flying. The neighborhood kids trailed in his wake.

"*Helen the Melon, Helen the Melon!*" they chanted, dancing toward me.

It was reassuring to be popular with a cat and a bunch of little kids. I climbed off the bike, gathered Mickey under one arm, and sat on the front steps next to the letter box.

"What's that?" Danny asked, as I slid a brown envelope from my school bag. Mr. Jackson's instructions had been clear. The envelope was not to be tampered with. We were to take it home and hand it straight to a parent.

"It's from the Queen," I said, trying to prize the seal open without inflicting visible damage.

I loved how the kids believed everything I said. They bowed their heads while I unfolded the paper and read the withering assessment:

> *Helen often thinks and acts in a manner beyond her years but shows little ability to discipline her concentration. Missing the point of a matter in hand can result in confused thinking later, as often happens in her arithmetic. She has done well at language but must persevere with maths and organise her study more methodically. Spelling needs improvement.*
>
> *Number in Class: 21. Place in Class: 18*

There would have been more dignity coming last. Being third from the bottom implied I'd tried and failed. I hoped this meant Mr. Jackson would put me out of my misery, kick me out of the clever class and demote me to a grade where I could be the middle of the middle.

"What does she say?" Donna asked.

I was about to crumple it up and toss it into the shrubs, but a dotted line loomed from the bottom of the page; PARENT'S SIGNATURE. Mr. Jackson had given the impression anyone who didn't return a parentally signed report would be crucified on the school rugby field and left to the seagulls.

"Who, the Queen? She wants me to have lunch with her at Buckingham Palace."

"Will you say yes?"

"I'm too busy."

"Can we come to your place?" Danny asked.

"Not today," I said, stuffing the envelope back in my school bag.

Mickey padded after me as I pushed my bike up the driveway and under the house.

"I hope you've been studying methodically," I said to Mickey as I let my bike collapse against a stack of shovels and rakes.

The cat fixed me with his soft, kind gaze that radiated into my brain. He lowered his haunches onto the concrete and curled his tail around his front feet. The extra toes gave him the appearance of wearing slippers.

You'll always be top of my class. he beamed.

"Oh, Mickey!" I said, crouching to embrace him. "Where would I be without you?"

We parted ways at the fishpond. Mickey glided off to his new cabin. It wasn't as good as the original. It had no veranda, but it did the job.

In the kitchen upstairs, Mum hunched over her Imperial

typewriter. She flattened a sheet of carbon copy paper between two rectangles of creamy stationery.

"Can you think of ways a wife can greet her husband when
he arrives home from work in the evenings?" she asked.

"Are you writing a comedy sketch?"

"No, dear," she said, feeding the wad of paper into the
roller. "Just a little piece for The Women's Page."

I dropped my school bag on the floor and headed for the
pantry.

"This sort of thing's very popular with women readers,"
she called, pecking at the keyboard with her manicured index
fingers.

"Place his slippers beside an armchair next to the fireplace,"
she read as she squinted through her reading glasses. *"Pour
his favorite drink and have it waiting for him on a tray (prefer-
ably silver or silver plate). Make sure his evening newspaper is
folded and in pristine condition. If the newsprint is wrinkled, give
it a quick iron with the heat set low."*

I sank my teeth into a stale scone and wandered back to
the sink.

"What do you think?"

"Hardly the sort of stuff you wrote when you were a general reporter," I said, choking down a glass of water. Our
town supply had a harsh flavor.

"I know. But those were the war years."

Back when she was covering court cases and council
meetings, she'd had a glimpse of the so-called *real* world and
the men who controlled it. She'd witnessed how the male hi-
erarchy operated. Her stories were about people wielding
power, not vacuum cleaners.

"Is Veronica paying you for this?"

Mum shrugged and flicked a flake of skin off her palm.

"Pin money."

*Bathe the children and have them dressed in pajamas, prefer-
ably asleep in their beds, before he arrives. This gives you time for*

*a quick dust and vacuum. Straighten rugs. Put books and toys
away.*

"Can't you go back to general reporting?"

"That's a full-time job," Mum replied, narrowing her eyes
in a puff of cigarette smoke. "There's no way a married
women with children would be offered something like that."

*"When a man returns from eight long hours at the office, he
does not want to be troubled with petty domestic tensions. No matter how challenging your day has been, slip into attractive lounge-
wear; comb and spray your hair, apply a light layer of makeup,
dab scent behind your ears. When you see him walking up the
front path, open the front door to welcome him with a smile and a
peck on the cheek."*

"You never peck Dad on the cheek."

*"If you have a wireless or record player, put on romantic music.
Make sure the mouth-watering aroma of a hearty evening meal
fills the air. Whichever meat you're cooking, serve him the largest,
juiciest slice."*

I couldn't work out if Mum was being serious, ironic or
something in between.

"Never mind, dear. It's just a job. If the editor likes this
piece, Veronica says they'll let me cover *The Bride of the Year*."

"You told me that's a cattle show."

Mum tapped her cigarette ash on the edge of a saucer.

"Look, if women want to relive the greatest day of their
lives by dressing up in their wedding gowns and parading in
front of adjudicators, who am I to judge?"

Her tone was flat and unconvincing.

"What happened, Mum? Are you okay?"

She didn't answer. Her attention was focused on the keyboard, smashing everything she'd raised me to believe in.

"What's that?" she said, pointing her cigarette at the rumpled brown envelope lying on the floor next to my schoolbag.

"A bill, I think. I found it in the letter box."

"Leave it on the hall table for your father to open. By the way, have you been dyeing your hair?"

My feet screwed to the floor. I felt my cheeks turn red as traffic lights.

"No! Why?"

"At the theater the other night, I overheard Pauline say, "there's a bottle blonde if ever I've seen one." She was looking at you. What have you been up to?"

"Nothing!"

Seething with guilt, I swept into the hallway and shoved the envelope under a pile of bills. My knees were shaking as I ran out the back door and called for Mickey.

The sun was sinking over the lip of our glen. Pink cats' whisker clouds streaked across pale sky. I went in search of my cat.

"Mickey!" I called. He seemed to come to his name, at least when he felt like it.

A spiral of sweet-scented smoke rose from the incinerator. I approached the rusty oil drum and raised my hands to capture warmth from the fading embers in its belly.

The clothesline groaned with dew-drenched washing. Sheets and undies would survive the night, but my bellbottoms were sacrosanct. As I pulled them off the line, the bamboo behind the incinerator rustled. Mickey bounded toward me and sprang into my arms.

"Whoa boy!" I said, patting the soft *M* on his forehead.

The whirr of a motor echoed across the valley. Any vehicle arriving in our street was a big deal. Mickey tensed in my arms as a black Holden sedan crunched over the gravel. Its chromium grill was fixed in a permanent grin. A red light glowed like a jellybean on its roof. A police car. Cops only visited our street if they were lost.

Police made me nervous. They were probably aware of my criminal career. Not so long ago, I'd fallen into bad company. Her name was Shona and her family ate sheep's tongues from a can. Shona once talked me into nicking a rose-scented eraser from Woolworths. I was hopeless at stealing. On our way out, the store manager stopped me and asked what I had in my pocket. I said nothing. He must've been stupid, or kind, because he let me go.

Becoming a thief made me sick with guilt. There was no choice but to eat the eraser in the shadows of my bedroom that night with only the fairies for witnesses. I wouldn't recommend an eraser diet. It tasted bland and plasticky, and nothing like the smell. On the upside, it didn't kill me—though I may yet die from the lingering effects of ingesting perfumed plastic.

More alarming than the prospect of my getting arrested was the thought of Mum or Dad being slapped in jail. People were always taking their flamboyant quirks the wrong way. Cops would find their artistic chitchat offensive, especially in a town like ours, where we were all expected to be two dimensional clones. Noeline and Bill (alias Athol) Blackman wouldn't last five minutes behind bars.

The police car slowed down outside our place. A ball of barbed wire coiled in my chest. What if our entire family was arrested? Would they send us to different jails?

The police car coasted to a halt at the bottom of our driveway. It sat there, as if wondering what to do.

A dog barked. Mickey struggled against my hold. His whiskers twitched forward at a sparrow hopping across the grass under the clothesline.

The police car started up again. Mickey dived out of my arms and lunged at the bird. As the sparrow spun into the air, the cop car did a U-turn and parked outside the Ds' house.

I ran back inside and pulled the school envelope from the mail pile on the hall table. Taking a fountain pen from the little drawer under the tabletop, I unfolded the report. The nib hovered over the empty space labeled PARENTAL SIGNATURE.

Dad's handwriting was cramped and weird. It was easy to copy. He was the only dad I knew with two first names. Back when he was a little boy, my father was given a jacket with lots of buttons. For no reason in particular, people started calling him Billy Buttons. They soon forgot his formal name, Athol. It was too hard to remember anyway. Billy was shortened to Bill, a name that stuck with him for life. Only those closest to him knew his real name.

I smiled down at the row of freshly inked letters marching like ants across the dotted line: "*A. Blackman.*"

I was now a thief, liar, and a forger.

Chapter Thirty-two

THE BOY WHO'S KIND TO CATS

A frenzy of buds shivered on the magnolia tree and raised their pink lips to kiss the pastel sky. Jasmine spilled over the rose bushes. Crimson and white daphne flowers infused the air with sweet-scented nostalgia for a time that was simpler, more benign.

Hardly anyone noticed I'd been skipping dance classes, apart from Margaret. When I told her I needed to spend time with Mickey and the neighborhood kids, she didn't mind. Her Mum wanted her to give up dancing and join a Catholic youth group.

The more I stayed away from dance class, the less I worried about my big bones and all the other things I loathed about my appearance. The strategy worked until Mrs. Harris rang Mum one Saturday morning. To her credit, Mum kept her cool. She rattled the receiver back on the hook and said Mrs. Harris needed me to show up for the final performance of The Magical Fairy Garden Spectacular that afternoon. Apparently, Mrs. Harris had tried to give my part away, but none of the other girls wanted to be a mud puddle.

I dragged the beige leotard and its crumpled brown cloak from the depths of my wardrobe. The outfit was depressingly small, like something for an eight-year-old. I sat on the bed, forced my thighs through the leg holes, and draped the cloak over my shoulders.

My body was no longer a weightless spirit that danced in unison with my thoughts.

"Have I got fatter?"

"All the women in our family have long waists," Mum said. "You've stretched a bit, that's all."

"Are you sure?"

"This cloak could do with an iron, though. Here, let me freshen it up. Go play under the house for a while. You spend so much time down there. What *is* it you get up to?"

"Um . . . photography."

I'd become an expert liar, like a crook on *Perry Mason*.

"You don't have a camera."

"No, but I like all the other stuff . . . developing and printing photos like Dad."

She was sucked in. I seized the chance to sneak a lump of the previous night's cottage pie from the fridge and head down for a cuddle with Mickey on the darkroom sacks. A shaft of pale, bright light beamed through the open doorway and played on Mickey's stripes. His coat was taking on a sheen of health. The cat raised his head so I could stroke the favorite spot under his chin. His sinewy neck was fleshing out into soft folds.

After lunch, Mum presented me with the mud puddle outfit. The body suit had a line down the back where she'd let the seam out an inch. The brown cloak was smooth as river silt.

When she dropped me at the Memorial Hall, I told her not to stay. I made my way past a noisy rabble of parents, grandparents, sisters, and brothers to the dressing room backstage.

An apparition in a gold flowing robe floated toward me.

"You're late," Pam said.

The Magical Fairy Garden Spectacular went down well with the audience. They clapped in the right places and were patient when the tape recorder jammed.

A supernova of calm settled over me as I walked to the center of the stage and lay down curled up in my cloak. My last performance was going to be my best. Consumed by the music, I danced with every cell in my body.

When Pam, ecstatic with glee, killed me at the end, every-body cheered. I didn't mind they were happy to see me dead on the floor. Any ambitions I'd had to conquer the dance melted under Pam's pose of triumph. Accompanied by a crescendo of Tchaikovsky music, Mrs. Harris, Pam, Margot Fonteyn, and the others pirouetted away on a cloud. I was free.

There was no point hanging around for fruit punch and sandwiches. I changed back into my bellbottoms, duffle coat, and headband and waited outside on the curb for a sky-blue Zephyr.

"How was it?" Dad asked, leaning across from the driver's seat to push the passenger door open.

"I'm not going back."

"Let's do something to celebrate," Dad said after a thoughtful pause.

As we drove down Devon Street, I didn't know what to ex-pect. Dad's idea of celebrating could range from looking at mountaineering boots in the outdoor shop to investigating suspicious gas smells. I could hardly believe my luck when he turned right toward the post office and pulled up outside the Pink Flamingo milk bar. The neon flamingo light flickered in the window.

"We haven't been here for ages!"

The Pink Flamingo was one of our favorite hangouts. Back when I was young and cute, Dad took me there most Friday afternoons for a lime milk shake in a big metal beaker. It made me feel so grown up.

"I thought we should make up for lost time," he said.

A group of boys clustered around the jukebox. Some perched on high stools, others leaned against the machine as though it was their private property. Two taller boys had Elvis haircuts. A couple of younger ones had the new Beatles style, with their hair growing over the backs of their collars.

Dad had strong opinions about young men with long hair.

They were unkempt and unmanly, according to him. He was too much of a gentleman to say anything out loud, thank goodness. One boy sat on a stool in front of the jukebox with his back to us. His dark hair was slicked back, short and he was wearing a denim jacket.

Ignoring the jukebox boys, Dad and I settled in a window booth. Dad sat with his back to the jukebox, so he could observe people out on the street. My bellbottoms squeaked against the red vinyl seat as I sat opposite him, in full view of the jukebox. Dad passed me the yellowing menu sealed inside sticky plastic. He needn't have bothered. I knew the thing inside out.

"What would you like?"

"Strawberry milkshake," I said, recalling the slimming, health-giving qualities of strawberries.

"How about something to go with it?"

Did cows eat grass? Warm rivulets of saliva coursed through my mouth.

"A banana split, please."

Bananas were fruit, after all. Dad ordered the same for himself, except with an iced chocolate in a tall glass instead of a milkshake.

The jukebox was playing "I Wanna Hold Your Hand."

"That's a Beatles song, isn't it?" Dad said.

Though Dad was interested in all kinds of music, I didn't want to encourage him to be trendy. If I'd told him the song was three years old and therefore ready to be archived in a time capsule, he would probably have been intrigued. Had I gone further and explained the Beatles were transitioning to a more complex period, combining poetic lyrics with undertones of classical music, as demonstrated in "Eleanor Rigby," he might have become fascinated, which would have been embarrassing. Our generation's music belonged to us.

A pale man with oily hair and a dot of bandage on his chin planted a pair of canoe-shaped glass dishes on our table. Two blobs of vanilla ice cream rose like giant breasts in front of me. Half a banana, sliced lengthwise, curved around the base of the breasts, which were smothered in red jam and chocolate sauce. It was topped off with a spectacular swirl of whipped cream, a glazed cherry, and two pink wafers.

"How's Mickey?" Dad asked.

"Great," I said, lifting an elongated spoon to excavate an ice cream mound. "I wish Mum would let him inside, though. It's not fair."

"I understand, but this is—"

"I know, a difficult time for her," I parroted. "At least she's got a job."

The Beatles were getting louder.

Dad's eyebrows rippled in a thunderous line. He took a large handkerchief from his pocket and dabbed his lips.

"I can't hear myself think," he said, rising from his seat. "Someone had better turn that rubbish down."

"Don't! *Please*, Dad *no!*"

He sank back into his seat and hoovered iced chocolate through his straw.

"It's not rubbish, Dad," I said, leaning across the table to pat his hand. "It's music!"

A jukebox boy pointed at me and laughed. A blob of strawberry milkshake landed on my lap, reminding me to never wear pale pants again.

"Who's your boyfriend?" he called, cupping his hands around his mouth.

Dad pretended not to hear. Or maybe he was going deaf.

"Bit old for you, ain't he?"

For the first time in my life, I was ashamed to be out with him. The boy in the denim jacket stood, touched the other kid's shoulder, and said something to him. The loudmouth shrugged and settled down to suck on his bottle of Coke.

"Aren't you going to finish your milkshake?" Dad asked.

Only if it's flavored with deadly nightshade, I thought.

Dad reached for the wallet inside his breast pocket.

"Excuse me, Mr. Blackman."

It was the boy in the denim jacket.

"I just want to apologize for the other boys," Shane said. "They didn't mean anything."

My father placed his wallet on the table and studied it briefly.

"Well, I don't suppose they can help it if they like pop music," Dad said. "It's a bit loud, though."

Shane shifted on his winkle pickers.

"I'll get them to turn it down," Shane said.

The young man gave me a nod so miniscule only the fly sitting on the lid of the sugar shaker would've noticed.

"I hear that boy's heading for trouble," Dad said as Shane strode back to the jukebox.

"That's not true!" I said, surprised by the vehemence in my tone.

"We don't want you going over to that house anymore," Dad said, as he stood up and headed for the door.

"I don't go there to see Shane."

"Stay away."

"Why should I? Shane's a good person. I know he is."

"And what evidence do you have to support that?" Dad asked, helping me into my duffle coat outside the front of the Pink Flamingo.

"He's kind to cats."

Chapter Thirty-three

DANCE
SPECTACULAR

"Who's that?" Danny asked.

I didn't mind the kids hanging out in my bedroom, provided they helped keep Mickey off Mum's radar.

"Margot Fonteyn," I said, tugging the photograph off the wallpaper and sending pins flying.

"Why's she dressed like that?" Deborah asked, teasing Mickey with a strand of red embroidery cotton. "Is she going to a fancy dress ball?"

"No, she's a famous ballet dancer," I said, ripping the image in two.

"Don't you like her anymore?" Danny asked.

Mickey snared the thread between his paws and teeth and rolled onto his back, kicking furiously. I loved how he behaved like a normal cat when the kids were around.

"I don't *not* like her," I said, scrunching the ballerina's image into a ball and tossing it at the wastepaper basket. "I don't want to *be* her. That's all."

"I thought you loved dancing," Danny said.

While he wasn't so rude to me these days, Danny took intense interest in my activities and motivations.

"How come your cat has extra toes?" Felix asked.

Mickey paused and blinked up at the boy.

"Everyone has something different about them," I said.

"Can I touch them?"

Felix was nervous of Mickey. He'd never approached the cat before.

Mickey raised an unarmed paw and flashed me a look that said *It's okay. The boy needs taming.*

"Extra toes make him a great climber," I said, as Felix dropped to his knees to rub Mickey's exposed underbelly.

Mickey squirmed under the boy's clumsy touch. Much as he was trying to be patient with Felix, I could tell he was planning to escape the boy's attention as soon as felinely possible.

"Tummy rubs are for when he knows you better," I said. "Try the spot behind his ears."

Felix understood. He sat back and withdrew while Mickey rolled onto his haunches and invited the boy to investigate his ears. Felix's face illuminated with delight and tenderness as Mickey leaned into his touch. Witnessing the transformation in such a reserved little boy was like watching the sun rise.

"Show us how to dance," Donna said.

"Let's go outside," I said, loosening the strings on my duffle bag. Mickey swished his tail and jumped inside.

Ever since Shane had rescued him from the well, Mickey had become fascinated with enclosed spaces. Boxes and bags were portals to comfort and safety. The duffle bag purred as I pulled the strings and hoisted it gently over my shoulder.

I detoured past my parents' bedroom and grabbed a bunch of brilliantly colored scarves from the bottom drawer of Mum's dresser. She hardly used them. They were glorious.

"We're going to dance! We're going to dance!" the kids chanted as they spilled across the bottom lawn.

I lowered the duffle bag and released Mickey onto the grass. He sprang gleefully into a fuzz of greenery. A breath of spring breeze set the hydrangeas whispering. The kids looked at me expectantly.

"This isn't dancing," Donna said.

"There's no music," Stacey added.

"Imagine you're a cloud floating through the sky at sunset," I said, handing her an orange scarf.

"And you," I said, giving Donna a silvery piece of fabric. "You're the wind."

"Can I have one?" Deborah asked, inspecting my pile of scarves through her thick lenses.

"Absolutely!" I said, handing her a pink paisley square. "You're going to dance with us?"

"Probably not," Deborah said, running the silken cloth through her hands.

"*I'm* going to dance," her younger sister said, taking a long yellow strip of fabric from the pile.

"But how can we do it with no music?" Stacey asked.

A thrush issued a trill of flute notes from the flame tree's bare branches.

"We don't need ordinary music," I said. "Just listen to the shush of the trees, and the birds sing. There's no better music than that."

A cobalt blue banner coiled on the grass. As I picked it up and wielded it through the air, Mickey sprang out from under the hydrangeas. Together, we twirled and skipped over the bottom lawn.

Danny stood on a mound of earth next to the cherry tree. Though he was doing his best to hide it, I could tell he was aching to join in.

"Here," I said, handing him a red scarf. "You're the sun, spinning around and sending out all the heat you can before the day ends."

The boy took the scarf. It hung limp in his hand.

"Go on!" I said. "You'd better get moving before the moon comes out."

Danny raised his scarf and carved a dramatic arc through the air.

"That's it!" I called. "Now, dance with your whole body."

Danny was a natural. A miniature Nureyev, he cavorted over the grass. Unable to resist, Portia followed him.

"I'm a star!" she called.

"I'm a cloud chasing the sunset!" Donna called after her.

Seeing his older sister dancing with joy, Martin took a green scarf from the pile and bounced across the lawn.

"I'm a kangawoo!" he cried.

"Who are you?" I asked Felix, who strode across the grass twitching a brown and cream banner with Mickey in his wake.

"I'm the keeper of the cats with extra toes!" he said.

"And I'm the helper," Linda said, tossing her curls and skipping after them.

The older girls lingered on the sidelines, bright-eyed with temptation.

"What the heck!" Donna said, surrendering to the joyous scene. "I'm the wind!"

"Come on, Deborah!" I called "Who are you?"

Deborah hesitated and nudged her glasses up her nose.

"I'm . . . the moon and stars and everything!" she said flourishing her paisley shawl.

A pearl button daylight moon rose above the bamboos as the kids leaped and twirled across the lawn with Mickey. I wanted time to stand still. Following their scarves into private worlds of freewheeling motion, the kids had never seemed happier, more themselves. I loved how the quiet ones, Felix and Deborah, loosened their limbs and became bolder, while the extroverts, Danny, Portia, and Donna, toned their movements down to merge with the impromptu pageant.

Embracing the spirit, Mickey used his tail as a scarf, holding it aloft as he pounced and whirled in circles around the children.

This was the real magical garden spectacular.

Chapter Thirty-four

FOREST OF
TINY RED TREES

"It's going to be a special Christmas."

Dad loved Christmas with boyish fervor. To him every Christmas was enchantment wrapped in jingle bell paper.

My shadow loomed over him as he crouched over a box of seedlings. Flowery tufts were unfurling on the flame tree above. A blackbird perched on a branch and cocked its head. I picked a stem of rosemary. Its sharp oily perfume tickled the back of my nose.

"It's months away," I said.

Mickey was delighted to encounter a human behaving like a cat. He wove around Dad's boots and burrowed holes around him through the soft dark soil.

"Not really," Dad said, smoothing over Mickey's craters with his trowel. "By the time these salvia bonfires come into flower, it'll be Christmas Day."

A plump worm writhed on a clod of earth. Mickey crouched and wriggled his rear end. He lunged, then recoiled at the touch of the squirming invertebrate.

"It's only a worm." I smiled as Mickey shook his paws and licked them clean.

Cat: 0. Worm: 1.

"This flowerbed will be the first thing visitors see as they come up the front path," Dad said, taking a handkerchief from the pocket of his paint-spattered khaki shorts and mopping his brow. "A forest of tiny red Christmas trees."

The new plants flopped on the soil like misfits at a dance.

I couldn't help thinking our festive callers were going to be far more interested in the Christmas cake Mum had just baked and stowed, precious cargo under a muslin cloth, in the pantry.

"Have you decided what you'd like from Santa this year?"

I shredded blue rosemary flowers off the stalk and let them float to the ground.

He was babying me, but there was no harm playing the game.

"I'd like him to let Mickey inside the house and be part of the family."

The blackbird swooped, snared the worm in its beak, and sped off like a spitfire.

Dad sighed and leaned on his trowel. He seemed the oldest, tiredest father in the universe.

Worm: 0. Blackbird: 1

Days melted into weeks as the school year dragged to an end. The clever kids were moving up to the co-ed school known as Spotswood College next year. I persuaded Mum and Dad to let me escape to Girls High. At the traditional, all-girls school, anyone with brains was siphoned into the A Stream to study Latin. I had no intention of learning a dead language. My parents reluctantly agreed to let me go into the B stream.

Nineteen sixty-six had been a year of shedding. Through it, I'd let go of people and things. My former crush on Friedrich from *The Sound of Music* had faded to mere embarrassment. Margot Fonteyn was no longer a goddess. I'd said goodbye to creative dance class and the clever kids. Margaret had disappeared into Bible class.

Jim was about to leave too. He'd finished school and was heading for the big smoke, Wellington, 240 miles away. A friend of Dad's angled him a manly job in the gas industry. Though a tinge of sadness hung over my brother's departure, nobody was surprised. Every teenager had to leave town or stay behind and have babies.

Shane was at an age where he'd have to go, too, unless he found a job at the abattoir or share milking on a farm.

I'd said goodbye to a large part of myself over the past year. I had no idea who was about to replace the neurotic, fanciful kid I used to be. Whatever happened, Mickey and his extra toes would keep me grounded. His wise voice and the steady heartbeat of his presence were sure to see me through.

An avalanche of Christmas cards choked our letter box.

"That makes 127 so far," Mum said, scribbling in her notebook. "Dammit! I forgot the Whistlers. Vera's always one step ahead of me."

Though some of the names were familiar, most of the cards had come from Mum and Dad's grown-up world, which excluded children who should be seen and not heard. To me they were Christmas ghosts, with varying degrees of taste in cards.

"Oh, well, that's the end of Douglas," Mum said, drawing a line through a name. "It's the second year in a row he's forgotten to send a card. And poor Aunt Carrie. There's no Christmas where she's gone."

Mum clunked her Imperial typewriter on the kitchen table.

"I'm on deadline. You can put those up if you like."

Mum's alter ego, Domestic Doreen, had morphed into a mega star in the Wednesday edition of the *Taranaki Herald*. Housewives craved Doreen's advice on everything from squeaky chairs to infestations of unidentified brown insects. Her tone verged on haughty when dispensing advice over the uses of castor oil, sodium bicarbonate, and white spirits. Doreen was not to be messed with. She was now in the throes of explaining Christmas pudding recipes and how to ensure the husbands had a carefree, festive season.

I stood on a chair and draped the recent cards over a

string on the wall. Covered in snowflakes and glitter, they were freakish reminders of *proper* Christmases people were enjoying in faraway America and Britain. While their nativity scenes were etched in ice and snowflakes, we were sprinting barefoot over burning black sand at the beach.

A large box of outdoor colored lights sat on the floor next to the piano. They were commercial grade lights, like the ones in Pukekura Park.

"I've rented them from the electricity department," Dad said, beaming with pride.

"I thought you were at war with Roy."

"He wants to borrow our tent, so he's letting me rent the lights."

"You're paying him money and he gets our tent for free?"

Dad shrugged and disappeared to spend the afternoon up his ladder, weaving strands of lights around the top and bottom verandas.

The clock was nudging toward dinnertime when we heard a gasping, groaning sound from outside the front door.

"Can somebody give me a hand?"

Jim and I hurried out to the veranda. We watched in awe as an enormous Christmas tree staggered up the front steps toward us. Under the wildly protesting branches, Dad's boots teetered on the edge of a step.

My brother grabbed the top of the tree and helped haul the thing up into the entrance hall. Grunting, they lowered the trunk into a bucket and weighed it down with bricks.

The tree filled the hall with piney magnificence.

"That's the tallest one we've ever had," Dad said, breathless with exertion.

The top branch bent under the fourteen-foot-high ceiling, like a giant inside a bus.

"Nothing a saw can't cure," Dad said.

"It's a great tree," I said, quietly wondering if it wasn't a little too great. People would have to fight past branches to get up the stairs.

The tree wobbled. With a wistful sigh, it lurched sideways toward the living room.

"We need bigger nails," Dad said, sloping off to find a hammer and string.

"No more nails in walls!" Domestic Doreen shouted from the kitchen.

Too late. It was a worthy cause.

Jim lifted the box of decorations from their cupboard under the liquor cabinet and placed them on the floor before the tree. Mary emerged from her bedroom to oversee placement of the baubles, fragile beauties that shattered if you looked at them twice. Broken baubles could leave painful glass shards in fingers.

Mary dusted off a decrepit angel. "This should be in retirement," she said.

Decorations were scarce and expensive. Those we had were treasured as visceral memories of Christmases past. The white pipe cleaners shaped like elves with felt hats were my favorite. Back when I was about seven, Dad and I bought them from Woolworth's one Friday night. It was a scandalous indulgence. As I lifted the elves from their box, they released a glitter storm over the carpet.

Mary climbed a stepladder to arrange the baubles at aesthetic intervals over the branches. Jim unwound a tangle of colored tree lights and plugged them into a wall socket.

"Jeez, there's a lot of duds," he said, counting the bulbs that refused to light up.

"Have you seen Shane lately?" I asked.

"Nah. He's hanging out with Troy."

"Do you know what he's up to?"

"Borstal, probably."

The pipe cleaner elf froze in my hand. Borstal was a place where bad boys were sent. It was one step away from jail.

"Why do you care?"

"I don't," I said, cheeks flaring. "Can I take over your museum? I mean, after you've left."

"No."

"I won't touch anything," I said, untangling an arthritic length of tinsel. "Promise. Not even the armadillo skin. *Specially* not the armadillo skin. Chopping up animals is disgusting."

I wasn't expecting a response from Jim. Most likely, he was going to storm off.

"You needn't worry," he said softly. "I've given up taxidermy."

His answer disarmed me.

"Why did you do it in the first place?"

My brother took a spare blue bulb from the box and rolled it in his palm.

"Guess I was looking for whatever it is inside us and other animals," he said.

"Their soul?"

My brother and I fell silent. Maybe the two of us weren't so different. We were both trying to find ways to make sense of life.

"Why should she have the museum?" Mary said. "I'm older."

"It's *my* museum," Jim said, unscrewing a dud. "Nobody's getting it."

"Can I just look after your stuff till you come back?" I asked.

The dud rolled off his lap onto a pile of spent bulbs at his feet.

"I won't be coming back."

The words fell heavily in my chest. How could Jim never come home? He could be difficult and scary, but I was going to miss him. Terribly. A mean spirit clamped the back of my throat and stopped me from saying a word.

"You're just going to leave all your junk in there like a crypt?" Mary asked.

Jim screwed in a fresh bulb where the dud had been. The new light glowed bright orange.

"It's not junk," he said.

Mary climbed to the top rung of the stepladder. Stretching up on her tiptoes, she placed the angel on top of the tree. It was a bit mangy, but it deserved the position of honor.

Dusk settled over the glen. The neighborhood kids appeared like sprites on the front lawn. Deborah bundled Mickey into my old pram and we went knocking on people's doors to torment them with our caroling. Mrs. D swayed benignly as we paid a clandestine visit to her back yard and sang "Away in A Manger" to my dodgy ukulele chords. Geraldine handed out perfectly formed mince pies. We scored lollies from Mrs. Gibson.

When Mickey became restless and threatened to jump out of the pram, I pointed up at the largest star in the sky, probably Venus.

"Santa's on his way," I said.

"Does that mean it's meow o'clock?" Felix asked.

"Sure does" I said. "We'd better get to bed."

"I'm not sleepy!" Linda wailed.

"Me neither!" Portia cried.

"Me stay up all night!" Martin sobbed.

"Only tired people cry like that," I said, looking at the older children for backup. "Besides, the sooner you go to bed, the sooner Santa will be here."

Stacey took her little brother's hand and guided him past the fuchsias up their path.

"Merry Christmas," she called over her shoulder.

"Come on, sleepyhead," Felix said, putting his arm around Portia's shoulders. "Let's go home."

"I guess that means us, too," Danny said, wiping Linda's tears with the back of his hand.

Watching the kids disappear, I felt a glow. They'd grown so much since I'd first met them. Felix had come right out of himself; Stacey wasn't so shy, and Donna was learning not to be cheeky all the time. As for Danny, his imagination was flourishing.

"Hey!" I called after them.

The children stopped and turned to look at me.

"I'm glad we're friends," I said. "So is Mickey."

"We are, too," Danny called. "Have a meowy Christmas."

As I turned to push Mickey's pram up the driveway, our house lit up with an unworldly glow. Dad's lights beamed from the top and bottom verandas, making our rickety castle glimmer with color. The place had never looked so magical.

This festive season was going to be special.

Chapter Thirty-five

THE
CHRISTMAS
FELINE

"Happy Christmas, boy," I said, squatting on a sack as Mickey devoured a sliver of contraband ham.

The first golden rays of Christmas morning filtered through the archway to transform his fur into a living kaleidoscope of amber, cinnamon, and ebony. Bathed in ethereal light, he licked the paint can lid clean.

He washed his paws and glanced up at me through eyes flecked with jade and topaz. They shimmered with ancient wisdom.

"You're the most beautiful cat in the world."

Mickey emitted a gracious squeak and climbed on my lap. He lifted a multi-toed paw and lowered it on the back of my hand. His musical purr surpassed the previous night's carol singing. It reverberated through my body in waves of pure love.

Upstairs, soft footsteps padded across the kitchen floor. One of the few rules in our family was that we had to wait till everyone was vertical before presents could be opened. At least somebody was up.

"Back soon," I said, kissing Mickey's M.

He sprang off my lap into his cabin while I climbed the concrete steps to the front door.

"Where have you been?" Mum said. "We've been waiting for ages."

"Just for a walk," I said, hitching my pajamas.

Jim, Mary, Mum, and Dad were circled like seagulls around the laden tree.

"Look who's home for Christmas," Jim said.

Fritz strutted across the carpet toward the pristine presents under the tree. We hadn't seen him for the past few days; he had no doubt been on one of his habitual walk-abouts.

"Stop him!" Mary cried. "He's going to pee on them!"

"No he's not," Jim said.

I wasn't so sure.

People open presents with techniques to reflect their personalities. Mary peeled the tape away with surgical exactness so as not to damage the paper. She flattened and folded the wrapping and put it aside for future use.

"What have you got?" I asked, craning over her shoulder.

She brandished a packet of pantyhose and a makeup bag. So grown up. Still, there was a chance I might also receive a token of my burgeoning womanhood. With a pang of disappointment, I realized my box-shaped present was too large to be lipstick or perfume.

Jim's gift dwarfed both of ours. A huge, boxy thing, it lurked under the lower branches. He was pretending to be cool, but I could tell he was desperate to find out what was in it. Like me, Jim was a compulsive tearer.

"Gee thanks," he said, ripping off yards of snowman paper to reveal a soft black suitcase.

It had rounded corners and a zip around the edges. The suitcase and the thought of him leaving filled me with sadness.

"I've always wanted a suitcase like that," he lied.

Unable to wait any longer, I dislodged my gift from a branch and shredded the jingle bell paper to reveal a cardboard cube, smaller than a shoebox. The carton contained a brown leather case with silvery trimming and the word VOIGT-LANDER emblazoned across the front. I wrestled with a stiff dome at the back. It popped open to reveal a glorious, gleaming example of twentieth-century technology.

"A camera!" I said, beaming up at Dad.

He was the only person who could have chosen such an elegant thing all the way from Germany. The camera was his way of inviting me into his world, of finding ways to step back from the uncontrollable aspects of life and become an observer.

It was the most grown-up present I'd ever had. Decades later, the camera remains an object of beauty. Though no longer used for its original purpose, it is a treasure to me. Its case is scratched, the leather worn in parts, but it remains a symbol of a father's empathy for a mixed-up prepubescent girl. It sits beside me on my desk as I type. Maybe someday I'll buy a reel of film—if any still exists—and use it again.

"Can we have Christmas cake now?" Jim asked.

"I suppose it's late enough to qualify as morning tea," Mum said.

We relocated to the living room where we oohed and aahed as she lowered her masterpiece on the low table. Gleaming with royal icing, white as our mountain's peak, the cake was topped with a tiny plastic Christmas tree.

"Domestic Doreen's favorite recipe," Mum said, sinking a carving knife through the icing and marzipan layers. "And I hope to God the fruit hasn't sunk."

Sunken fruit was the hallmark of housewifely failure.

"Oh, no!" she cried. "It's a disaster!"

"Not at all," Dad said, taking an outer slice covered with a generous layer of icing on the side as well as the top.

We all agreed the cake was a paragon of deliciousness.

As the morning slipped by, the heavy, comforting aromas of roast meat and steamed pudding wafted through the house.

"Sorry we're late," Aunt Lila said, helping Nana through the front door. "We had to stop to admire those salvias at the top of the path. They look just like little . . ."

Fritz exploded with yaps of joy at the sight of Nana. The old woman raised her walking stick to keep him at bay. Dad took her elbow and escorted her to the dining room while Fritz sniffed at her heels.

"That dog has ruined enough of my stockings," Nana said, easing herself onto a chair.

We pulled Christmas crackers, read the silly jokes aloud, and placed paper hats on our heads. Nana rested a jaunty yellow paper hat over her silver bun and chewed quietly. Her wrinkles were deep as mountain crevasses, but her rheumy old eyes were kind. Her finger joints were gnarled, and her hands crisscrossed with veins. It was hard to imagine she'd ever been young. I sometimes wondered which was older— Nana or the mountain.

Once we'd stuffed ourselves with chicken, ham, and potatoes, Jim marched us outside onto the top lawn. We looked up to see an apparition waving from the tower window. Dressed in red and wearing a Santa hat, the figure stepped out onto the roof over the top veranda. It flung a sack over one shoulder and flopped about in oversized gumboots like the ones our farming cousins wore.

"Merry Christmas!" Lila boomed down at us.

"And to you, Santa!" we yelled back.

Lila reached into her sack and pelted us with a hail of Macintosh toffees. Her sack was empty too soon. I sucked vestiges of caramel stuck to my teeth as we bundled back inside, where Mum was boiling sixpences for the pudding.

"Come on, you lot!" Lila called.

In less than a breath, our aunt had changed back into her cream linen frock with the tan belt and tailored shirt collar. We trooped after her into the living room, where she performed baffling card tricks. Her piece de resistance was *The Surgeon Who Chopped Too Much*. Blindfolded, we listened as Lila recounted the story of an operation that went horribly wrong. We waited in trepidation as Lila passed around *body parts*—a prune for an eye, a dried apricot for an ear, a string of sausages for the intestinal tract.

"What's *that* noise?" Mary said.

It sounded like the melodramatic sigh of a Victorian lady, followed by a rustling and shooshing of petticoats, and a thud on the floor. We tugged at our blindfolds and hurried to the entrance hall.

The Christmas tree lay on its side, decorations scattered. Clinging to the top branch just below the angel was an embarrassed gray tabby with extra toes.

"Your mother better not find out about this," Dad said, resurrecting the tree with as much haste as two whiskeys and several glasses of wine allowed.

Before the news had time to spread to the kitchen, Mickey and I escaped to Dad's vegetable garden. The cat stretched languorously under the tomato plants. I raised my camera, adjusted the lens to the closest possible distance, 3.5 feet, and pressed the shutter with a satisfying click.

That black-and-white portrait of Mickey was the first photo I ever took.

Chapter Thirty-six

BITTER HONEY

Scarlet flowers blazed on the branches of the Flame Tree. Every bright, vigorous blossom made a joyous declaration that I didn't need to worry about Mum anymore.

The holidays were over. Jim unraveled yards of cream-colored masking tape and sealed the museum door. He zipped up his new suitcase and left. His departure was sudden. Brutal, almost.

I wanted to tell him how happy I was he'd given up taxidermy, that underneath his prickly veneer beat a heart soft as fur.

The pain and rebellion burning inside him were palpable. Lila was correct in her reading. No *manly* job was going to change who he was. Jim was a creative soul, not a scientist.

There was no time for goodbye. While Mum and Dad dropped him off at the bus station, Mickey and I lay on the floor and peered through the crack under the museum door. I wanted to maintain the fragile connection with my brother. The familiar stench of dust and formaldehyde was oddly comforting.

Mickey followed me upstairs to my bedroom, where my new Girls' High uniform spread like crime scene evidence over the bed.

"Hurry up!" my sister called from her room.

Mickey sniffed the white buttons and dull blue pleated skirt. The navy-blue beret flopped like a crash-landed UFO on my pillow. Berets were compulsory at Girls High, though nobody except a Frenchman knew how to wear one. That was of no importance. Any girl caught bareheaded in public risked detention and public shaming at assembly.

Mickey's whiskers stiffened toward the hat. He crouched low on the eiderdown and prepared for ambush.

"Go on, boy. Kill it!"

"We're leaving in five minutes!" Mary shouted across the landing.

I climbed into the uniform. Its ugliness was weirdly comforting. Not even Sophia Loren would look attractive in it.

Mickey pounced on the beret. He dug his claws into the wool and snared the funny little stem on top between his teeth. I laughed.

"What are you doing?" Mary said, standing in my bedroom doorway.

"Getting ready," I said, putting on my headband.

"You can't wear that," she said. "Headbands are banned. Your skirt looks a bit short. Have you checked it?"

"A few weeks ago," I said, dropping to my knees. "I might've grown a bit since."

My sister orbited me to make sure the hemline touched the floor all the way around. Our fusty school board hadn't heard about the *swingin' sixties*. They insisted our skirts reach our knees.

"Only just," she said.

"Why does the school have this stupid rule anyway? Are they scared we're going wear miniskirts?"

A smile played across my sister's face.

"They want us to look respectable."

"Do they think if our skirts are above our knees, we'll be floozies?"

Mary shrugged.

"Or worse." I added. "Like falling pregnant before we're married."

Mary didn't answer. Falling—a girl always *fell*, she never *became*—pregnant out of wedlock was the worst thing she could do. Especially if the boy, or his Mum, decided you were a slut and refused to let her have a shotgun wedding.

Mickey shook the beret and tossed it like a frisbee across the room.

"Mum will be home soon," Mary said. "Better hide him."

I slapped the beret on my head, gathered Mickey up, and placed him on top of the books inside my new school bag.

"You'll lose that beret in the first gust of wind if you wear it like that," Mary said, handing me two brown hair clips.

My sister inhabited her uniform with ease. It was her last year at school. She'd found ways to wear her beret without looking ridiculous. She flattened it at the back and molded the front part forward to form a mini visor. Hairclips pinned either side kept it neat and close to her scalp.

I tried to replicate her style as we hurried to the basement. The clips slipped through my hair and the beret slipped sideways.

"You'll get the hang of it," she said, guiding her bike into the sunlight.

Mickey sprang out of my school bag and pranced into the basement shadows.

"Be good!" I called after him.

In books and movies, all the bad stuff happens when the weather closes in. It's the lazy writer's attempt to make external storms reflect the trauma and fraught emotions of fictional characters. Real life's never like that. All the greatest challenges I've had to face have invariably taken place in fine weather.

Pedaling hard to keep up with Mary, I ignored the singing birds and the gleaming ferns along the roadside. Though the sky was an eye-watering blue, I made a point of not looking to see if there was any snow left on the mountain. It was my first day at a new school. Nausea rose in my throat. I was grateful my sister was at my side, pedaling calmly along streets, under the giant Pohutukawa tree, across the bridge to Girls High.

We dismounted at the school gates.

"Hey! Where are you going?" I asked as Mary veered off to join a surge of older girls.

"To my classroom."

"Where's my classroom?" I shouted after her.

"Over there," she said, pointing over my shoulder.

I had yet to appreciate my sister was entitled to a rich and rewarding life of her own.

As Mary disappeared in a sea of berets, I wheeled my bike toward a dismal asbestos prefab. In the post-war baby boom, many schools addressed the shortage of classrooms with pre-fabricated, single-story blocks of two classrooms. Prefab designs eliminated the need for corridors and freed up funds for the construction of assembly halls and other showy buildings.

A lowly third former, I resented being stuck in a cold, drafty prefab while older girls swanned around in the grand brick two-story building, or the glamorous new sixth form block.

I parked my bike and climbed the prefab's rickety wooden steps to meet my new classmates. Unaware of the efforts I'd made to be with them, the B stream girls regarded me with wariness and suspicion.

It was a relief to be with pleasantly unambitious girls earmarked to become nurses and teachers before fulfilling their destinies as wives and mothers. Though not as technically smart as the A stream girls, they considered themselves a cut above the C streamers, who learned shorthand and typing so they could become secretaries.

Girls' High was a totalitarian state propped up by endless regulations. No walking on randomly allocated bits of grass, no loud talking on buses, no jewelry, no hair on collars, no swearing, no smoking. Any girl caught doing any of that stuff would be punished with detention or the strap. Having grown up with minimal restrictions and virtually no physical violence, I was intrigued to find out how rules worked for other people. The concept seemed laughable, so far.

Our first lesson was in a science lab. My interest was piqued when the teacher explained biology meant the study of life. An understanding of biology, she added, would make us more valuable housekeepers and mothers. The glamor of test tubes and Bunsen burners evaporated. Science might have been an escape route for Marie Curie, but she didn't grow up in a place where women were regarded as two-legged dairy cows.

Mickey didn't seem to mind waiting an extra thirty minutes for me to get home. He jumped off the front steps and galloped toward me with the kids chanting *Helen the Melon* in his wake.

"Can we do dancing?" Danny asked.

Mickey sprang into the basket on my handlebars.

"No."

Their little faces turned pale and blank.

"Tomorrow!" I called over my shoulder as I heaved the bike and its passenger past the overgrown privet hedge up the driveway. "I've got homework!"

"What sort of homework?" Donna called.

"French, and it's really hard."

"Is the king of France asking you to his place?" Danny called.

I didn't have the nerve to turn around and wave at the eight little faces down on the street. Not when they were so quiet and accepting of my rejection. As I rattled my bike into the basement, Mickey jumped out of the basket and trotted off to roll in the dahlia bed, leaving me to wallow in guilt. I'd betrayed those poor waifs.

Mum ran down the path toward me. I could tell something was wrong. She was wringing a tea towel in her hands. "We've got bees!" she wailed.

"Where?"

"In the attic. They're making honey."

"Is that bad?"

"It's a *nightmare!*" Mum turned and flapped the tea towel, which I took as an instruction to follow her. I dropped my school bag and trailed after her upstairs to their bedroom.

"Look!" she said, pointing at a large, dark stain running from the ceiling and down the wall above their bed. "It's dripping everywhere."

"Honey?"

"Of *course* it's honey!" she said, collapsing on the candlewick bedspread and convulsing with sobs.

The electric clock on their mantelpiece emitted a weary click. I touched her shoulder.

"Mum, it's only honey."

"No, it's *not!*" she cried, clasping her hand to her forehead.

"What's the matter?"

Afternoon sun played on the blue horses above the bed.

"I've lost my job," she whispered.

"What? But everyone loves Domestic Doreen."

"That's the point," Mum's voice was weak and quavery. "The Women's Page is so popular now, the editor's taking on a full-time Ladies Editor."

"You're going to apply for it, aren't you? You needn't worry about us. We can fix the evening meals."

"She's already hired Peggy Thomas."

"Peggy Thomas? The one you say couldn't write a road sign?"

"Yes, but she's single. A career woman," she said, rolling her eyes. "The editor says they need someone whose attention isn't diverted by family and domestic demands."

I stroked a curl back from Mum's forehead. The strands felt so fine and fragile.

"I can't stand the thought of doing nothing but housework all day," she sighed, pushing my hand away. "Honestly, I'd rather—"

"The editor's wrong. You could do that job in a coma."

Mum reassembled her composure. She propped herself up on her elbows and blew her nose on the tea towel.

"Anyway, I'm calling the bee man," she said.

"Who?"

"The man in the beehive house."

The elderly couple who inhabited a dwelling built entirely of hexagons were local celebrities. Adhering to their belief that people should live in a world with no right angles, their front door, every window, and every room was hexagonal in shape. Every now and then we visited their six-sided temple to buy large, rotund cans of honey. It made sense he'd be interested in our bees, or at least know somebody who was.

"He'll come and smoke them out and take the swarm away."

It was unbelievable the editor could be so stupid. Domestic Doreen was the talk of the town, especially since the addition of the subsection *Handy Health Hints*, in which Doreen explained with cheerful authority how to lance boils and perform home enemas. Doreen was an intelligent woman. She even dared advocate for joint bank accounts, which allowed wives to have access to their husband's salary (with his approval and under strict supervision, of course).

How could the newspaper editor fail to realize it was Domestic Doreen's unique writing style, her voice, that had sent the popularity of the Women's Page skyrocketing? Next to Mum, a mediocre hack had no chance.

Two days later, Mum announced she'd landed a job as an untrained kindergarten assistant. I hurried outside to find Mickey basking in his favorite spot under the dahlias.

He raised his tail in a friendly curve and followed me into Dad's darkroom. I sat on the sacks and beckoned him onto my lap. Mickey purred and ran his sandpaper tongue over my fingers.

"I don't get it, Mickey. She doesn't even like kids."

Chapter Thirty-seven

TIGER IN
THE SNOW

The B stream girls were in no hurry to get to know me. It was mutual. I was comfortable in the background, a neutral wallpaper against their adolescent antics.

My classmates and I had a couple of run-ins when I yelled at them for flicking ink at the French teacher, Madam LaRue, and for teasing a girl they called Wobbles because she was born with one leg shorter than the other.

Shouting at people was hardly a recipe for making friends, and the classes were dull. I gave up homework and went back to playing with Mickey and the kids after school.

My lack of sociability put me in an awkward situation when Aunt Lila invited me to bring Mickey and a friend to stay with her and Nana for a few nights over Easter. I didn't know anyone who qualified as a friend. Fortunately, although Margaret and I had drifted apart since we'd started going to different schools and she'd gotten tied up with Bible class, she was willing to give me another chance. No kid in her right mind would have turned down the opportunity to stay with my aunt. Lila curated every day to suit the tastes and enthusiasms of her young guests.

Simmering with excitement, Margaret and I bundled our bags into the back of Lila's Morris Minor. Mickey crouched under my duffle coat in a basket between us. Nana dozed in the passenger seat while Lila zoomed through streets at breathless speed.

Once we were safely out of town, I raised my camera and

took a shot of the wrinkles in the back of Nana's neck. Her silver bun was like a modern sculpture by Henry Moore. An old lady smell wafted from her paisley scarf.

The mountain loomed before us like a giant ice cream sundae.

"Snow's well down," Lila said.

I lifted a corner of the duffle coat. Mickey sprang out of the basket onto my lap. He sank his claws into my thighs. Every muscle in his body was taut.

"He's scared of being in the car," Margaret said.

"No, he's not. Look . . ."

Mickey sat like an Egyptian cat statue, straight and tall, his nose pressed against the window. He was mesmerized by the vibrant green dairy pastures unraveling outside.

"How are the mice?" Margaret asked.

"*Your* mice, you mean. Still having babies."

"Why don't you sell them to the pet shop?"

"I tried."

"You could give them away," she said, flicking her ponytail over her shoulder.

"Who'd want them?"

Margaret changed the subject and said she'd heard the clever kids were missing me. It was a lie, but a kind one.

Mickey loved every minute of the drive. As we puttered into Hawera, he stood on all fours and probed my nostrils with his tail. I flattened his hind legs to make him sit.

The township was smaller, flatter, closer to the mountain and therefore colder than New Plymouth. To our family, Hawera held regal status. Here Mum grew up and learned to sing in the Bel Canto Italian style. We glided past the Hawera Star building where Mum had spent the happiest four years of her life. Lila wound her window down a couple of inches so we could inhale the rustic cologne of our cousins' dairy farms.

With its racecourse and drab concrete water tower, Hawera looked like any hick hamlet. However, a disproportionate number of writers, singers, and musicians had sprouted from its unassuming streets to strut the national stage. How Hawera could have become the Florence of Taranaki was a mystery. There were no Medicis among the cheesemakers. The farmers were of no-nonsense Scottish and Irish stock and suspicious of anything fanciful. Perhaps a kiwi version of Professor Harold Hill from *The Music Man* launched himself on the place a generation back and opened its soul to creativity. Or there was something in the milk.

Nana and Lila's bungalow sat primly at the end of a drive lined with proteas and rose bushes. The cream weatherboards and orange tiled roof presented a façade of modest ordinariness. Mickey was in no doubt that he was welcome. He jumped out of the car, stretched his front legs first, then the hind ones, and trotted up the steps to the front door.

"What's that?" I asked pointing at a mysterious box hanging in the porch.

"A bird house," Lila said. "Aunt Myrtle's boyfriend gave it to us."

The bird house itself wasn't familiar, but I recognized the faded lettering on its side, TEA. The plywood was straight from Mickey's first cabin.

"The Jigger?"

"Mmmm," Lila nodded. "No idea why he thought we needed it. Plenty of trees around here for birds to live in."

Margaret, Mickey, and I settled in together in the icy spare bedroom. Margaret chose the bed underneath the etching of thatched cottages, while Mickey and I took the one next to the window. Lila warmed our beds with hot water bottles, but Mickey and I hardly needed ours.

Next morning as we scooped porridge and brown sugar from our bowls, Lila asked her usual question.

"What do you feel like doing today?"

Her inquiry was 100 percent genuine. If we'd said we wanted

a party, Lila would have scoured the neighborhood for kids and thrown one. Beach swims in the rain, seaweed baths, egg white facials—anything was possible.

"Do you think Mickey likes snow?" Margaret asked.

Two hours later, the Morris Minor was through the gates of the National Park and toiling up the mountain slope. Mickey's whiskers stiffened as we snaked past ice-trimmed waterfalls through colonnades of native trees dripping with snow. I snapped a photo through the window. As we climbed higher, the mountain's stately peak grew larger and more defined. The motor groaned and whirred.

"Steady, girls," Lila called, revving up around a steep corner.

The car gasped to a halt outside the toilet facility in the parking lot. Lila slid out of her seat and strode to Nana's side of the car. An icy blast burned our cheeks as she opened the door and handed the old woman her walking stick.

"I'm never going to be that old," Margaret sighed as Lila took Nana's elbow and guided her to the ladies' room.

"Me neither."

"What'd you do for your birthday?"

I'd pretty much ignored my thirteenth birthday. Mum was exhausted with her new job at the kindergarten. She stayed up late to sew me a new headband in black-and-white op art fabric, which was too tight. Dad gave me a copy of *The Hobbit*, which I liked, but not as much as *The Lord of the Rings*.

"Some little kids came over."

"How little?"

"You wouldn't like them. They're a nuisance."

Mickey dug a stealthy claw into my thigh.

"Did you have cake?"

"Just a cream sponge from the supermarket, and some used candles from last year."

Margaret caressed her ponytail like it was an animal she'd tamed.

"Do you realize in the year 2000 we'll be forty-six years old?" Margaret was too smart at math for her own good.

"There's never going to be a year 2000," I said, holding Mickey to my chest to bathe in his warmth. "The world will have blown up by then."

Margaret folded her fingers into a cat's cradle on her lap. "You bring gloves?" she asked.

"No," I said, pulling my orange headband over my ears.

I knew Dad would have killed us if he found out we were cavorting on the mountain in our town clothes.

"Wanna snow fight?" Margaret asked.

Mickey flattened his ears and slunk off my lap onto the rubber mat at my feet.

Margaret and I climbed out into a world of profound silence. We stood awestruck at the mountain's glistening peak, so close I wanted to reach up and touch it.

I raised my camera. There was no hope of capturing this majesty. Compared to the mountain's age and size, we were nobodies. It existed in a timeless zone beyond measurement. Aloof in its chilly magnificence, the great, silent mound was indifferent to our presence.

Below us, a patchwork of pastures stretched toward the tiny blob of New Plymouth nestled on the edge of a bulging coastline. The lives people were so engrossed in down there didn't matter a bean. We were little more than fleas on the back of a giant presence we had no hope of understanding.

"Let's build a snowman!" Margaret cried, leaping across the crisp white carpet.

I left the car door ajar in case Mickey changed his mind and decided to come out. Building a snowman turned out to be harder than it looked. My fingers turned red and stung with cold. Our creation resembled a drunk kitten more than the dignified snowmen of Christmas cards.

The snowman's pebble eyes slipped and gave him a mournful air. I was rustling about in a patch of scrub searching for snowman nose material when a glorious mountain lion bounded toward me.

"Mickey!" I cried. "You like snow!"

My cat didn't like snow, he adored it. He bounded across the crystalline playground, pounced on unsuspecting clumps of grass, and burrowed tunnels in the soft powder. He didn't seem to feel the cold at all.

"Where's your Nana?"

We hadn't seen the old girls for ages. I gathered Mickey up and carried him toward to the restrooms.

"There you are!" Lila said, as if we were the ones who'd been missing. "Time to pack up."

Nana clutched her arm and hobbled back to the car.

Margaret and I piled snow onto the windscreen and bundled into the back seat. Mickey shook his whiskers dry, licked his many toes, and settled between us.

On the way back down the slope, Lila switched the car engine off to see how far we could go without the motor running. We swooshed and swerved downward at exhilarating speed, narrowly avoiding collision with the astounded driver of an upcoming van. The Morris Minor took on a life of its own, hurtling silently through the gates of the National Park to rest beside a paddock of startled cows.

"Do you want me to restart the motor?" Lila called over her shoulder.

"No!" we cried in unison.

"Better get outside and push."

Margaret and I rose to the challenge. We shoved the old Morris Minor along the road until it reached the top of a gentle incline. As the car gained momentum, we ran to catch up and jumped into the back seat. After the third go, the car rolled to a halt by a patch of scruffy land. A Morris Minor is surprisingly solid. We couldn't push it any farther.

"Hmmm, blackberries," Lila said.

She climbed out of the driver's seat and opened the trunk.

It was a treasure trove of spades for scooping horse manure off roads for her garden, sacks for gathering wild mushrooms, buckets, towels, and a rug for picnics.

"Here you go," she said, handing us each a bucket.

"Will the farmer mind?" I asked.

Lila didn't honor the question with an answer. We scrambled over a barbed wire fence and filled our buckets with luscious berries. Meanwhile, Mickey, with graceful, calculated steps, approached a nearby jersey cow, who was chomping on a clump of grass. The cow, sensing the cat's presence, lifted her head to regard him through large, curious eyes.

We laughed as Mickey pounced around the cow's hooves, swishing his tail and weaving around her legs.

"Careful, Mickey," I called. "She might kick you."

The docile cow seemed amused by Mickey's attention, however. Emboldened, Mickey darted in front of her towering legs, inviting her to pursue. His new friend obliged, trotting behind him with a rhythmic beat of her hooves on the damp grass.

Every now and then, the cow tried to tag Mickey with her large, rubbery snout, but the nimble cat managed to elude the larger animal's touch. Together they performed a harmonious dance of feline grace and bovine tranquility. We could have watched them play together all day, but Lila was anxious to get Nana back home.

I called Mickey back to the car. He meowed goodbye and retreated from his newfound companion, leaving her to resume her grazing.

Like every visit with Lila, it ended too soon. A few days after Margaret and I were back home, Mum answered the phone at the bottom of the stairs. It was Lila. She said Nana had caught a chill on her kidneys while we were up the mountain. It didn't sound good.

Chapter Thirty-eight

TALENTED CRIMINAL

Dad had a backlog of film to develop, so he let me take mine to Teeds Pharmacy. A full week passed before Mr. Teed was ready to hand over the fancy envelope with prints inside.

Mr. Teed oversaw all the black-and-white processing, so he would have seen my prints. I was too nervous to open them in front of him.

"Are they any good?"

The pharmacist's gaze drifted to the Coppertone poster beside the entrance to his shop. It showed a little girl at the beach with a puppy tugging her pants down. Though it was meant to be cute, the image unsettled me.

"Not bad, for a beginner," he said, sliding an envelope of prints into a brown paper bag.

I cycled home at demonic pace. Panting for breath beside the fishpond, I tore at the paper bag. Mickey curled his tail around my calves. I opened the envelope and emitted a mournful moan.

"What's the matter?" Dad said, emerging from his darkroom.

He'd taken charge of the household since Mum had gone away to Hawera for a couple of nights. She was helping Lila and her sisters look after Nana, which was weird. Lila usually managed on her own.

"They're *terrible*!" I said thrusting the envelope at him. "Nana's all blurry. And *this*—we're in a snowstorm!"

Dad's eyebrows undulated as he examined the prints.

"Well, you were up the mountain," he said. "A little snow's to be expected. You just moved the camera slightly. They're a bit overexposed. But your composition's good. And *this . . .*"

He held up the image of Mickey.

"Now *that*'s a photo. It captures your cat's personality, and your love for him."

I blushed. Mickey arched his back as I bent and stroked him from the crown of his head to the tip of his tail.

"Would you like to learn how to develop and print your own film?" Dad asked. "I could teach you. Only if you're interested . . . but you seem to have talent."

The word landed like a great golden sun in my chest. Photography was an unusual hobby for a girl, but if I had *talent . . .* in anything . . .

Mickey froze and pricked his ears.

"What's wrong, boy?"

My gray tiger scuttled away to disappear under leafy fronds in Dad's pumpkin patch. His ears had tuned into the sound of our car rumbling up the drive long before we'd heard anything.

The car door slammed. Mum was pale as buttermilk. She ran to Dad and sobbed into his neck.

I felt awkward standing there watching Dad rock her in his arms and kiss her hair. It was strange witnessing raw adult emotion.

"Did Nana die?" I asked.

Mum said nothing. She lifted her head from Dad's shoulder and nodded.

They didn't want me there. I wandered off to the pumpkin patch, where Mickey was waiting. My knees felt weak. I sank to the ground. The cat climbed onto my lap and snuggled under my chin. He stayed still and let me weep into his fur. There was no one in the world I loved more than Mickey.

"If we hadn't dragged Nana up the mountain, her kidneys would be fine and she'd still be alive," I sobbed. "I killed her!"

On top of being a forger and a shoplifter, I was now a murderer.

At the tea party after the funeral, the cousins were unsuspecting. I overheard one of them say she'd succumbed to a little bit of cancer in her lady parts. Someone else shook his head and mumbled about eighty-six years being a good run.

Mum was shaken to the core. At night, she sat beside the gas heater worrying the skin off her hands. In daylight hours, she buried her grief in the job she loathed. Her boss, a younger formally qualified kindergarten teacher, treated her like a slave. She insisted Mum arrive an hour early every day to open the building and set equipment up in the various play areas. At the end of the day, Mum had to mop floors and clean the toilets. Whenever a child had an *accident* involving either end of their digestive system, it was Mum's job to clean up.

Mum invited Lila to move in with us. We were all taken aback when my aunt said no. She valued her independence, thank you. Independence seemed a poor second to living with us.

We weren't wealthy. It just looked that way to some people because of the house. They didn't understand how desperately Mum and Dad struggled to keep the place from crumbling around our ears.

Almost every evening after dinner, the walls echoed with anxious discussions about money. If Dad lost his job, and that seemed more likely by the minute, we'd have to survive on the wages of an untrained kindergarten assistant.

However, even the darkest night can have glimmer of starlight.

A few weeks after Nana's funeral, Mum dressed up in her tweed suit. Her hat with the jaunty feather tucked in the brim, white gloves and patent leather handbag added the finishing touches. We waved her off to Hawera to see a lawyer along with her five surviving sisters and two brothers. As her parents

had owned three farms, it made sense the properties would
be divided equally between the eight surviving offspring.

Mum was subdued when returned from her trip.

"Are we rich?" I asked.

"You wouldn't believe it," she said, slumping on a kitchen
chair and taking a packet of Matinee from her handbag.
"Edgar and Walter are getting a farm each. The third farm
will be divided up among the six sisters."

"A sixth of a farm," I said, able to do math for once.
"Doesn't that mean we're rich?"

"It makes my lazy brothers rich," she said, studying the
cigarette smoke as though her dreams were evaporating into
it. "Simply because they were born with an appendage between their legs."

"You'll be able to pay off the house now, right?"

Mum hooded her eyes. Even in the depths of disbelief and
bitterness, she could be a movie star.

"It's barely enough to pay off a fraction of our debts."

That night, I woke to a terrible yowling from under the
house. I jumped out of bed and hurried outside into the moonlight. Mickey's silhouette appeared from behind the incinerator. He limped toward me and crumpled into my arms.

"You've been in a fight!" I cried. "Who did this to you?"

My chest imploded as I examined his injuries. His nose
was scratched. His right ear was torn. None of this would
have happened if Mum had let my best friend stay inside
with me. It seemed so unfair.

Chapter Thirty-nine

ELVIS IN
UNIFORM

As the school term wore on, I identified the outcasts and hovered around them. We were all freaks for different reasons—too fat, too pimply, too smelly. A girl called Diane, the daughter of an oilman from Texas, had thick glossy hair and teeth so white other girls said they were false. Diane was too new to work out who the rejects were. She upended the status ladder for a while by hanging out with us.

I was neutral about other girls anyway. I had Mickey. He was all I needed.

Mum cheered up faster than we'd all expected. She bought an old Ford Prefect and rattled off in it to the kindergarten every morning. Later in the day, she regaled us with horror stories over dinner.

"Sniveling Steven pooed in the block corner again today," she said, spooning mounds of mince on toast. "And HRH pretended not to see it."

HRH was code for Mum's boss. Though HRH was twenty years Mum's junior, she insisted on queenly treatment. HRH always arrived late at work to shut herself in her office while Mum wrangled the preschoolers.

"I hope you asked her to clean it up," Dad said, raising an ironic eyebrow.

He was in a good mood because Mum was letting him and George do a day hike on the mountain's foothills, known as the Ranges. Having retrieved his outdoor gear from where she'd dumped it behind the woodpile under the house, he'd promised never to do anything risky again. His backpack was already half filled.

Money talk was now taboo, thank heavens. After dinner, Dad tucked a tea towel into his belt and rattled dishes in the sink, which was big of him, considering he was a man with a proper job (for now). Mum poured a gin for herself, and a whiskey for him.

Mary took off to watch *Dr. Kildare* and have a sleepover with Melissa. They were in love with Richard Chamberlain. He did nothing for me. I stood at the window and watched her cross the street. She and Melissa were inseparable. If only I had a friend like that . . . then I realized I did. He had a tail and extra toes.

Outside, a ribbon of orange sunset arced across the sky above the glen. It was too spectacular to ignore. I went outside and called for Mickey. He trotted toward me and sprang into my arms. The scratches from his fight were fully healed. We checked for silhouettes in the kitchen window. Mum and Dad would be listening to a record in the dining room by now. Mickey and I trotted across the street and up the Dooley's path.

"Where've you been, strangers?" Mrs. D. said, opening her back door with a flourish. "Come on in. Shane's just back from the wharf."

She flattened a sheet of newspaper on the floor and spooned a lump of fish on top of Situations Vacant. Mickey assailed the slimy mound.

Her daughters hovered in the doorway.

"Time for bed, girls," she said, pouring herself a beer from a half gallon jar. "Put your nighties on. Want one?"

I shook my head.

"Go on. Just a half," she said, pouring amber liquid into a second glass. "You're a teenager now, aren't you? And we've got something to celebrate"

The beer was sour and bitter. I tried not to gag.

"Shane! Come here!" she shouted over her shoulder.

The second gulp of beer was no better than the first. I plotted a path to the kitchen sink where I could toss it down when she wasn't looking.

"He's in his bedroom," she added. "Let's go get him."

I was grateful to have an excuse to abandon the glass and follow Mrs. Dooley to the hallway.

"Come out!" she called, hammering on Shane's door. "Someone's here to see you."

The door glided open. It was Shane, but not Shane. His Elvis hairstyle had succumbed to a razor cut. He was taller, dignified, in a khaki uniform.

"They need lots of boys like him in Vietnam," Mrs. Dooley said. "It's a great career. He might even get a medal."

Unspeakably handsome, Shane bent and scooped Mickey off the floor.

"You're going to war?"

Shane didn't say anything. He and Mickey touched noses.

"Is Troy going with you?" I said, wondering if Shane's Ghost Train friend had talked him into it.

"Didn't you hear about Troy?" Mrs. D said. "He's been arrested."

A sharp breath caught the back of my throat. I'd never known anyone who'd been arrested before.

"What did he do?"

Shane scratched the M on Mickey's forehead and pretended not to be listening.

"The cops say he stole a motorbike," Mrs. D said.

"Where from?"

"Oh, some boy down the road. What's his name? Rick Gibson."

A wave of nausea washed over me. Maybe it was the beer.

"We need to go," I said, unraveling Mickey from Shane's embrace.

I clutched Mickey to my chest and ran down the Ds' steps.

War, war, war. I couldn't believe Shane was signing up for Vietnam. If he was doing it to escape Troy's bad influence, the price was way too high. The thought of Shane getting shot like one of the soldiers on television was . . .

We arrived home to hear Andy Williams crooning from the television. Through the crack in the living room door, I saw Mum gazing wistfully into her gin. Smuggling my fugitive down the hallway and up to my room was a breeze.

I needed Mickey to sleep with me that night. Dad would be heading up to the Ranges before dawn. Though he swore they wouldn't be going near the snow this time, he and George were unstoppable old fools, according to Mum.

After I switched the bedside light out, my beloved pet and I curved into each other's shapes under the eiderdown. The night was moonless, velvet black, and still.

For the first time in ages, a shimmering appeared high in the corner on the wall above my door. I watched in awe as the glistening particles sparkled and spread down the wallpaper.

It was glorious. Unbelievably wonderful.

The fairies were back.

Chapter Forty

GREEN VELVET CUSHION

Henry the Fifth's battle raged around me. We were struggling to get through the breach. Masonry crumbled around me. Dying men wailed at my feet. My comrade, Shane, stretched out his hand. I reached for him. Just as our fingers touched, he tumbled backwards under a shower of arrows.

A sword stabbed my neck. An arrow hit my chin. Another landed under my ear.

"*Ow!*" I yelled, pushing Mickey off me. The cat yowled. Claws unsheathed, he lunged at me again. "Stop it!"

I pulled the blankets up to shield my face. The cat had gone crazy.

Ears flattened, he scratched and growled. I fended him off again. He refused to go away.

"Okay! I give up," I said, rolling out of bed.

Mickey lowered his tail and signaled for me to follow him. He scampered downstairs past the museum to the kitchen door. I rattled the handle. The door was jammed shut from the inside. A sickly smell drifted through the keyhole.

I knew what it was straight away. Gas.

Mickey and I hurried back down the hallway, through the living room to the kitchen's other entrance. That door was sealed too. Without thinking, I summoned every ounce of energy in my body and rammed the door with my shoulder.

The stench of gas was overwhelming.

I ran forward. Mum knelt in front of the oven. She was bent over with her head resting on a green velvet cushion. I turned the gas off and helped her up off the floor. Her joints were loose and compliant under her dressing gown.

"What are *you* doing here?" she said, rolling her eyes with annoyance.

A wave of fresh morning air rolled in as I opened the windows.

I held Mum tight and sobbed into her shoulder.

"Mickey told me you were here."

Chapter Forty-one

A Rather
Special Cat

"She won't have to go to the looney bin, will she?"

Dad plonked his hiking boots beside the fireplace and peeled long woolen socks off his feet.

Mickey sprang onto Dad's lap and curled into a letter C.

"She just needs rest."

"If Mickey hadn't made me get up this morning, she could have died."

Dad smiled in his world-weary way and caressed the cat's spine with soothing strokes.

"That's the irony," he said. "It's mostly natural gas coming into peoples' houses these days. It wouldn't have sent her to sleep."

"Killed her, you mean?"

"Suicides aren't so common since we stopped adding carbon monoxide to town gas."

"Natural gas is explosive, though, isn't it? If she'd lit a cigarette the whole house would've blown up."

Dad's hand stopped and trembled over Mickey's fur. The *click clack* of Mum's stilettos echoed down the hall.

"Are you talking about me?" she asked.

A slash of scarlet lipstick stood out against her teased-up hair and black mascara. Daubs of rouge glowed like hot suns on her cheeks. In her crimson velvet gown and marcasite earrings Mum looked like a goddess.

"You gave us a fright," Dad said.

Mum arranged herself in a stately pose.

"I'm terribly sorry. I seem to have given the wrong impression."

Dad and I waited for her to elaborate.

"I was simply . . . doing research."

"Research?!" Dad retorted.

Mickey bounced off Dad's lap to lick himself under the table.

"Yes, David's written a wonderful little play for the Repertory Society," Mum said in a tone reserved for kindergarten kids. "About Sylvia Plath."

"The poet," I said. "The one who . . . ?"

"Yes, that's the one, dear. He's calling it *My Head, My Oven.*"

Dad crossed his arms in gloomy silence.

"It's a great part," Mum went on. "I thought I'd have a crack at auditioning for it. You remember I told you about Method Acting, Helen?"

I nodded.

"Well, I just wanted to find out how it feels."

"To kill yourself?"

"You didn't think for one moment I was serious?" Mum said, tossing her curls and gliding toward the Waterford crystal glasses.

"You could have died!" I yelled.

My voice echoed around the kitchen. Mum stood still, assembling her thoughts.

"Don't be silly, dear. Nothing happened, did it?" As she slid a pair of glasses onto the table, her gaze drifted to Mickey sitting on my feet. "He is rather a special cat, isn't he?" she said.

To my astonishment, my mother bent over and enfolded Mickey in her arms. "You have magnificent markings, don't you, puss? And my goodness! What do we have here? Extra toes!"

Chapter Forty-two

PACIFIC OVERTURE

After weeks of heavy rain, a cool breeze rolled moisture-laden clouds away. Trees opened their branches to the opalescent sky. Raindrops glistened on leaves. Pale blue rosemary flowers filled the air with luscious perfume.

Inside the walls of our dilapidated castle, a similar miracle was taking place. Our mother had set aside her long-standing feline aversion to embark on an unexpected transformation.

"I've always kept my distance from cats," she said, nestling into a living room armchair. "The claws and sharp teeth frightened me. After a while, I let my fear become prejudice. I never missed an opportunity to tell people cats can't be trained to sit or heel. Compared to dogs, I thought cats were aloof."

As if to counter her argument, Mickey sprang onto the armrest beside her and, using his mittens, kneaded the floral cover in a soothing rhythm. My mother drew a breath and glanced sideways. I half expected her to lash out and swipe him to the floor for damaging the upholstery. Instead, I saw something shift inside her. She exhaled and lowered her shoulders.

"I'll be making a new cover for this chair in a year or two anyway," she said, offering him her hand. "There's a new fashion for gold brocade coming in."

I felt a surge of delight and relief as Mickey nuzzled her fingers.

"His fur is so soft," she said, tickling the soft spot under his chin. "Listen to that music box!"

My purring tiger buried his head in her palm.

"We got off to a bad start, and I'm sorry about that," Mum said. "Mickey means a lot to you. He's helped you through a difficult time. I was so wrapped up in other things, I didn't understand."

"That's okay," I said.

"Let's put some meat on those bones," she said, lowering Mickey to the carpet.

Tail aloft, he trotted after her into the kitchen. She ladled a spoon of fresh ground beef onto a chipped saucer and placed it on the floor beside the stove.

The gold flecks in Mickey's eyes flashed. He raised his tail in a question mark.

"Come on puss," she called in a tender tone.

The cat bowed politely. He pointed his whiskers forward and padded across the linoleum to lick delicate circles around the saucer rim.

"He eats like a gentleman," Mum said.

Thrilled as I was to witness the tender scene, a single question blazed inside my head. There was never going to be a perfect time to ask it. "Can he stay in my bedroom?" I blurted. "Please?"

Mum considered the spoon in her hand.

"He knows how to get outside when he needs to," I added.

She turned to rinse the spoon under the tap. The fridge sighed as Mum gazed through the kitchen window across the glen. It was impossible to tell what she was thinking.

"Well, I suppose he's earned his place as part of the family," she said.

I cried out and rushed forward to latch my arms around her neck.

"Thank you so much!" I said through happy tears. "You're not going to regret it."

Mum and Mickey spent a lot of time together after that. He supervised her efforts at the sewing machine. In the evenings, he climbed on her lap and nestled into the folds of her skirt while she was knitting. Her eczema improved to a point where she wondered if feline fur might have a healing quality. I could hardly believe my ears one night at dinner-time when she decreed every household should have a cat.

Fritz wasn't so keen to begin with. After a few teeth-baring encounters, he settled down, however, and the animals formed a truce. Cat and dog spent hours curled up in a yin yang circle in front of the gas heater.

School wasn't so terrible anymore. I gave up fighting the rules, the uniform, and everything else. One lunchtime when I was eating honey sandwiches in a state of numb compliance, Miss Allen the English teacher approached. She asked if I'd be interested in running dance classes during lunch hours. I said yes right away. Once we got started, I was impressed by how eager the girls were to become fountains, autumn leaves, and avalanches.

After school one day, Mickey and I were in the kitchen for our usual afternoon snack.

"Have you heard about the fancy new food from Italy?" Mum said.

She grated cheese on a chopping board, then rolled out a layer of puff pastry.

"Here's the important part," she said, spreading the pastry with Vegemite.

"It's called pizza," she said, sprinkling the cheese on top.

Much as I was proud of her insistence on keeping up with trends, I wasn't going to let her get away with this one.

"Isn't it just a version of cheese on toast?"

"Not at all!" she said, arranging tomato slices and ham in artful shapes on top of the cheese. "It's *exotic*. One of these days, the whole country will be eating pizza."

She was starting to sound as crazy as Dad was about his gas. Mum tossed a handful of ham onto Mickey's plate. He devoured it in a few gulps.

"When's the audition for David's play?" I asked.

"*My Head, My Oven*? He couldn't finish the revisions, poor thing. Writer's block."

"He's not a real writer anyway. How can he get blocked?"

The oven emitted a puff of smoke as she opened its door and slid the pizza under the grill.

"He couldn't work out how to end it on a hopeful note."

"It was never going to be a laugh a minute," I said, easing the lid off the biscuit tin.

"David wants to be an angry young man like Joe Orton, but I don't think he's angry enough," Mum said. "Kitchen sink dramas may be all the rage in New York and London, but our townsfolk aren't going to part with hard-earned cash for a night of misery when they could see *Oklahoma!*"

"*Oklahoma!*? Hasn't the Operatic Society done it already?"

"What's that I smell?" Dad said, striding across the linoleum. "Cheese on toast for dinner?"

"Pizza. It's Italian."

"Mum says they're doing *Oklahoma!* again this year."

"No, I didn't," she said peering through oven's murky glass window. "I was just . . ."

Dad settled on a chair and rattled the pens in his breast pocket.

"You haven't heard the announcement?" he said.

"I have less than no interest," Mum said, lifting the pizza from the oven.

It didn't look so bad now the cheese had melted and browned around the edges. Maybe the Italians were on to something.

"I'll give you a clue," Dad said, standing up and disappearing into the living room.

"Dinner's ready!" Mum yelled.

The piano oozed tones of high romance through to the kitchen. Mum and I stood still, transfixed by the liquid longing tones of "Some Enchanted Evening."

"*South Pacific!*" Mum said with a wistful sigh as she lowered the pizza onto the table. "A wonderful musical. Call your sister down, will you?"

The music stopped.

"You know there's an outstanding role for a contralto in it," Dad said, beaming from the doorway.

Mum clutched a tea towel to her throat and placed a hand on the back of her chair as though her knees had forgotten how to support her.

"Bloody Mary!"

"None of your fancy mezzos," Dad said. "She has to be a genuine contralto."

"It's such a great character role," Mum said. "I was born for it. When's the audition?"

"Saturday a week."

"What's that smell?" Mary said, coming through the hallway past the museum.

"Pizza."

"What?"

"It's *Italian!*"

"Are there any parts for people my age?" I asked.

A distracted cloud crossed Mum's face.

"Yes, but you'd have to speak French."

I sank back into my seat.

Fritz trotted across the linoleum to curl up with Mickey in front of the gas heater.

I couldn't help feeling excited for Mum.

"You'll be a fantastic Bloody Mary," I said, chomping into the pizza.

A cool wisp of doubt threaded through my words. Mickey raised his head and blinked. He knew what I was thinking.

What if she didn't get the part?

Chapter Forty-three

MAESTRO MICKEY

The weatherboards held their breath on the day of Mum's audition. Birds forgot to sing. Bloody Mary was more than just a character part. The chords of her iconic solo *Bali Hai* opened the entire musical.

I called for Mickey. He wasn't on the front steps or under the house. After a frantic search, I found him inside, sitting on top of the piano.

"Isn't he funny?" Mum said. "Most cats hate music, but this one walks over the keyboard when I'm not playing. He likes my voice too."

"Really?"

"Yes, my contralto is so low I think it reminds him of purring."

I went to the kitchen and put the kettle on.

"*Stingy bastard!*" Mum scolded in a harsh, unfamiliar voice.

"You okay?"

"Don't mind me, dear. It's just Bloody Mary trading with sailors on a Pacific Island. *You like, you buy?*"

"Does she swear like that on stage?" I asked, placing a mug of instant coffee on top of the piano next to Mickey.

"Well, yes. She's upset because a marine called Lieutenant Cable rejects her daughter because she isn't white."

"A racist?"

"He gets killed anyway."

It sounded like *South Pacific* might have something to offer townsfolk who voiced certain views about Maoris and Polynesians, not to mention the Indians and Chinese who'd migrated to our country not so long after our own pioneering ancestors.

"Where does Bloody Mary come from?"

"She's Tonkinese."

Mum and her fellow thespians took pride in adopting fake accents and exotic costumes.

"Isn't there a Tonkinese woman in town who'd like to play her?"

Mum flattened the sheet music against the piano stand.

"Hardly, dear. Tonkin belongs to North Vietnam. We're at war with them."

She cleared her throat and leaned closer to the page and began to sing.

The notes reverberated up my spine. It was a cross between a prayer and a magic spell, an incantation.

"Are you dressing in character?"

"I'm not tempting fate this time," she said, lifting Mickey off the piano and snuggling him into her twin set (the pearls were fake but looked the part).

"You can be my lucky charm," she said to Mickey.

He blinked up at her.

She brushed her lips on his forehead *M* and gathered up her sheet music.

"Good lu—" I called after her.

Mum swiveled on her heel.

"We don't use that word in the theater!"

"Sorry, I forgot. Break a leg. Break two of them!"

The afternoon dragged. I peered over the hedge into Geraldine's kitchen. Her window was dark and lifeless.

My fears were confirmed when her three kids showed up on the doorstep.

"Where's your Mum?"

They stood open-mouthed, more lost than usual.

"Gone for a swim in the Pacific," Felix said.

I was about to send them away when their five friends arrived, breathless and bright with anticipation.

"Can we play charades?" Danny asked.

Mickey and I followed them down to the bottom lawn.

I was impersonating Mary Poppins, holding an imaginary umbrella aloft when a dazzling figure waved from the veranda. Her vivid yellow sarong gleamed in the afternoon light.

She flapped a long shell necklace at us and treated us to a full-blown performance of Bloody Mary at the height of her powers.

Mickey, the kids, and I ran up the steps to witness the spectacle at close hand. Mum's eyes were circled in black eyeliner. Her front teeth were blacked out, and her hair scraped up in a fake bun.

"Dorothy the wardrobe mistress insisted I try a few things on."

"Did Geraldine audition?"

"Who? Oh, yes. Terrible chest notes."

"Did Eric give you any hints?"

Mum twirled the shell necklace.

"He said there's only one woman in this town who can play Bloody Mary."

Her face erupted in a triumphant smile, then launched into song. in her rich velvet voice.

Mickey sat entranced at her feet as she wove a spell of mystery and longing around us.

As she reached the final note, Mum bent and scooped Mickey up to nuzzle her neck.

The kids and I cheered as Mum and Mickey bowed before us.

"This is one lucky cat," she said.

Chapter Forty-four

WILDCATS AND ROSES

Mickey bore little resemblance to the emaciated stray we'd brought home from the Gasworks a year earlier. His fur was plush and glossy. He was bulging around the middle, probably because of the extra treats Mum kept tossing his way. She even talked about putting him on a diet, which was a ridiculous idea for anyone, let alone a cat.

The cast for *South Pacific* included the usual suspects. After his success as the king in *The King and I*, Roy was so stagestruck he accepted the minor part of Professor. Closer to home, Geraldine was overwhelmed by professional and domestic demands. She declined the offer to be a second-row nurse in the chorus.

It was widely agreed *South Pacific* was the best musical in the Operatic Society's long history. A *Taranaki Herald* critic issued a personal invitation to Mr. Rogers and Mr. Hammerstein to visit our town to see one of the finest interpretations of their work. The season was extended by a week.

Bruce the dairy farmer made an excellent Emile de Becque and Stephanie Fields did her usual bright young thing as Nellie Forbush. David from C. C. Ward's received well-deserved accolades for his interpretation of the racist marine, Lt Joseph Cable. Beryl Dickson from the bank was praised for her role as Bloody Mary's daughter, Liat.

The moment Mum stepped on stage, however, something shifted. The theater's atmosphere changed. As her voice soared to the back of the gods, people knew they were witnessing something extraordinary. The coughers and the candy paper scrunchers fell silent as she filled the auditorium with the magnetism, humor, and pathos of Bloody Mary.

Whether dancing, trading insults with sailors, or casting a hypnotic spell as she sang about her special island, Bali Hai, Bloody Mary summoned a profound response from her audience. Emotion rose in chests. Hairs sprang to attention on the backs of necks.

After the curtain went down on closing night, our hands were sore from clapping. As the man who was married to Bloody Mary, Dad was mobbed in the foyer. While he chatted to Mum's new fans, he pressed her coat into my hand.

"Take this backstage to her, would you?" he said. "She must look after her vocal cords."

Clutching her coat, I ran through the brisk night down the side street to the back of the opera house. I squeezed through the stage door and wove around exuberant sailors. One of them, Stewpot, smiled and pointed at a door with Mum's name on it.

The door creaked open to reveal a tiny room, not much larger than a wardrobe. A dim bulb hung from the ceiling. It cast an amber glow over a small wooden table strewn with brushes, greasepaint sticks, and a tangle of hairpins. The scent of old costumes, makeup, and excitement mingled in the air.

My mother—a least a version of her—sat at the table and leaned into a small mirror.

"You were magnificent!" I said, thrusting the coat onto her lap.

"Was I?" she said, massaging dollops of cold cream into her face. "I think my hand movements could have been better in Happy Talk. Did they look like birds from where you were sitting?"

Mum was always her harshest critic.

"Of course they did!" I said, squeezing her shoulders. "They were like seagulls floating over a beach."

Once the cast had shed their makeup and costumes, they all gathered at the fanciest new restaurant in town, La Scala; *NZ's Most Attractive Fully Licensed Restaurant where dining is NOT expensive—we eat here ourselves.*

To keep some of his overseas oil men entertained, Dad invited them along too. Expectant guests trotted across a copper-plated ornamental bridge spanning an artificial stream just inside the entrance. La Scala was my personal wonderland. Space age, copper trimmed lights hovered from the ceiling.

Frank Sinatra crooned *Strangers in the Night* to low-slung chairs lounging around the bar. The striped awning over the counter issued a bright invitation, but I was too young to approach the barman in his scarlet waistcoat.

A waiter escorted us across the crimson carpet through a jungle of indoor plants to a large round table. A grand piano stretched like a leopard on a rostrum behind us.

I followed the aftershave lure of an American oilman and took at seat next to him. Aware that a thirteen-year-old kid was the ultimate dud at an adult dinner table, I tried to make myself invisible. The oilman smiled politely and turned away.

"Hello there," David from C. C. Ward's said, sliding into the seat on my other side. "Is this chair free?"

Across the table, an enthralled Eric sat next to Mum. Resplendent in her new satin evening gown with the high Chinese collar, she was a magnetic force. A hibiscus flower blushed from behind one ear as she breathed gin and Dior over Eric. The flower was fake, but a perfect match for her scarlet fingernails and lipstick. Dad, pink with pride, draped his dark jacket with silver buttons over the back of his chair and adjusted his houndstooth cravat.

The oil man was busy falling in love with Stephanie Fields on his other side. David tried to be polite, but I was too embarrassed to say much. After his performance as Lt. Cable, my opinion of him had changed. He was a true artist. His job as an evening fabric salesman was simply to keep him in Weet-Bix.

"Are you going to finish your play?" I asked.

"*My Head, My Oven?*" he said, studying a ribbon of cigarette smoke curling toward the ceiling. "I hit a wall."

"Writer's block? You should keep going. You've got talent."

David shrugged and ground his cigarette into a red glass ashtray.

The adults took care of themselves while I perused the menu. As if life wasn't complicated enough, New Zealand had converted from pounds and shillings to decimal currency a few weeks earlier, on the tenth of July. The government aired jaunty television ads kept saying dollars and cents would be a breeze. They lied.

Despite La Scala's claims, their prices (all main dishes came with vegetables included) were scandalous. Sirloin Steak was 85 cents (8/6), for heaven's sake. That said, the steak was a bargain compared to Chicken Martini at $1.00 (10/-). They probably didn't put real Martini in it either. I ordered the cheapest item, grilled lamb cutlets for 80 cents (8/-).

After the main course, Eric rose to his feet and tapped a teaspoon against his glass. Raucous dinner guests sank into amiable silence.

"I'd like to congratulate you all on the biggest box office success we've ever had," Eric said. "Would our lead performers please stand."

Applause erupted as Stephanie, Bruce, David, and Beverly arose to smile and wave at the adoring crowd.

"Ah, but we're missing our most talked about star," Eric said.

Mum dipped her head and took a gulp of red wine.

"This production's Bloody Mary will be remembered for decades to come. Noeline, please . . ."

Mum stood up to resounding cheers. *Speech! Speech!* echoed across the room.

"It's been an honor to perform with you all," she said. "We created something wonderful together."

Something wonderful? Deep down she was still hurting from last year's rejection.

"Thank you, Eric, and everyone for all your hard work. I won't say I look forward to working with you again because it'll probably never happen. We're in an ephemeral world. This production will now become a collection of memories for us, and for those who enjoyed our performances."

As she was about to sit down, she paused and raised her glass.

"I'd like to propose a toast to you all. And I have an absent friend who deserves a mention."

People straightened in their seats. If Noeline Blackman was conducting a secret liaison, the whole town wanted to hear about it.

"There are times when our animal friends seem to know more than we do. I'd like to pay tribute to a cat who showed up at the right place at the right time. He began life unwanted and unloved but now he's part of our family. I call him my lucky charm. Please raise your glasses to Mickey."

The restaurant reverberated good-natured cheers for Mickey.

"You have a cat?" David said, turning to clink his wine glass against my Coke. "I have three. You must come and visit us some time."

It was my first introduction to the global network of remarkable, often offbeat people who love cats.

Of all La Scala's offerings, Tropicana Deluxe was my favorite. Half a coconut shell filled with fruit salad and topped with whipped cream (50 cents, or 5/-). As I waited for it to arrive, the oilman stood up, hammered his knife against a glass and cleared his throat. Curious faces turned in his direction. They assumed he'd had too much Asti Spumante.

"I don't know if y'all heard the news, but this seems as

good a time as any," he drawled. "Y'all know we've been wildcat drilling for oil off this beautiful coast of yours for a long time now. Well, just a few days ago, we found natural gas out there."

He wasn't drunk, just confident in that American way. The restaurant rumbled with interest.

"It's a massive field beyond anything we were hoping for. We reckon there's enough to fuel this entire country for several decades."

A patter of applause from a corner near the toilet doors.

"And see that man across the table there? Bill Blackman stuck with the notion there'd be decent amounts of natural gas in this region for the past twenty years. I know some of you thought he was crazy . . ."

A rumble of good-humored acknowledgment emanated from the bar.

"But we just found out he was right all along."

Dad studied the tablecloth and beamed.

"This man before you isn't a gasworks manager," the oil man continued. "He's a visionary."

Cheers echoed across the restaurant. The oil man urged Dad to his feet.

"Thanks, Jerry. I'm honored by your words, but tonight isn't about gas or me," he said, stepping up to the piano.

Dad unleashed a flourish of chords, riveting in their familiarity. Mum hurried to his side. She drew a breath and cast a conqueror's gaze across the room.

By the second line, the entire restaurant was singing along to "Bewitched, Bothered and Bewildered."

Chapter Forty-five

APPLY WITHIN

A volcanic pimple sprouted on my nose. The zip on my bellbottoms refused to close at the top. I wasn't the only one. Mickey's undercarriage was drooping. His sleek stride stiffened to a waddle. I told him not to worry. We were magnificent.

The orange headband snapped. I tossed it in the incinerator. The peroxide bottle ran out. I stopped bleaching my hair.

Though Mickey and I reveled in his newfound freedom to roam the house, his fascination with the tower was a worry. He spent hours sitting at the bottom of the ladder gazing up at the trapdoor as if it was a portal to heaven. If anyone went up and forgot to close the trap door on their way down, he'd surely find a way to shimmy up there. It would be mouse Armageddon.

I phoned Margaret and asked her to come over one Saturday morning. We went under the house and tore the side off a cardboard box. I opened one of Dad's old paint cans with a nail and skimmed the hardened skin of enamel off the top.

"That's a weird color," she said.

"Chartreuse. Nothing wrong with it. What should I write?"

"Looks like lime green to me," she said, taking the brush from my hand.

Margaret emblazoned FREE WHITE MICE on the board. Her lettering was tidier than anything I could've done. It was an excellent sign. We carried it up to the kitchen. Mickey sat neatly under the table while Mum bent over a library book.

"Lovely, dears," she said, glancing up from *The Feminine Mystique* by Betty Friedan. "But you make it seem political."

Margaret and I exchanged looks. Ever since Mum had given up the kindergarten job to write a weekly Arts column for the newspaper, everything was *political*. On the upside, her eczema had disappeared.

"We're just trying to give mice away."

"Those words imply you want mice liberated from their cages to wander the streets. You need to add APPLY WITHIN. This is a fascinating book, by the way. You must read it."

Mum exhaled smoke through both nostrils and dismissed us with the turn of a page.

Mickey raised his tail and followed us back under the house.

"This makes no sense," I said, squeezing a wobbly APPLY WITHIN underneath Margaret's perfect lettering.

"Nobody will see it anyway. There's no traffic on Bracken Street."

"You're right. Let's put the sign on Cutfield Road," Margaret said.

Though convinced our mission was doomed, I played along with Margaret to keep her happy. We placed the sign on top of a pile of bricks out on Cutfield Road.

It turned out half the town was desperate for a free white mouse. By weekend's end all forty-two had disappeared to grateful new homes.

The mouse exodus was swift and seamless, apart from one glitch. On the Sunday morning, a distraught woman returned a mouse complaining it had no tail. She insisted on swapping Tail-less for a *proper* mouse. Just as I was about to succumb to the idea of keeping Tail-less forever, a little girl with tawny braids fell in love with him. I threw in the mouse cage and wheel to go with him. Tail-less and my mouse phase were gone for good.

That night, I unlatched my window and lay in the dark with Mickey snuggled beside me on the pillow.

"Did I wake you?" Mum said, bursting into the room.

A shaft of light from the landing stung my eyes. Mickey shook himself awake.

"I've been thinking about your future," she said, switching my bedroom light on and lowering herself onto the edge of the mattress. "Life's so difficult for women. You must have a career to back you up."

"Are you a women's libber?"

"I'm not about to burn my bra, if that's what you're thinking. Not that your father would notice. He's more interested in high pressure natural gas pipes these days. A woman must be qualified in something."

"What could I do?"

"You're good with children. Teaching?"

I shook my head. Mary was to head to teacher's training college the following year. That was her specialty.

"Nursing?"

"Yuck!"

"What about journalism? You know, I spent the best four years—"

"*No way!*"

"Times have changed. You can't expect a man to look after you."

If I told her I wanted to be a spy like Emma Peel in *The Avenger*s, I knew she'd laugh. I cast about the room for hints. Books, old toys, a pile of clothes on the floor. It was the same as any kid's bedroom—apart from the camera.

"Photographer."

"You mean, weddings?"

"No! A hardcore news photographer. I'll go to Vietnam."

Mum was taken aback.

"But we don't know anyone in Vietnam, dear."

"Shane's there."

She drew an almost inaudible gasp.

"You're not keen on *that* boy, are you?"

"Course not. I'll take photos of the war. People will see how stupid it is and make it stop."

Mum fumbled in her pocket for a cigarette. She couldn't find one.

"It's political," I added.

Mum crossed her legs.

"Well, I suppose you could take one of those self-defense courses," she said at last. "Are you sure you're up for it? Photographic gear's awfully heavy."

"No worse than a school bag."

She lapsed into silence. I turned on my side and pulled the sheet up around my ears to indicate the conversation was over.

"But what about your vision, dear? How is your sight, by the way?"

I rolled onto my back.

"See that light switch over there?" I said, considering the options.

"How many do you see?" she asked.

If I lied again and said there were two switches, Mum would take me back to Dr. Hughes. He'd sign me up for more surgery. My parents would fuss over me, I'd get a few weeks off school, and wouldn't have to take responsibility for anything for at least six months. It had appeal.

I scrunched my eyes and concentrated on the light switch. How many could I see in all honesty? I was about to say two, maybe three, when Mickey stretched his paw out to comb my hair. His touch was tender, comforting, reassuring.

"One. Just one."

The lines of concern softened on Mum's face.

"Are you serious about photography?"

I stroked the gristle under Mickey's chin and nodded.

"All right. I'll ask Veronica if she can give you a holiday job in the photographic department at the newspaper."

Chapter Forty-six

CAT OF A DIFFERENT COLOR

As the mountain surrendered to spring, icy white fingers crept down its pleats and crevices. Snow melted and gurgled through streams. Knobby-kneed calves hobbled over vibrant green paddocks.

The humid air was heavy with anticipation. It seemed everything on the lush, fertile land was aching to be born.

Down on the bottom lawn, jasmine flowers filled the air with bitter-sweet longing. I plucked a stem and put it in a jar beside my bed.

"You'll like this," I told the fairies.

Next morning, my bedroom window creaked on its latch and drifted open. A cool breath caressed my face. It was dark outside. I lay on my back and watched the milk truck's headlights slide across the tangled forest on my walls. The engine rattled and groaned over gravel. Tokens tinkled from empty bottles; quarts and pints clattered against each other inside their crates.

That was when I felt it. The pre-dawn air was sharp with urgency. Something was different.

Hurry up! I need you.

Mickey's tone was serious and clear.

I reached for the comforting mound of his feline body. Blankets sagged in an empty hollow where he usually slept. The space was cold, lifeless.

Alarmed, I sat up. The scar inside my left eye pulsed tight and dry.

Don't waste time! the voice said, louder this time.

"Puss! Puss!" I called into the shadows.

The milk truck cleared its throat and sputtered out of our street.

I rolled out of bed, hitched up my pajama bottoms, and padded down to the kitchen. Mickey's saucer was in its usual place, licked clean.

Fritz lay comatose on the rag rug in front of the fireplace. His feet twitched; his lips curled back in phantom chase.

"Have you seen Mickey?"

The dog raised an ear. His dream was too engrossing to leave.

I strode past the museum—a mausoleum for Jim's absence—to the back door. A ringlet of smoke rose from the incinerator in the pewter light.

"Mickey!" I yelled into the bamboos. A blackbird sang a triumphant arpeggio. Its mocking delight sent goosebumps down my arms.

A shy, egg-yolk sun peeked over the rim of the glen. Streaks of gold dripped over rooftops and trees. Across the street, a black-and-white cat melted under Mrs. Finkle's gate.

A boy's silhouette appeared around the side of our house.

"She's up!" Danny called, beckoning his friends.

The neighborhood kids were always up early. They knew to play outside until their parents rose. Their upturned faces were hopeful, untouched, as they gathered around the back steps.

"Where's Stacey?" I asked.

"Sleeping in."

The kids were sprouting faster than onion weed. The seams on Danny's tiny shorts were begging to burst. Donna twirled in a *new* nylon frock inherited from her older sister.

Not to be outdone, Geraldine's offspring were decked out in freshly sewn garments for summer. Deborah and Portia's floral prints rippled on the breeze. Felix, an elongated crazy mirror image of his former self, stood to one side. His tailored gray shirt drooped from his coat hanger shoulders.

"Can we have a mouse?" Donna asked.

"They've all gone."

"Where's your cat?"

"Have you seen him?"

My eye scar pulsed. What if they'd found Mickey lying in a gutter and couldn't summon the words to tell me?

Donna and Martin shook their heads. The others stared at the ground.

"Bet he's under the house." Danny said. "Let's go!"

Chilblains throbbed on my toes as I skittered after them over the cold concrete path.

I paused at the basement entrance and scanned the neighborhood. A distant rooster crowed. Brutus issued throaty barks from his cage across the street.

Come ON!

Danny sank to his knees next to the front tire of Dad's Zephyr.

"Nothing here!" his voice echoed into the car's underbelly.

"Mickey's cabin's empty," Deborah said, pink-cheeked with concern.

The scar in my eye ached. I leaned against the darkroom door. It groaned open. An aroma of raw earth and photographic chemicals enveloped me.

The room was darker than a moonless night. I fumbled for the familiar shape of Dad's workbench to hold me steady till my eyes adjusted.

"What's in there?" Danny said.

The boy pushed the door wide open behind me. A triangle of light illuminated an extraordinary sight.

Bewildered, confused, I rubbed my eyes.

On the floor in the far corner of the darkroom, a striped cat nestled on top of a pile of sacks.

"Mickey?" I wavered. "Is that you?"

The cat raised his head and blinked at me in slow motion. Dust particles hovered between us.

His purrs reverberated off the darkroom walls. This was an older, better fed version of the cat we'd brought home from the gasworks last year. Mickey, who'd helped me find a place in the world. The same cat who'd taught me life had no meaning until I could love something beyond myself.

The same cat. Only different.

I ran forward and dropped to my knees beside Mickey. He dipped his head so I could stroke the *M* on his forehead. My whole body began to tremble.

"Mickey, I never knew . . ." I said, hot tears of joy streaming down my cheeks.

I lowered my gaze to the four tiny creatures burrowing into the soft folds of Mickey's abdomen.

Blind and helpless, they writhed in a tangle of scrawny legs and claws. Their noses were pink as Christmas baubles, their eyes sealed like envelopes. With ears flattened against their skulls, they resembled tiny spacemen recently arrived on Earth.

Their fur was sparse and damp. Three kittens sported gray stripes and Ms on their foreheads like their mother. The smallest hardly seemed to belong to the same family. Its fur was black and white. I raised the kitten's delicate paw between my fingers and counted the toes. Six on each front foot. A polydactyl.

Chapter Forty-seven

COSMIC LULLABY

Under Mum's instructions, Mickey and the kittens were relocated to a cardboard box and placed beside the gas heater in the kitchen. After dinner, Mum settled at the kitchen table and rolled two sheets of newsprint with carbon paper sandwiched between into her Imperial typewriter.

"Off you go," she said, waving her cigarette in a tender circle. "I'll keep an eye on them."

Upstairs, I lay on my eiderdown and listened to the comforting *plunk plunk* lullaby of her keyboard echoing off the kitchen walls.

As I stretched and yawned, a four-legged silhouette appeared in the doorway.

"Mickey!" I cried as the cat landed with a thud on the blankets. I gathered the soft folds of my pet's body to my chest. A symphony of purrs reverberated through my torso and down my arms.

Evening shadows rippled across the wallpaper. A glint of light flashed from the corner in the ceiling above the door. It expanded to encircle us and encompass the room. The cat and I drew a simultaneous breath.

"Meow?" I asked.

Mickey stopped purring and considered my question.

"Meow," came the answer at last.

Cat and girl, we embraced the meow, surrendered to the shimmer, and let ourselves melt into the particles.

Mickey and I shed our physical bodies and became weightless spirits, limited only by the size of our thoughts. The cat expanded to become the size of a giant tiger. I climbed on her back. Together we dissolved through the ceiling and floated across the night sky.

We smiled down at Mum bent over her typewriter, and Dad at his desk sketching webs of natural gas pipelines across a map of the North Island. Fritz sat at his feet and twitched an ear. The dog sensed our presence but didn't bark.

Mickey and I wafted past Mary's bedroom window. Her swaying form danced in the arms of an imaginary man to Engelbert Humperdinck crooning "The Last Waltz" from her portable record player.

We sailed high above the glen, bestowing kisses on the cheeks of eight sleeping children and surrounding them with golden halos of protection.

Swifter than thought, we floated on the night breeze to hover over the gasworks, where Mickey's story began.

We swept above twinkling streetlights, across the curve of coastline to the port and sugarloaves jutting out from the sea.

Releasing hurt and fear, Mickey and I sailed higher, our hearts unfurling with love for the people and places below.

A dark, majestic pyramid rose from the farmland. A wafer biscuit moon illuminated Mt Taranaki's snowy shoulders. Mickey and I couldn't resist the mountain's call. It drew us in to become part of every rock, fern, and sparkling stream.

We felt no fear. Only infinite love, and a sense of belonging to everything in the Universe. With Mickey, my guide and avatar, I could do anything.

WHAT HAPPENED AFTERWARD

Whenever I return to New Plymouth to visit my sister Mary, I invariably find an excuse for us to drive around the old neighborhood. The house looks much smarter these days. There's no peeling paint and sixty-foot ladders. If I half close my eyes, though, I can see Mum waving from the kitchen window.

After her Bloody Mary triumph, she became a regular arts columnist for the local newspaper. In generous-hearted interviews and reviews, she encouraged artists, both visual and performing, to have faith in their abilities and to nurture their talents to the full. Dad's two trees, The Lovers, still stand on the top lawn. It doesn't take much imagination to see him striding across the grass, hedge clippers in hand, humming Mahler.

Though he preferred to stay out of the spotlight, he took enormous pride in the development of gas fields off our coast. As a council employee, Dad received none of the wealth associated with such finds, and minimal recognition for his visionary contribution. He did, however, become successful enough to hire a troupe of Irishmen, professionals in their trade, to paint our house.

Mary left town to study at teachers' college. It wasn't long before the mountain drew her back to New Plymouth, where she was a respected primary school teacher for many years. With husband Barry, she raised three children and remains a well-loved member of the community. I'm eternally grateful for her steady support through the decades.

As Lila predicted, our brother Jim struggled to enjoy work in the gas industry. After years of wrestling with his identity, he finally came out. Jim started up New Zealand's first (and only) gay television channel, Triangle TV, which continues today as the community channel FACE TV. Sadly, dear Jim succumbed to esophageal cancer at the age of sixty-six. He is buried alongside his beloved Old English Sheepdog, Tasha, in the shadow of Mount Taranaki. I am and always will be proud of him.

Shane returned from Vietnam restless and disorientated. He tried working on building sites, but the machinery noises sometimes triggered panic attacks. Dad encouraged him to put his military fitness to good use, working as a mountain guide and assisting with rescues. Shane took to the calling with enthusiasm, basking in nature's healing while helping others.

Margaret and I lost touch, but I heard she summited the mountain—a tremendous feat I have no hope of attaining.

Though the glen is still the same shape and houses are speckled about it in the same order, a lot has changed. A two-story modern house has appeared on the bottom lawn, and the bamboos have been beaten into submission.

The valley no longer echoes with joyous cries of children chanting *Helen the Melon*. My young friends are now well into middle age, and I occasionally hear whispers of the lives they created for themselves. I was enormously happy Danny contacted me to say he was enjoying a wonderful career as a theater director, a vocation inspired, he believes, by our first dance classes on the bottom lawn.

If you want to learn more about happened to me, you could start by reading my books *Cleo*, *Jonah*, and *Bono*.

As for Mickey, she continued to guide me through my teenage years, reminding me to keep an open heart and live in the meow. Mrs. Finkle across the road took one of the kittens and christened him Thistle. Veronica from the newspaper adopted the largest one, whom she named Scoop. David Carrington from C. C. Ward's took the third kitten and christened her Mary after Bloody Mary. It looked as if nobody wanted the black-and-white runt with extra toes— until Mum's heart melted. She named the kitten Sylvia, after Sylvia Plath. After all, Mum said, clicking her needles in front of the gas heater, two lucky cats are better than one.

ACKNOWLEDGMENTS

If I was a cat, I would have been born with extra toes. How else could I have landed wonderful publishers such as Michaela Hamilton in New York, along with Jude McGee and Georgia Frances King in Australia. It's a joy working with talented, generous women who *get* me. You're my guardian angels and I love you.

Jude, I can't thank you enough for rescuing an unwanted manuscript from a slush pile more than 10 years ago. *Cleo* was later published in more than eighteen languages.

Michaela, your devotion to cats launched me on many adventures, including fostering a charmer named Bono. Thanks for making *Cleo* a New York Times bestseller, for publishing multiple editions of my books—and, just when I'm about to retire with Jonah and a book of crosswords, asking for more.

Buckets of gratitude to my agent, Anne Hawkins of John Hawkins & Associates in New York, for your sharp-eyed perspective. My promise to introduce you to a wallaby in Australia holds firm. Thanks, too, to clever Moses Cardona for finding international markets for my books.

Writing about cats and the impact they've had on my life has introduced me to extraordinary people in publishing around the world. Some, including Martina Schmidt of Austria, Manami Yasui of Japan and Edy Tassi from Italy, have become close friends. Thank you for your support and friendship through the years.

Chairman of Australia's ABC Ita Buttrose believed in my ability to write long before I could. Back in the early eighties when I was a grieving solo mum, magnificent Ita published my columns in the *Sunday Telegraph* and encouraged me to write for a global readership. Ita, you're an inspiration to women of all generations.

Meanwhile, Philip has once again endured cohabiting with

me in book-writing mode. Thank you, dear adorable man, for listening to me read chapters aloud on our Friday night drives to Phillip Island. Your observations are tactful, generous, and (nearly) always spot on. The bottomless mugs of tea are life savers. Our crazy cat Jonah is an invaluable chief editorial assistant. Every morning he herds me upstairs to my study and yowls till I settle at the keyboard. You two are the best.

While I was writing *Mickey*, our younger daughter Kath fostered a shy tabby called Mishie. Kath's devotion to Mishie reminded me how profoundly a rescue cat can transform a young person. Kath and her boyfriend Alex subsequently adopted Mishie, who was later joined by a handsome ginger feline, Sebastian. Thanks, Kath, for reading the first draft of *Mickey* and claiming to have enjoyed it more than any of my other books.

Much to our delight, our family expanded in other ways while I was writing about Mickey. Born in the depths of Melbourne's Covid lockdown, Lydia and Ramon's baby Alice brings unimaginable joy. A baby's chuckle is the happiest sound.

Thanks to my sister Mary. I treasure your gentle presence, our phone calls across the Ditch, and shared memories of our magical childhood.

When embarking on writing *Mickey*, it was clear the fairies would have to be included, but I was nervous. Nonphysical beings aren't my genre. Heartfelt thanks to dear friend and laughing buddy Reverend Ian Turnnidge of St Andrews Uniting Church for encouraging me to delve into Celtic mysticism. And for never doubting the importance of the unseen.

Spectacular, rugged Phillip Island reminds me of Taranaki when I was growing up there. A shout-out to our island soul mates, including Pete Smith, Heather and Manny Fahnle, Jayne Menensdorfe, Cryss Plummer, Lois Gaskin, Carol and Colin Brewster, Lindy and Greg Antippa.

Big Kiwi hugs to Mano Thevathasan, Sir Roderick and Gillian Deane and Bronwyn Croxson for our shared love of Taranaki. And to brilliant friends Professor Deirdre Coleman, and Diane Jungman, along with Susan and Richard Francis Bruce for your unwavering encouragement.

Through the pandemic, Melbourne had one of the longest lockdown periods in the western world. During those years, the heartbeat of our Prahran neighborhood grew stronger. Love to Heather Leviston next door, to Angus and Hannah (who are forever fostering animals) on the corner, and to my lifetime friend, Honorina Sihin.

I don't know how we'd have managed without daily injections of good coffee. Big thanks to Joey Charbel, Vittorio Murdaca, Olly, Ruby and the team at Full Steam for beaming smiles and always remembering my order (long black, hot milk on the side). Across the road, at Beyond Organic, Dean Burke, Andrew Purnell and staff enrich our community with laughter and great food. Shout out to Dean for the fabulous gluten-free toasties he conjures up for me most lunchtimes.

Kate Lister of Mindbody Integration saved our sanity and joints with regular zoom Pilates throughout the pandemic. Philip, Jonah and I became addicted to your sessions.

Special mention goes to Danielle Gray in Tasmania. After a ferocious bidding war in Kensington Publishing's auction to benefit relief efforts in Ukraine, Danielle won one of my hand-knitted beanies. I'm embarrassed to say how much she ended up paying for my humble craftwork. Danielle's daughter, Georgie, is a talented artist who delights Jonah with her portraits of him. Thanks Danielle, Georgie, and Charles, for your generous hearts.

Purrs to book sellers and long-time readers around the world. Thanks, Maureen Riesterer, for reading my stuff for decades—and for the exquisite baby clothes you've made our granddaughters. Ongoing appreciation to Cindy Code, Jeff Erlitz, Julia White, Susan Hatch, Nisa Briggs-Kelly, Abbey

Hartevelt, Wendy Joy, Jon Hollinsworth, Kirsten Hicks, Kathryn Hobson, Tamar Beaman, Jessica Davis, Emma Lawson, Julie Thomson (who uses my Christmas pudding recipe every year), Rebecca Woodmore, Lise Porter, Beth Echeverria, Jeanne Powers, Rachel @portsmouthcatsitting, Nina McCabe, Kathy Quirk, Lyn Crow, Barbara Briguglio, Alison Roberts, De-Anne Dean, Rarita Cotae, Ruth Vant, Te Jonssen, Gemma Ellis, Cath Richards, Genowefa Ela Kochajk, Cynthia Garrett, and countless others. My books exist because of you.

The deepest bow of love, respect and gratitude goes to Mickey, the lucky cat with extra toes.